GEOFFREY CHAUCER

Geoffrey Chaucer.
from the Occleve MS.
reproduced from the copy in the possession of Mr. John Munro.

EMILE LEGOUIS

PROFESSOR OF ENGLISH LITERATURE
IN THE UNIVERSITY OF PARIS

GEOFFREY CHAUCER

TRANSLATED BY

L. LAILAVOIX, M.A.(LOND.), L.ÈS.L.(PARIS)

*Senior Assistant Lecturer in French
at the Victoria University, Manchester*

NEW YORK

RUSSELL & RUSSELL

1961

PUBLISHED 1961 BY RUSSELL & RUSSELL, INC.

BY ARRANGEMENT WITH E. P. DUTTON & CO.

LIBRARY OF CONGRESS CATALOG CARD NO: 61-12126

The frontispiece is taken from the portrait in the Occleve MS., and is reproduced by the courtesy of Mr. John Munro, from the copy in his possession.

PRINTED IN THE U. S. A.

PREFACE

An English professor, to whom I mentioned, soon after
its appearance, M. Legouis' book on Chaucer and its
admirable verse translations, replied, with true British
bluntness, that he did not care to read Chaucer in French
verse, and that he would wait for an English translation
to be published. This original opinion, no doubt inspired
by a perusal of the many insipid modernisations of Chaucer
produced in the eighteenth century, together with a desire
to bring within the reach of the English reading public a
work, which embodies all the discoveries of recent criticism in a form both palatable and attractive, led me to
undertake the translation of this work. But the characteristic pronouncement of the English professor remained
in my mind, because it showed that he did not appreciate
the importance of those translations in the history of
Chaucerian criticism abroad, and I resolved to explain in
a preface why they deserve more than a curt dismissal.
They represent the latest endeavour, in a long line of
critical appreciations, to initiate the French public into the
knowledge of the art of Chaucer. I propose here to make
a brief survey of these appreciations, and to show the
varying fortunes of Chaucer in the country whence, in
youth, he gained both his inspiration and his training.

I

If some lucky student of Chaucer discovered a little bit
of manuscript five inches square, on which Guillaume de
Machaut had penned a few graceful lines addressed to the

English poet, commending him on his progress and his achievements, the history of Chaucerian criticism would not be any the richer. I am not referring here to that relationship between the two poets, which is becoming more and more obvious every day. I wish to suggest that such references as that found in Eustache Deschamps, who was also a pupil of Machaut, may interest the biographer of Chaucer, but do not prove that Chaucer was appreciated as a poet in France in his day. Unless we take the epithet "grand translateur" to be more than a statement of fact (and it would not be anything very flattering then), we can dismiss it as a pretty piece of flattery on the part of Deschamps, who would not have minded seeing some of his verse woven into the garland of a poet, whose reputation in his own country was becoming greater every day. At the date ascribed to the ballad by the critics, let us say about 1386, Chaucer, the man, was no doubt known of a few in France, such as Machaut and Deschamps, and the acquaintance may even have been of his own seeking. But Chaucer, the poet, was not looked upon as a master of verse, as a creator, from whose works anything could be learnt. Nay, leaving aside the question of language, which might have proved an impossible obstacle to most (although Leblanc declared later that Chaucer had made the reading of the old French poets easier for him), it is doubtful whether Chaucer, " the English Homer, " " the Father of English poetry," could have had any influence on French literature whatsoever.

He lived at the end of the fourteenth century. The decadence of French poetry had already begun and continued during the whole of the fifteenth century. It was exhausted, stifled out of existence by the maze of convention and allegory. It was dying from that very ideal

to which Chaucer strove to add a new lustre, and which
would have proved his undoing also but for his tendency
to realism, and the great good fortune that was his, of
creating for England a literary language, and being the
first to use it for poetical purposes. Had he lived in France,
what sort of fame would have been his? Think of the
hapless Charles d'Orléans, labouring in his English prison
to compose, after the same ideal, delicate poems of un-
reality, in which the convention to which he was a slave
forbade him to recall the things that made his heart heavy,
his father foully murdered, his mother driven by sorrow to
a premature grave, his brother unjustly detained, and the
pitiful state of his own dukedom, which had to be sold piece
by piece to pay his gaolers. That was between 1415 and
1440, not many years after Chaucer's death. But during
the duke's absence things had been moving in France,
patriotism was born in the stricken land forsaken by its
rulers and harried by the English soldiery, and with it a
new ideal which threw open the gates of the secluded
temple, and let in the rumour of life with its cries of
anguish and its shouts of joy. When Charles d'Orléans
returned with his volume of pretty verses, he found they had
aged like himself, and that the courtly wooing of imaginary
beauties seemed a little ridiculous to these new Frenchmen.
He shut himself up in his château of Blois, and spent his
time fondly collecting and arranging his rondeaus and his
chansons. But the men outside had no use for them, and
they lay forgotten after his death for three centuries, until
an erudite abbé discovered them, as one discovers the
mummy of an ancient Egyptian ruler. Of influence he
had none, for one cannot describe as such the curiosity
which made a few nineteenth-century poets delve in his
dust for complicated poetical moulds.

That is why Chaucer, who paid allegiance to the same ideals, could not have been any more fortunate. Even his masterpiece, *The Canterbury Tales*, with their wealth of observation, their humour, their sympathy, their truth, would not have been listened to very long in France, for they only retold stories and legends which tradition had made familiar. The novelty of Chaucer's handling of these topics was only to become apparent much later, in England as well as in France, at a time when the topics themselves had become obsolete, so that the historian of Chaucerian criticism in France must not hope to find traces of literary influence, but to see what notice has been taken of Chaucer there, when the bare knowledge of his name gives place to an appreciation of his works and to estimate the quality of this appreciation. I hope to show that such marks of interest were not wanting in France, and that Frenchmen, once the name of Chaucer had fairly established itself among them as that of a great writer, lost no time in finding things out about him, and even ran English critics very close in the recognition of his rare merits.

II

The feuds which separated England and France during the first three centuries following Chaucer's death, the loss of the English provinces in France, and the growing literary ascendancy of the latter country during that period, are probably the causes which explain the lack of intercourse between the two nations and the appalling ignorance of English life and literature proudly displayed by the French in those days. But for all that, we ought not to overlook one solitary instance of a Frenchman who

was well acquainted with Chaucer and counted the
Canterbury Tales amongst his favourite books. This was
Jean d'Orléans, Comte d'Angoulême, brother to Charles
d'Orléans, " the courtly maker." Brought to England as a
hostage after the treaty of Bezançais, the treachery of the
Clarence family, who saw in him a never-failing source of
profit, kept him in prison from 1412 till 1445. He was
thirteen years old when he came; he only departed at the
age of 46, bent and old before his time. During this long
captivity, he learnt to speak fluently the language of his
conquerors. Books were his only solace, and Charles
d'Orléans kept him well supplied. A catalogue of his
library, made soon after his death, in 1467, mentions " Ung
romant, en Anglois, rimé," which is a copy of the *Canterbury Tales*. So fond was the Count of this work that he
had indexed it in his own hand. The manuscript, with
his own annotations, can be seen to this day at the
Bibliothèque Nationale in Paris.

Whence came this copy? Jean d'Angoulême was
entirely dependent on his brother Charles for money, for
clothes, and for books. It is therefore more than likely
that Charles sent him the *Canterbury Tales*. But the poet
was also imprisoned in England from 1415 till 1440, and
must have come by this copy during his own captivity.
Among the gaolers who had him in their keeping during
that period was William Pole, Earl of Suffolk. The poet
lived with him in his castle of Wingfield between 1432 and
1436, and it is said that friendly relations existed between
the earl and his prisoner. Now, this William Pole had
married, in 1431, Alice Chaucer, grand-daughter of Geoffrey
Chaucer. Is it far wrong to suppose that it was during
his stay in that house where tradition made poets welcome,
that Charles obtained that copy of the *Canterbury Tales*,

which found its way some time after into this brother's
library ?   Be this as it may, the golden goose of the Clarence
family had a pretty taste for literature, and should be
remembered as the one Frenchman in the fifteenth
century, who read and appreciated Chaucer.

Is it necessary, *à propos* of Chaucer, to pillory once more
the " grand siècle " for its neglect of English letters and
its contempt for that " isle abominable " and its language,
" the barbarity of which . . . prevented its being taken
into account " ?   The English after all were as much
responsible as the French for this state of affairs: they too
readily forgot their own language abroad, and to speak
French was looked upon by them as a sign of refinement.
Moreover, it was far more difficult for France to form an
adequate estimate of foreign literatures, not because of the
barrier of language, nor on account of religious or political
antagonism, but because of the literary supremacy which
she enjoyed and which brought writers of all countries to
Paris, as to a shrine from which a chosen few derived that
enlightenment, which was to cure their minds of their
native roughness.   In fact, the discovery that there were,
outside France and apart from the ancients or the classical
Italian poets, in England of all countries, writers of merit,
must have caused the French as much surprise as might be
aroused in our day if an astronomer idly peering at the
moon, discovered at the other end of his telescope, a score
of living men, scurrying down the slopes of an extinct
volcano.   This discovery, however, was made, and Chaucer
was one of the first to benefit by it.

Readers of Louis Moréri's *Grand Dictionnaire Historique*,
published in 1674, must have experienced no little surprise
in finding amongst the list of " Geoffroys " the name of one
" Geoffroy Chaucer, called the English Homer on account

of his fine verse." It was but a short notice, the first to be found in a French book since Froissart mentioned the poet in connection with the negotiations at Montreuil-sur-Mer, but it may have awakened curiosity and made some readers wonder who that Chaucer was, whom they found so unexpectedly associated with the greatest poet of all times.

There was, however, one person, to whom the name was not perhaps unfamiliar, or who must have become acquainted with it very soon after it was mentioned in Moréri's dictionary. And this the last perhaps from whom we should expect it, for she lived in a fanciful world, far removed from the realities of other men, a world where the heroes of Greece and the warriors of Rome spent their time in sweet dalliance at the feet of their ladies, a world of gallantry to which she led her friends, who in their turn christened her Sapho. Her real name was Madeleine de Scudéry, and we are told that towards the end of her life, forsaking that country of *Tendre* and its perfumed roads, the map of which she and her friends had drawn, forsaking Clélie and Cyrus and Célamire, she spent her days in studious concern, translating Chaucer into French. Dryden says so in his preface to the *Fables Ancient and Modern*, written in 1699, and he had it from a friend of his, a lady who was in touch with some of Madeleine's admirers.

Several objections suggest themselves at once, which are not however insuperable. Mademoiselle de Scudéry was then ninety-two, which is an age when most people have ceased to care about their own, let alone about a foreign literature. But we know from an English traveller in France, Dr. Martin Lister, who saw her in 1698, that her mind had not lost any of its vigour. Again, she had to learn English in order to read Chaucer, and old ladies are

wont to say, long before they reach ninety-two, that their
learning days are over. But was not Mademoiselle de
Scudéry known as " la Première Fille du Monde " and
" la Merveille du Siècle de Louis Le Grand " ? She who
could speak Italian and Spanish when she was still in her
teens, may have found the study of English exhilarating at
nir ety. We are not aware that she ever came to England,
but her works, according to her own testimony, had been
translated into " Italian, English, German, and Arabic "
(letter to the Abbé Boisot, March 6, 1694), and had won for
her in England both applause and friends. It is not impossible that amongst those who attended her famous
" Saturdays " at her house in the Marais in Paris, there
was one English person who initiated her to the charm of
Chaucer and helped her to read him. She was looking for
new pastures; the style which she had originated lay dead,
traversed by the sarcasms of Boileau, and one would like
to imagine that, had she lived longer or known Chaucer
earlier, there was that in the English poet which might
have led this brilliant lady to transplant into French soil
that love of reality, that intuition of the motives of men,
that sympathy which is never dupe and yet never stinted,
qualities which France was not to realise definitely for
another century and a half.

III

So far we have only come across curious and isolated
instances of Chaucerian knowledge, which reflect credit on
those in whom they are found, but show plainly that the
reading public had not as yet caught the name nor realised
the importance of Chaucer. This was to come a little later,

thanks to the sudden interest shown by the French in
English literature, an interest which, according to some
critics, was determined by the awful religious rent, which,
at a stroke of the pen from a confessor-ridden king, threw
out of France thousands of her most virtuous and hard-
working citizens.   Many took refuge in England, and not
unnaturally began to study the literature of their adopted
country.   They were in close touch with the Hague, where
they poured their newly acquired knowledge into an ever
increasing number of reviews and journals.   These found
their way into France and were the means of spreading
English ideas and letters.

Such is the explanation generally given, but it over-
looks two or three causes which ought perhaps to have
been put in the front rank.   The Revocation of the Edict
of Nantes did open up a channel (and a crooked one since
it must needs go *viâ* the Hague), along which information
concerning English literature might flow into France.
But, just as it is impossible to graft a cherry-tree on a
pear-tree, because of the different nature of their saps,
likewise this foreign influence could only become active
when a demand had arisen for the kind of nourishment
which it offered.   This presupposed a weakening of the
classical ideal, which had so far held complete sway.
The quarrel between " Ancients " and " Moderns," Bayle's
Dictionary and Fontenelle's *Entretiens* and *Eloges*, are
sufficient evidence that at the end of the seventeenth
century a new spirit was at work in France, that the study
of " moral man " would soon cease to have an exclusive
claim on thinkers and writers, that men had opened their
eyes on the world around them and would take an increasing delight in the observation not of man in the
abstract, but of man in the mass, of nature, of social

conditions in France and abroad, and of foreign literary creeds and productions. That is the important fact; the migration of the French Protestants is only secondary.

One other factor in this evolution, which has not been given the place it deserves, is the increasing number of Englishmen, who, towards the end of the seventeenth and at the beginning of the eighteenth century, journeyed to France, carrying with them first-hand information, which they were only too ready to impart. We saw that through them a report of Mademoiselle de Scudéry's doings had been circulated in England, and we advanced the theory that they were probably also responsible for her attempt at translating Chaucer into French. Unless of course she was indebted for her tardy acquaintance with English literature to some of the Catholic refugees, who, fleeing with James II. from the wrath of their countrymen, founded at Saint-Germain a miniature English court, which must have been a sort of neutral ground where the Saxon met the Gaul in friendly converse.

But since Chaucer was the starting point of this argument, let us see how the theory, here objected to, works out in his case. The *Journal Litéraire*, a Protestant paper printed at the Hague, contained, in 1715, a short notice announcing the forthcoming edition of Chaucer by Urry. Two years later, the same periodical published an anonymous article entitled *Dissertation sur la Poësie Angloise*, at the end of which the writer expressed his regret at not having dealt with Chaucer, but proposed to do so on the appearance of Urry's edition. His promise, however, was never carried into effect. According to Joseph Texte's oft quoted theory, the knowledge of Chaucer revealed in these two articles ought to have found its way into France. Yet, so far as can be ascertained, the name of Chaucer was not mentioned in France, in any book, article, or other printed document until 1740, twenty-three years later, when there appeared a short notice concerning him, in the eighteenth edition of Moréri's Dictionary and in the Abbé Prévost's paper, *Le Pour et Contre*. I know very well that Chaucer's case cannot disprove a theory, which embraces the whole of English literature, but at any rate that theory does not prove Chaucer's case, and that is merely what I wished to point out. If it be objected now that the bare announcement of Urry's edition was not likely to be picked out by the French public in preference to other matters, I shall beg the reader to remember that the article on English poetry, where Chaucer's name occurred, was a long and thoughtful study, which must have attracted considerable attention. But if this last argument even be taken from me, the fact will nevertheless remain, undeniable and certain, that the first notice describing Chaucer's achievements did not come from the Hague but was written in France, and owed nothing whatever to the Protestant element.

The best proof, however, that the " gazettes " at the Hague were not solely responsible for the popularity of English ideas and literary models in France during the eighteenth century, remains to be given. Because of that modification of ideals and that awakened curiosity referred to above, the French, in spite of their dislike for travelling and their proverbial hatred of the sea, of their own accord sought in England confirmation of their newly acquired point of view. It is important to note that those who came to England to study the foreign creed were not only literary men of the second rank such as Le Blanc, Suard, or Morellet, but writers like Prévost, Voltaire, Montesquieu, and Buffon, who were to exercise such a profound influence on French thought during the century. I do not mean that the Dutch periodicals were not read in France and that information of the kind required was not sought in them, but merely that this need was anterior to them, and very soon, if not immediately, satisfied itself without the help of any mediators.

It seems, moreover, that the honour of having first aroused the curiosity of the French with regard to England belongs to a Swiss, Béat de Muralt, and not to the Protestant refugees. His *Lettres sur les Anglais et les Français*, written in 1694-95, were only published in 1725, but they were known and talked about long before that date. They came upon the French like a thunderbolt, and incensed their national pride to an incredible degree by the assertion they contained, that English literature was superior to French literature, and English character and intellect correspondingly finer. The passionate discussions originated by Muralt's letters provided the impetus needed to start the French upon their inquiry. Once this had been given, they worked strenuously to gain as rapidly as possible an acquaintance with a nation which prejudice had caused them to ignore. Two men, whom the fear of prison had driven to England, quickly realised the possibilities of the rôle to which circumstances had seemingly appointed them, and became the chief purveyors of the new taste. The Abbé Prévost, the resourceful founder of *Le Pour et Contre*, was one; Voltaire, the apologist of English scepticism and philosophy and the author of the *Lettres Philosophiques ou Lettres Anglaises* (1734), was the other. The change of attitude was so sudden and so complete that very soon it was enough for anything to be English to gain instant favour. In 1736, if we are to believe Voltaire, men of letters had already become familiar with English, and this is cor-

roborated by the number of grammars and methods which
began to appear, all designed, of course, to facilitate the
acquisition of the language. Wait yet a while and a
tyrannical public will insist on their plays being written
" in the free manner of the English stage," and their novels
" translated from English," or at any rate wrought in the
English style. Chaucer, along with his countrymen,
benefited by this " engouement," and his name is one of
the first to appear under the pen of French critics.

The great initiator, Prévost, who made it his business
to chronicle for the benefit of his countrymen whatever
seemed to him curious or characteristic in the manners
and thought of the English nation, seems to have become
acquainted with Chaucer rather late. He referred to him
in *Le Pour et Contre*, in 1740, but that was only an incidental
notice. When he took up the management of the *Journal
Étranger*, in 1755, the public had already become familiar
with the name of Chaucer through the dissertations of
Yart, Trochereau, and Chauffepié: it behoved him to
show that this remote province of English poetry was
not unknown to him. As it happened, Cibber's *Lives
of the Poets*, containing an account of Chaucer, had
recently been published, and presented some facts
which had not been seized upon as yet by any French
commentator. This served as a basis for the article,
which was further indebted to the more liberal criticisms
of Dryden. No signature appeared, but the date, circumstances, and style, all point to Prévost as being the
author. This contribution marks a great advance over its
predecessors, and brought Chaucer one step nearer to the
French public, for it included a translation of twenty-four
lines taken from the Pardoner's Prologue. True, these
were part of a longer quotation given by Cibber, which

of course dismisses the assumption that Prévost might have
read the *Canterbury Tales* in the text.   But what matters
where the lines came from ?   This quotation of Chaucer by
a French writer, even deprived of the merit of priority,
has an importance all its own, since it is the first to appear
in French type for the benefit of French readers.

The indefatigable Abbé Prévost then had been fore-
stalled, and his article was even perhaps suggested to him
by three contributions, which had already made known in
France the principal facts of the poet's biography.   The
first was by the Abbé Yart, who, in 1749, published a sort
of miscellany containing poems by Philips, Swift, Pope,
and, among some critical appreciations, Addison's *Account
of the Greatest English Poets*, and Lady Mary Wortley
Montagu's *Progress of Poetry*.   It was in two volumes and
entitled: *Idée de la Poësie Angloise, ou Traduction des
meilleurs Poëtes Anglois, qui n'ont point encore paru dans
notre Langue* . . . Chaucer was only mentioned in an
explanatory note, suggested by one of Sewell's remarks in
his life of John Philips, to the effect that Philips had studied
Chaucer and Spenser in order to enrich his vocabulary.
Yart was obviously influenced by Addison's and Lady
Montagu's adverse criticisms, quoted in the second volume.
" The language of Chaucer," he said, " has become so archaic
that the English themselves have great difficulty in understanding it " (vol. i. p. xix.).   Fortunately, Yart's investigation did not stop there, and the second and enlarged
edition of his *Idée de la Poësie Angloise*, published between
1753 and 1756, shows that he had made good use of
Dryden's preface in the interval, and attempted to read
and even to translate Chaucer.   This progress reflects
great credit on the Abbé and on the soundness of his
judgment.   The seventh volume contains a " Discourse

on Tales," a " Life of Chaucer," and a translation of
Dryden's " Palamon and Arcite."   In the " Discourse,"
Yart refers to the indebtedness of Dante, Petrarch, and
Boccaccio to Provençal taletellers, and quotes Dryden's
opinion that Chaucer borrowed both from the originals and
from their Italian imitators.   He gives further a personal
appreciation of the *Canterbury Tales*, which, not unnaturally, appear to have shocked the good Abbé's sense
of propriety.   It is curious and worth quoting:

" What is really original in Chaucer is the diversity of
the characters who relate the tales . . . he painted from
nature their characters, their dress, their virtues, and
vices, but nevertheless his portraits are so strange, so
peculiar, his characters so unpleasant and indecent, his
satire so cruel and profane that, despite the artistic concern
which guided me in my translation, I cannot hope to have
made them bearable. His other tales are even more licentious
than anything our poets have ever written; I shall therefore
leave them to the obscurity of their antiquated language."

This first impression made by Chaucer on a French
mind is particularly interesting. Too much importance
ought not to be attached to the strictures which Yart,
as a priest, was almost bound to make upon the
immorality of the Tales, but the opening sentence, with its
keen perception of Chaucer's originality, ought to be
remembered, for this point was lost sight of until Taine, in
that brilliant piece of work, his *Histoire de la Littérature
Anglaise*, brought it to light again in a happy comparison
with the methods of Van Eyck.
Yart also had been at pains to find some French writer
with whom to compare Chaucer, and with unerring judg-

ment had selected La Fontaine. "Do not look," he says, "for more originality in Chaucer's poems than in those of La Fontaine, but if originality of invention was denied them, they both made up for it by the genius they displayed in the details, a greater merit perhaps than that of invention." One may regret that the Abbé did not carry further a comparison, which is perhaps more appropriate than the one with Ovid, as suggested by Dryden. The Latin poet was capable of a sensuousness and passion recalled by Boccaccio rather than Chaucer; his refinement was the sort of delicate plant which does not grow in the vigorous furrows of a newborn literature, but is the product of a complicated and already exhausted civilisation, seeking an exceptional pleasure in the expression of fastidious longings. But La Fontaine was, like Chaucer, an amused spectator at the comedy of this world; like him, he could see the medley of motives, good and bad, which make up every human action, and his fables are as broad and as true a picture of humanity as the *Canterbury Tales*. The comparison, however, should not stop there, for La Fontaine possessed a sense of humour too, which was in no wise inferior to that of Chaucer. We have only to remember the gentle irony, tempered by sympathy, the humour, to put it in one word, which gives such perfect little pieces as the fable entitled *Le Chat, la Belette et le Petit Lapin* a width and fullness, equalled only by life itself:

> Du Palais d'un jeune Lapin
> Dame Belette un beau matin
> S'empara. . . .

Collections of poems by modern English writers were very much in vogue in the early days of the "anglomanie," but the compilers, in their desire to give something which had not been published before, did not always select the

most representative. They were probably too new to
their task to be able to separate the chaff from the wheat.
Still, this method had its good points, since it had led Yart
from John Philips to Chaucer. It was the same kind of
fortuitous association which put Jean Arnold de la Berlière
Trochereau on the track of Chaucer. In his *Choix de
Différens Morceaux de Poësie, traduits de l'Anglois,* he
gave Pope's *Temple of Fame,* together with the foreword
where the poet acknowledges his debt to Chaucer.
Trochereau felt that he could not let this name pass without some explanation, and he related everything that was
known about the English Homer. His account, chiefly
derived from Dryden, is a little dull, and its lack of
freshness may be due to the influence of Pope's dis-
couraging lines, which he quotes at the end and probably
endorses.

Chaucer had by now gained a sure foothold in France.
What proves it is that his name began to appear in
dictionaries and encyclopædias. It is well known that these
were the treasure-houses where the eighteenth century
stored all its information and even its seditious ideas.
Pierre Bayle, for instance, had used this kind of publication
as a vehicle for his sceptical opinions, and his *Dictionnaire
Historique et Critique,* read and sifted by an eager public,
had supplied the enemies of tradition and dogma with their
most valuable arguments. In a revised and enlarged
edition of this dictionary, brought out by Chauffepié in 1750,
we find a long article devoted to Chaucer, which did not
adduce anything new to what was already known in France,
but which was valuable nevertheless, because it quoted the
appreciations of English critics as far back as Ascham
and Sidney, and further gave a complete list of the poet's
works, not unnaturally including some now recognised as

apocryphal, together with Dryden's and Pope's modernisations. This useful contribution was largely indebted to
the article published in the *Biographia Britannica* in 1748.

This last compilation also inspired the anonymous
writer of the *Journal Anglais*, which was started in 1775.
It is significant both of the importance attributed to him
by the editors, and of the regard entertained by the public
for the English Homer, that the first number should have
been devoted to Chaucer. The article covered eight pages
and laid under contribution not only the *Biographia
Britannica*, but also Lydgate, Cibber, and Dryden, whose
comparison of Chaucer with Ovid was published in the
same paper in 1777. This is the most complete account of
Chaucer ever given in France; the author is sufficiently
familiar with the facts to be able to keep them down, and
to provide a commentary which is always sound and sometimes original. He is the first to compare Chaucer with
Marot. Moreover, the portrait of Chaucer, with which he
concludes his article, shows such a true appreciation of the
poet's personality, that neither the biographical discoveries
of the nineteenth century, nor the interest displayed by
later commentators, have produced a more accurate and
sympathetic piece of criticism. Here it is in full:

" There existed in this great man's character a mixture
of gaiety, modesty, and gravity, which rendered him
equally suitable for court or town and made him a favourite
in good society. His mind was pleasant and subtle, his
judgment healthy and sure. He was a sincere and honest
critic, more prone to kindness than to severity, and more
inclined to excuse and cover up the faults of the writers, his
contemporaries, than to expose them. He was superior
to his times and desired to elevate them to his level. His

fame as a poet is patent, and his country has ratified this
judgment. It is impossible to over-estimate his antique
and lasting grace, nor the clearness of his style in a language which, since the thirteenth century, has undergone
so many changes. . . . His virtue was on a par with his
talent. He was a faithful and constant friend. In short,
he was a philosopher in the true sense of the word, that is
to say he was a moral and accomplished man."

There is a sort of flowing grace about this portrait
which covers up all the little bits of information, gathered
from many quarters. These are so judiciously arranged
that they seem to fit in naturally one with the other.
Scanty as were the particulars at his disposal, the portrait
drawn by the anonymous writer is complete. It is a
delightful piece of literature, and recalls the felicity of that
past master in the art of portrait painting, Saint-Simon.
True, the physical traits are lacking which give such
relief to the Duke's work, but I am not sure that their
absence does not endow the picture with a remoteness and
charm eminently suitable for a moral portrait.

We have now completed our survey of Chaucerian
criticism in France during the eighteenth century, and it
seems to us that French critics on the whole, and behind
them a portion of the French public, did rather well by
Chaucer, especially if we take into consideration the double
difficulty of language and archaism, which made him, to a
large extent, a sealed book for them. Freed from the prejudice which prevailed in England, and which represented
Chaucer's English as obsolete and uncouth, and so affected
adversely the opinion that people had of him, they brought
to the study of Chaucer a freshness of impression and a
sincerity which were too often lacking just then in his

English critics.   They refused their adherence to Addison's
and Pope's adverse criticism, in spite of the authority which
these writers enjoyed in France, and with rare literary
instinct turned to Dryden for a more appreciative criticism
of the poet's writings.   Further, the few extracts we have
given show that they could go beyond Dryden even and
form for themselves an estimate, so true and penetrating
that more recent criticism has only upheld it.   Compare
with this the severity of English writers of the same period.
It would not be fair to quote Addison's lines, since they
were written in 1694 and therefore do not belong to the
eighteenth century.   Moreover, according to Pope's
testimony, they were a youthful concoction, which did not
correspond to the essayist's later opinions.   But pretty
generally Chaucer baffled English critics during the century,
and because they felt him fast slipping from them, they
were inclined to underrate him.   Even Dryden, who
protested so eloquently against the contempt in which he
was held, cannot help saying that " he is a rough diamond
and must be polish'd e'er he shines."   And his laudation
had so little influence that in a contemporary dialogue,
which represents him in converse with the shade of
Chaucer in one of the coffee-houses of hell, Chaucer is made
to say, " . . . you have done me a wonderful Honour to
Furbish up some of my old musty Tales, and bestow modern
garniture upon them. . . . I must take the freedom to tell
you that you overstrain'd Matters a little, when you
liken'd me to Ovid, as to our Wit and Versification."   This
fairly represents English opinion in the eighteenth century,
and leads one to wonder whether Chaucer, barring one or
two glorious exceptions, was any more read in England
than in France.   The greatest of the day, those who
supplied the majority of their countrymen with literary

PREFACE xxv

tenets, do not escape the reproach.   They either exhibited absolute indifference or treated the old poet with superior benevolence.   Pope's lines to the effect that the rapidity with which a writer's language becomes obsolete causes him to be neglected and soon forgotten, are well known:

Our sons their fathers' failing language see,
And such as Chaucer is shall Dryden be.
An Essay on Criticism.

But whereas Pope, in his melancholy dictum, only referred to the language, Dr. Samuel Johnson, the great literary dictator, the Boileau of the century, went further and condemned both subject and style:

" The works of Chaucer, upon which this kind of re-juvenescence has been bestowed by Dryden, require little criticism.   The tale of the *Cock* seems hardly worth revival; and the story of *Palamon and Arcite*, containing an action unsuitable to the times in which it is placed, can hardly be suffered to pass without censure of the hyper-bolical commendation which Dryden has given it in the General Preface."—*Lives of the Poets* (Life of Dryden).

This was written in 1779, four years after the appearance of Tyrwhitt's admirable edition of the *Canterbury Tales*. Horace Walpole, the eccentric founder of Gothic romance, was no less incapable of appreciating Chaucer at his true worth.   To a friend, who offered him a first edition of Chaucer for the small sum of a guinea, he declared that, although a Goth, he was a modern Goth, and preferred Chaucer in Dryden, or in Baskerville than in the original garb.

Thus, Chaucer was little appreciated and little read in the Augustan age of English literature.   The French read him even less, no doubt, but whilst his countrymen were anxious to modernise his verse and rejuvenate his thought, in order to bring him down to their standard of taste, French critics gave him a generous welcome and showed him a reverence, which was perhaps of greater intrinsic value, and, in any case, testified to a truly liberal conception of the art of criticism.

IV

The eighteenth century had approached English literature with a feeling of curiosity, which made all and sundry welcome. The nineteenth century, more conscious of its aims, only admitted authors likely to help in defining and developing the new tendencies. Instead of a host of English writers finding indiscriminate favour in France, only a few were studied, foremost among them Walter Scott, Ossian, Shakespeare, and that was the beginning of a real influence. Chaucer had no grist for the romantic mills and so passed from the public rostra to those minor tribunes, where learned men discourse on literary merits. At the hands of these specialists, a great many things concerning him, which were still obscure, or had been over-looked, received a proper amount of attention. This investigation was started in England, but the French did their fair share of it. They left aside the questions of language and text, for which they were not competent, and confined themselves to the study of sources and influences, to the interpretation of Chaucer's art and personality, a task for which their habitual penetration and worldly wisdom made them pre-eminently suitable.

Two sure signs there are that Chaucer, at the beginning

of the nineteenth century, was gradually passing into the hands of the schoolmen. To start with, the new literary gods did not know him. There appeared in 1813 a very good article by Suard in the *Biographie Universelle*. The writer, who was evidently acquainted with the work of his predecessors, shows by his allusions to *Troilus and Criseyde* that he must have read Chaucer in the original. In the same year, a certain Dubuc published *Les deux Grisélidis, Histoires traduites de l'Anglois, l'une de Chaucer et l'autre de Mlle. Edgeworth*. This book marks a further step in the evolution of French criticism, facing at last Chaucer's text. Dubuc, after comparing one of the many modernisations current in England in the eighteenth century with Chaucer's own poem, was so struck with the originality of the latter, that he felt compelled to give a translation of it, which is both complete and accurate. But Suard, by the bulk of his work, belongs to the eighteenth century, and Dubuc is practically unknown. Who are the leading writers in 1813? Madame de Staël and Chateaubriand, and their genius could find no inspiration in Chaucer. Strangely enough, they both referred to him, Madame de Staël in 1800 and Chateaubriand in 1836, but in such a way as to prove that they knew next to nothing about him. This indifference of the new literature to Chaucer, contrasting with the increasing interest taken in him by the schoolmen, is curiously emphasised by the rebuke administered to Chateaubriand for his ignorance of the poet by Villemain, the head of the modern school of critics. The other evidence of this specialisation is found in the mutilations to which the articles dealing with Chaucer, in the eighteenth-century dictionaries and encyclopædias, were submitted during this period. If we want to find out anything about the " English Homer " we must now turn to the specialists and consult their books and magazine articles. They are very numerous, and make one wonder that foreign critics should have been able to penetrate so deeply into the heart and mind of a poet who bears such strong marks of his times and nationality. But sympathy is the safest of guides, and they had none other in their patient researches.

Between 1813 and 1830 hardly anything interesting was produced in the way of Chaucerian criticism. France followed the fortunes of her flag on the battlefields of Europe, and found England against her almost at every point. To the strained and often interrupted political relations corresponded a weakening of literary intercourse. Moreover, French universities were being organised, and not until that was completed could a systematic study of English literature begin. But take the period between 1830 and 1908: what a wealth of critical output, what a conscientious investigation of England's literary history! I counted between those dates no less than forty books, articles, or notices dealing with Chaucer, which works very nearly at the rate of one per year. They are not all of equal value, of course, but it must be admitted that this is a remarkable achievement. There are indeed many French authors of note who have not been so well done by.

It is not possible to review here all these appreciations. The catalogue, moreover, has been made—and definitely made—by Miss C. Spurgeon, to whose book we refer below. But the most important of them may help to show that French critics, although perhaps not curious enough at times of the biographical and philological problems attached to the name of Chaucer, amply made up for it by that other kind of inquiry, which through his work explores a man's mind and heart, finds out what is topical or local in his utterances, what belongs to all times and all nations, and thus pieces together the history of human thought.

Villemain, that eloquent professor and lecturer, who retraced to admiring audiences the history of the literatures of France, England, Italy, and Spain in the Middle Ages, could not fail to see the importance of Chaucer. He had made his own Madame de Staël's theory that literature is the mirror of society, and Chaucer, ". . . than whom," he says, " no one painted better the Middle Ages," told him much about the customs, feelings, and thoughts of that period.   He perceived the weakening of mediæval ideals implied in his mocking descriptions of monks and knights; he saw the many evidences of his sympathy for Wycliff, and realised the novelty of his multifarious pilgrimage.   The lectures were published in book form in 1830.   Eight years later appeared in the *Revue Française*, under the name of E. T. Delécluze, a long and thoughtful article of twenty-nine pages devoted to Chaucer.   The author had a particular admiration for the *Canterbury Tales*, and in order to make them better known among the French public, he gave a detailed analysis of each, and translated the whole of the Prologue, which had never been done in French before.   With H. Gomont rests the honour of having written the first book on Chaucer published in French.   It contains an abundance of material, and the facts are carefully chosen.   Gomont dealt at length with the *Canterbury Tales*, and translated the whole of the " Knight's Tale," but his estimate of Chaucer too often lacked sympathy, and in that respect was a long way behind that of Villemain or Delécluze. Leaving aside the clumsy rendering of the *Canterbury Tales* given by the Chevalier de Chatelain in 1857, we come at last to Sandras's remarkable volume, entitled *Étude sur Chaucer considéré comme imitateur des Trouvères*, and dated 1859.

It would be difficult to overrate the importance of this work, which probably initiated much of the later criticism both in England and in France. Dr. Furnivall looked upon it as the most valuable contribution since Tyrwhitt, and he who was the founder of the " Chaucer Society " had every qualification to pass a correct judgment. Sandras, who placed Chaucer between Aristophanes and Molière, was the first to establish on proofs his indebtedness to the literature of France and, in particular, to the two parts of the *Roman de la Rose*.   The following extract explains clearly his standpoint:

" The names of two French poets characterise very well to my mind the genius of the father of English poetry.   In his allegorical and chivalrous poems, Chaucer adopted the style brought into favour by Guillaume de Lorris; in the Canterbury Pilgrimage, satire was the predominant element, and its gibes were directed against the same objects which had exercised the erudite and merciless humour of Jean de Meung."

Taine's account of Chaucer in his *Histoire de la Littérature Anglaise* was not inspired by Sandras, since he had already contributed the substance of it to the *Revue de l'Instruction Publique* in 1856, but it would be interesting to see to what extent the original article was modified by Sandras' thoughtful study.   However, Taine had too much personality and too original an outlook upon literature to be influenced by any one.   Nothing could excel the brilliance of the pages he devoted to Chaucer.   He pointed out, amongst other things, his superiority to Boccaccio, whose taletellers are mere phantoms and nonentities, so different from the robust flesh and blood painted by the English poet.

No less illuminating was M. Jusserand's appreciation of Chaucer in his *Histoire littéraire du peuple Anglais,* which appeared in 1893. Its eighty pages count amongst the most discerning ever written on Chaucer, particularly those where he sums up the qualities of the poet's temperament, humour, sympathy and common sense.

The fact that they only deal with Chaucer incidentally, forces me to exclude a host of minor notices from various authors, amongst whom I should like to mention Messrs. A. Baret, A. Filon, J. C. Demogeot, L. Morel. They belong to that admirable body of French professors, who, through their patient and unostentatious efforts, have brought English studies in France to the level of true scholarship, and also have produced from time to time contributions which, for accuracy, soundness of judgment and breadth of treatment, are second to none. Moreover, were not Villemain and Taine nurtured in the same institution as they? This book is another instance, and not the least, of what is being done for English literature, and for Chaucer in particular, in the French universities. Who has retold better than M. Legouis the birth and growth of Chaucer's talent, the help and hindrance which his foreign models proved to him, and the final efflorescence of his genius when he had discovered, after years of groping, a subject where he could express his many-sided nature to his own satisfaction? There is something intensely pathetic in the successive efforts of the learned poet to assert himself, and the chapters of M. Legouis' book, describing each attempt, with its mixture of gains and failures, are like the acts of a dramatic composition which is being unravelled before us. But this book marks yet another advance, and one that we cannot praise too highly. It was designed for a wider public than had been the wont since criticism parted from literature and became a distinct province. Nothing was neglected to make the information accurate, but it was clearly desired that erudition should not be the obvious feature of this book. And in order to remove the last obstacle to a full appreciation of the English poet, copious verse translations were given, not in a modern form, but in a metre resembling as nearly as possible that of the original, and in a language just archaic enough to preserve that quaintness which charms a modern ear in Chaucer's verse, without, however, presenting those linguistic difficulties which prevent the present day reader from enjoying to the full Balzac's *Contes Drolatiques*, for instance.

True, we had the admirable translation of the *Canterbury Tales* published in 1908 by a group of French professors, but although wonderfully accurate, it follows the movement of the Chaucerian sentence too closely not to be a little disconcerting, and, in any case, it deprives it of that ease and grace which alone could recommend it to the general reader. That such is not the case with M. Legouis' translations any one who cares to consult the pieces given in the appendix can see for himself.

V

Thus, Addison's complaint that

> . . . Age has rusted what the Poet writ
> Worn out his Language and obscur'd his wit,

is now sufficiently disproved, for Chaucer, far from receding into the dimness of a forgotten past, has become a real and living presence among us, and his art, overstepping the national boundary, found in France some of his most sympathetic admirers. It would be difficult, in fact, despite the deep imprint made by French literature at one time or another on the literatures of her neighbours, to find a single French poet of similar antiquity having met in England with the same favour, with the same abundant proof of genuine appreciation as Chaucer has in France. If the records of Froissart and Montaigne even were drawn, despite their lasting influence on English letters, I doubt whether they would be found to equal Chaucer's. Taking Miss Spurgeon's book as a basis, I divided all the Chaucer references which this author mentions under four heads, namely:

a. Books, articles, or notices containing appreciative criticism (A.C.).

b. Giving facts of his life (F.L.).

c. Showing that the author had read the whole or portion of Chaucer (R.C.).

d. Giving part or whole translations of some of his works (T.W.).

In order to find out exactly what belonged to each of the three periods, which I outlined as corresponding to three different stages of the evolution of Chaucerian criticism in France, I distributed the references between the following dates: (1) 1749-1800, (2) 1800-1830, (3) 1830-1908. Here is the result of this inquiry:

	A.C.	F.L.	R.C.	T.W.
1749-1800	7	6	2	2
1800-1830	2	3	3	2
1830-1908	40	18	19	14
	—	—	—	—
	49	27	24	18

xxxiv   GEOFFREY CHAUCER

These totals speak for themselves. They prove beyond a doubt that "noble Geffroy Chaucier" has at last won from the French that full measure of admiration which he gave them unstintedly, and perhaps nothing would have pleased him better than the favour he now enjoys in the home of the troubadours and " courtly makers," which was a little his home also.

The main facts of this preface were derived from Miss Spurgeon's excellent Doctorat thesis *Chaucer Devant la Critique* (Paris, Hachette et Cie., 1911), in which she has summarised some of the results of the most scholarly and exhaustive study of Chaucerian criticism embodied in her *Five Hundred Years of Chaucer Criticism and Allusion*, now in the press. I cannot, however, make her responsible for my conclusions, which differ substantially from hers. I wish further to express my gratitude to her for the interest she has taken in this translation, and for the invaluable help she has rendered me at all the stages of my undertaking.

I have to thank Messrs. A. Rose and J. Marks, two students in the French department at the Victoria University, for kindly compiling the index.

L. LAILAVOIX.

CONTENTS

CHAPTER V

THE " CANTERBURY TALES ": SOURCES AND COMPOSITION

CHAPTER VI

THE " CANTERBURY TALES ": A LITERARY STUDY

GEOFFREY CHAUCER

CHAPTER I

THE POET'S BIOGRAPHY

I. Life of Chaucer. II. His character. III. Relation of his
work to the history of his times. IV. His patron John of
Gaunt.

I

In October 1386, in a law-suit between two noblemen over
a coat of arms, one of the witnesses was described in the
curious French of English law-courts as " Geffray Chaucere,
Esquier, del age de xl. ans et plus, armeez par xxvii. ans."
This is the most positive information we possess as to the
date of the poet's birth, and doubt may even be expressed
as to its reliability, because the ages of the other witnesses
were set down most inaccurately in the document.   On
the face of it, however, his recent biographers, after checking
this indication by the known facts of his life, are agreed
to fix the date of his birth about the year 1340, rather
earlier than later.   This places him in the generation of
Froissart and Eustache Deschamps, and makes him a
contemporary of Charles V., King of France, of the children
of Edward III., King of England, and in particular of that
John of Gaunt, Duke of Lancaster, his patron, the dates
of whose birth and death thus correspond with his very
nearly.   He was probably born in London, in Thames

Street, a road which is parallel to the river and where his father owned a house and tavern. Nothing of any special account is known about his ancestors. The name, however, tells us much. Chaucer is the French " chaussier," which means shoemaker or rather hosier. This nickname used as a surname reveals in all probability a French origin on the father's side. Moreover, the Christian name of the poet's grandfather was Robert, and the name of Geoffrey given to the poet had been introduced and popularised in England by the Angevin dynasty with which it frequently occurs.

The Chaucers, however, were hosiers no longer in the fourteenth century. For two generations at least they had belonged to the guild of " vintners " in the city. In 1310 Geoffrey's grandfather, Robert, had been made a collector for the port of London of the newly established customs on wine agreed to by the merchants of Aquitaine. As to his father, John, he seems to have been a prosperous vintner with friends at court. On the 12th of June 1338, before crossing the sea in the retinue of Edward III., who was going on an expedition to Flanders, he obtained some letters of protection rendering his property exempt from all suits in his absence. In 1348 he was appointed deputy to the king's butler in the port of Southampton. He died in 1366. We know that his wife's name was Agnes, and that she was related to a certain Hamo de Compton. She displayed as much haste as the Wife of Bath, and married again soon after her husband's death. But it is not certain that John Chaucer was only married once, nor that this Agnes was the poet's mother.

What a curious medley of merchants, sailors, tavern-keepers, and customers of all kinds there must have been, streaming in and out of the vintner's house! The child's first observations were not lost to the poet, and helped him to picture accurately the various trades of the city. Even when he wrote the *Canterbury Tales*, his early mercantile impressions came back to him over thirty years of court life. There are details which become peculiarly interesting if we think of his up-bringing. He shows an accurate knowledge of the mixing of wines which was practised then, although the offender ran the risk of being put in the stocks for it. He speaks of the heady fumes of the white wines of Lepe, near Cadiz, mixed with the wines of Bordeaux or La Rochelle. What he saw and heard in his childhood was not all lost.

But no trace whatever remains of his more formal education. We do not know the school he was sent to. His name does not appear on the registers of any of the Oxford or Cambridge colleges, although legend will have it that he attended one or the other of the universities, or even both in turn. But despite this lack of information, one is much tempted to connect him with the universities. To begin with, it is the easiest way of accounting for his learning and wide reading at a time when books were scarce and not easily accessible. Later, when he personified the love of science, the character he chose was a book-loving clerk of Oxford, to whom he is supposed by many to have ascribed, as we will see, one of the most memorable incidents of his own life. Besides, what a vivid picture of places and customs in his *Miller's Tale*, which introduces to us the courteous Nicolas, so versed in astrology and a consummate player of the psaltery, which describes his little room fragrant with flowers at the Oxford carpenter's where he lodges, and his love affair with the lively Alison. Again what realism in the presentation of those two Northumbrian clerks, with their dialect and broad accent, who appear in the *Reves Tale*, sent by the warden of their college to superintend the grinding of the crafty miller of Trompington—

> nat fer fro Cantebrigge,
> Ther goth a brook, and over that a brigge,
> Upon the whiche brook ther stant a melle,
> And this is verray soth that I yow telle.[1]

There can be little doubt that Chaucer, at some period, was in close touch with university life, both on its serious and gay side; one is even tempted to believe that he himself led that life for a time. The difficulty is, however, since he was employed at the court so early, to find room for a preliminary sojourn at Oxford or Cambridge. The earliest documents we possess show him in the service of the Duke of Clarence, the third son of Edward III., and he was then not much more than seventeen. In two fragments of a household account-book of the duke's wife appears an entry to the effect that in April 1357 a complete suit was supplied, for a sum of seven shillings, to one " Galfridus Chaucer," to wit a *paltock* or short cloak, a pair of red and black breeches, and a pair of shoes. That is the costume of a page, and it is obvious that at this date the young man had already entered upon his career as a courtier. His father's friends at court, the charm of two bright eyes in a still childish face, a precocious mind, and the gallantry of some early love-poems—many reasons can be found to explain the presence of the vintner's son in the princely household. In all probability he became known as a poet very early, and there is nothing to prevent us from believing quite literally the words of his friend Gower, who represents him as the disciple and clerk of

[1] *The Reves Tale*, ll. 1-4.

Venus, having " in the floures of his youthe "[1] filled the country with his ditties and merry songs in honour of the goddess.

When therefore the page is transformed into a soldier, and in 1359 goes campaigning into France in the following of the Duke of Clarence,[2] one is tempted to picture him very like that young poetical squire whom he described in his pilgrimage—

> With lokkes crulle, as they were leyd in presse . . .
> Embrowded was he, as it were a mede
> Al ful of fresshe floures, whyte and rede,
> Singinge he was, or flaytinge, al the day, . . .
> *He coude songes make and wel endyte.*

Were they not both just twenty, were they not " as fresh as is the month of May ? " Did they not both ride through Artois and Picardy, and why should not Chaucer, just like the squire, have displayed prowess in order to win the favours of his lady? Making all due allowance for whatever is convention or literary reminiscence in the portrait of the squire—some of the traits are derived from Guillaume de Lorris,[3] and through Guillaume de Lorris from Ovid [4]—it is yet very significant that Chaucer alone endows him with the gift of poetry. The coincidences are so many, that in painting his squire, it is quite inconceivable that the poet did not think of himself.

The campaign was not a glorious one. The King of France, Jean le Bon, defeated at Poitiers and brought to

---

[1] *Confessio Amantis*, lib. octavus, ii. 2943.

[2] From " the new Chaucer item " discovered in the Exchequer Accounts, it appears that Chaucer was still of the Duke's retinue in 1360. (*Modern Language Notes*, March 1912.)

[3] *Roman de la Rose*, ed. Fr. Michel, ll. 2185-2221.

[4] *De Arte Amandi*, bk. i. l. 595.

London as a prisoner, had, in order to free himself, consented
to the cession of all the Plantagenet possessions to Edward
III. But his son, the dauphin Charles, having repudiated
this treaty, Edward invaded France in order to force her
to carry out the clauses. But his progress was checked
by the town of Reims, and for seven long weeks the English
besieged it in vain. Froissart's account, whilst giving
prominence to the individual prowess of a few of the
English combatants, does not conceal the failure of the
expedition. All we know of what befell the poet in that
war is that he was one of a detachment which went as far
as *Retters* (Rethel), and that he was taken prisoner during
an encounter. He remained a captive until March
1st, 1360, when the king paid sixteen pounds sterling
for his ransom. From the fact that about the same time
Edward III. paid similar, or even larger, sums for the sake
of recovering certain chargers, it has been inferred by
some that the young soldier-poet was of no great account.
But as a matter of fact the sum set down for the ransom
of Chaucer, supposing that it represents the whole of the
money disbursed, is not inconsiderable, and would amount
to something between £160 and £240 in our money, which
would tend to show on the contrary what a high value was
put on the poet's services.

Not a single angry word can be found in Chaucer's work
against the enemies that had captured him. Who knows
but that his supple and adaptable mind did not turn this
mishap into account, and that he did not make good this
opportunity of perfecting his knowledge of the French
language and literature? By a curious coincidence, the old
poet Guillaume de Machaut was in all probability at the same
time shut up in Reims, besieged by the English, and was
training there in the art of verse-making a youth, destined

to make illustrious the name of Eustache Deschamps.[1] Although we are unable to assert that Chaucer met either of them, one would like to picture the young English prisoner brought into contact at that early date with him who was his earliest master in letters, and with that other, who later became by turn his pattern and his praiser. In any case why should not Chaucer's acquaintance with Machaut's verse date from this temporary propinquity?

Did Chaucer return to England with the king after the peace of Bretigny, or did he remain behind in France? Or was it then that, having decided to follow letters as a vocation, he went into residence at one of the English universities? There is a blank here in his biography; we can find no trace of him between the years 1360 and 1366. At the latter date John Chaucer died, and his widow married again almost immediately. As to Geoffrey, it seems as if he too had wedded just about that time, for the documents begin to mention a certain Philippa Chaucer "una domicellarum cameræ Philippæ Reginæ," and the name of this lady-in-waiting will henceforth be frequently associated with his. After the queen's death, in 1369, Philippa joined the household of the Duke of Lancaster. If we admit the very plausible hypothesis which identifies her with Philippa Roet (or Rouet), a daughter of Sir Payn Roet of Hainault, we have at the same time an explanation of the favour in which she stood with the queen as her countrywoman, and later with the Lancastrians. For her sister Catherine, the widow of Sir Hugh Swynford, first a governess to the children of John of Gaunt, became the duke's mistress about 1371, perhaps earlier, and his third wife in 1396.

[1] G. de Machaut, *Poésies lyriques*, edited by V. Chichmaref, 1909, vol. i. p. xlix.

Chaucer's marriage, judging by the many remarks he
makes on the misfortunes of matrimonial life in general,
and by a few direct allusions to his own, does not seem
to have given him unalloyed happiness. He complained
of the harsh voice which pulled him out of bed every
morning by shouting "*Awak!*" [1] It was not only by his
late rising, we must admit, but also by his loose morals
and amorous verse, that the poet may have alienated a
companion, of whose shrewish nature we seem to get
sundry glimpses. As a matter of actual fact we know
nothing of her. Even her sister, despite the glamour of
her life and the fact that she founded a royal line (King
Henry VII., first of the Tudors, was descended from her
through her son John of Beaufort), is a somewhat indistinct
figure. One chronicler labels her an adventuress, whilst
Froissart, on the other hand, courteously calls her " une
dame qui scavoit moult de toutes honneurs."   In any case,
after Chaucer had become a widower in 1387, he gave
himself out as having full practical knowledge of " the
sorwe and wo that is in mariage," and shuddering at the
thought of falling again " in swich dotage " [2]—a mere
conventional joke current at the time, says Professor
Kittredge, from whom it is always unsafe to dissent;
but if Chaucer's verse were nothing but convention, it
would not deserve very deep study. Besides, it is hard
to reconcile much respect for the deceased wife with such
trifling under certain circumstances. A mournful widower
is not likely to tell a friend: " It is foolish enough to
marry once; it would be sheer madness to do so twice.
Believe me, for *I* know. Read my *Wyf of Bath*,
wherein thou wilt find the condensed results of my own
experience." Chaucer's verse-letter to Bukton is nothing

[1] *H. of F.* i. 560.   [2] *Lenvoy a Bukton.*

if not personal. But there can be little doubt that Chaucer's marriage proved singularly useful to him in a worldly sense, and contributed to his fortune. He was no sooner married than favours began to shower on him in the shape of pensions, titles, grants, missions, remunerative posts, and sinecures. During the twenty years of his married life, his worldly prosperity was uninterrupted.

In the month of January 1367, the king granted him an annuity of 20 marks for life (about £200 of the present currency), and described him as " dilectus valettus noster." From a valet of the king's household he rose to be, a year or two later, an esquire of less degree, *armiger* or *scutifer*, and the office allotted to him, as described in an old manuscript, was one well designed to suit a poet. The duties of the thirty-seven squires attached to the king's household, consisted in drawing to the Lords' chambers within court winter and summer, in afternoons and evenings, there to keep honest company after their cunning, in talking of chronicles of kings, and of other policies, or in piping or harping, singing lays or martial deeds.[1]

With his ready imagination and well-stored memory, Chaucer was admirably suited for such a post. His talent as *conteur* and poet had no doubt already met with much appreciation. He was asked by the Duchess Blanche of Lancaster to translate Guillaume de Deguileville's *Prière à Notre-Dame*, and he turned it into fine English verse. But he was above all the clerk of Venus, the poet of human love. To this period belong no doubt the early "Balades, Roundels, Virilayes,"[2] unfortunately lost, and with which, according to Gower, "The lond fulfild is

[1] *Life-Records of Chaucer*, part ii. p. xi. Chaucer Society, 2nd series.
[2] Prol. of *Leg. of G. W.* Text B. l. 423.

overal." [1] Chaucer was here following the lyrical novelties of Machaut, whose " dits " he also took as models in 1369, to mourn the good Duchess Blanche, who died of the plague in that year. To that same period belongs in all probability his famous translation of the *Roman de la Rose*. He is at this time entirely under the influence of French masters.

His life, however, did not remain sedentary for long. In the same year; 1369, he obtained advances of money to equip himself for a military expedition to France. The English were trying to regain the vast possessions, which they had lost through the clever policy of Charles V. of France, backed up by the valour of Duguesclin. But what interests us more than his obscure part in this futile campaign, is that in 1370 he started upon a series of diplomatic missions, of which we can trace no less than six in the course of eight years; they took him to France, to Flanders, and even to Italy.

His Italian missions deserve especial attention. The first one in particular marks a memorable date in his poetical career. On the 12th November 1372, Chaucer, the king's esquire, was appointed a member of a commission, together with a certain James Provan and John de Mari, a citizen of Genoa, to negotiate with the Duke and merchants of that city, who were anxious to select an English port where they could found a commercial establishment. Chaucer visited Florence and Genoa, and may have stayed about six months abroad. Of this journey, from which the poet learnt much, as we shall see later, no other official particulars are known. But it has long been assumed that when he made the Oxford clerk say, in his Tales, that he had heard the story of Griselidis at Padua from Petrarch

[1] *Op. cit.* l. 2947.

himself, Chaucer was only commemorating what had happened to himself. As a matter of fact, in the year 1373 Petrarch, declining in years, had just left Arquà for Padua, and was then, as testified by his correspondence, engaged upon a Latin prose version of "Griselidis," the last tale of the *Decamerone*, which he read to some friends. Though much doubt has been lately thrown on the meeting between the two poets,[1] it remains possible. Anyhow, whether historical or legendary, it symbolises the first literary intercourse between England and Italy: it is the first ray of the Renaissance lighting upon an English imagination. Chaucer must have wished to visit Italy again, after his return to England. The opportunity soon occurred, and we find him, four years later, negotiating a sort of military alliance with the Duke of Milan, Bernardo Visconti, and the famous English " condottiere," the formidable " aguto," Sir John Hawkwood. The details of the negotiation are not known, but the object was to seek aid for John of Gaunt, who was engaged on an expedition against France and vainly besieging Saint-Malo. That is how, from May to September 1378, Chaucer, in the company of Sir Edward Berkeley, paid a second visit to Italy, the object of the journey being this time Lombardy.

If Chaucer's missions to France are of lesser literary significance, the importance of the points he had to nego-tiate may be a surer indication of the favour he enjoyed. In February 1377, he was sent with others to Montreuil-sur-Mer to arrange a treaty of peace with France, and it is in connection with this that his name occurs in Frois-sart's *Chronicle:* " Si furent envoyet . . . du costé des Englès, messires Guichars d'Angle, messires Richars Sturi et

---

[1] *See* especially the article by Mr. Mather, *Mod. Lang. Notes,* 11, p. 419.

Jeffrois Cauchiès." [1]   Less than a year later, in January
1378, after the death of Edward III., he was again on a
mission intended to arrange a marriage between the reigning
king, Richard II., and the daughter of Charles V. of France.
The negotiations however failed in both cases.

The draughts of the moneys, sometimes considerable,
granted to Chaucer on these various occasions, have been
preserved, but he had gained meanwhile some rewards
of a more durable nature " in secretis negotiis domini
regis." The year 1374 was particularly profitable to him;
the Duke of Lancaster, on the one hand, granted him, out
of his own revenues, a pension of £10, in consideration of
services rendered by him and his wife, and on the other,
the king himself, who had just made him a grant of a pitcher
of wine daily, appointed him to a fixed and remunerative
post. In June, Chaucer was made comptroller of the
customs and subsidy of wools, skins, and hides in the Port
of London. His duties, it is true, were heavy. He had
to keep in his own handwriting the account-books of his
office, and had to be always in attendance, except when
engaged on the king's service elsewhere. There were,
however, some compensations inherent to the post: he
was for instance granted, soon after his appointment,
the whole of a fine worth about £800 paid by a certain
J. Kent, who had sent some wool to Dordrecht without
paying the duty. Although " the secret business of the
king," as already shown, often called him away during the
four years which followed his appointment, he became
nevertheless, through it, closely connected with the City of
London. He had returned a grown-up man to the surroundings of his childhood. In the same year, 1374, he

[1] *Œuvres de Froissard*, ed. Kervyn de Lettenhove, Bruxelles,
1869, tom. viii. p. 383.

took up a house situated above the fortified gate of Aldgate, the lease of which was granted him by the corporation for the term of his life.   It was here, no doubt, that he wrote his translation of the *De Consolatione* of Boethius, and his unfinished allegory of the *House of Fame*, where we get a description of him returning straight home, after his hard work at the office, to bury himself in his beloved books; here also that, later on, he composed his *Parlement of Foules* and his great poem of *Troilus and Criseyde*.[1] Pampered by Edward III., who in 1375 granted him the profitable guardianship of two orphans, Chaucer enjoyed unchecked prosperity throughout the inglorious years in which his royal patron gave himself up to senile excesses, and retained his worldly advantages after the latter's death, on June the 21st, 1377.   Neither the troubled times of Richard II.'s minority, nor the plagues, nor the terrible peasant rising of 1381, seem to have affected his fortune any more than his equanimity.

The old king once dead, Chaucer was not long in winning the favour of his grandson, helped no doubt by the Duke of Lancaster, who was then all-powerful.   Our poet was a wary courtier.   He flattered Richard II. by writing his *Parlement of Foules*, which is an allegory of the young king's betrothal to Anne of Bohemia, daughter of the Emperor Charles IV.   That was in 1381.   Chaucer ingratiated himself thereby with the new queen.   Was it as a reward that he obtained in May 1382, over and above his first post, the office of comptroller of the petty customs in the port of London, a real sinecure, for he was allowed to exercise it by deputy?   Queen Anne, who is well known

[1] *Troilus* was formerly thought anterior to the *House of Fame*. Mr. Lowes has recently shown that it was very probably written last, in 1382.   (*Publ. Mod. Lang. Assocn.* 23, p. 285.)

for having introduced into England the fashions of the
Continent—the sharply-pointed poleine shoes, the high and
crescent-shaped hennins, the dresses with long trains—
combined with this fancy for eccentric luxury, a taste for
sentimental poetry. She admired in Chaucer's verse the
tender passages, and disapproved of the satire upon women,
which under the influence of Jean de Meung and Boccaccio,
he had introduced into his *Romaunt of the Rose* and *Troilus
and Criseyde*. It was very likely in 1385 that she invited
the poet to redeem his sins by writing the *Seintes Legende
of Cupide*. Chaucer at once set to work on his *Legend of
Good Women*, to which he wrote a pretty prologue, where,
under the guise of allegory, he indulged in eulogies of the
queen, and softly whispered to the young king some useful
advice of wisdom and clemency. We have a right to
surmise that the grateful queen had something to do with
the favour granted to the poet on February the 17th,
1385: he was henceforth allowed to fill by deputy his
principal office of comptroller of the customs of wools,
skins, and hides. This was a respite he had long yearned
for, and the day when he got it must have been one of the
happiest of his life. This favour was closely followed by
a fresh distinction, for in 1386 he was selected a knight
of the shire of Kent, and in this capacity sat in parliament
from October 1 to November 1.

This month of October marked both the climax and the
collapse of his public career. The parliament in which he
sat proceeded vigorously against the Duke of Lancaster's
party, and demanded of the king that the duke should be
stripped of his power. A council of regency, composed
of eleven members, was appointed, at the head of which
was Gloucester, Richard's other uncle, and the political
enemy of Lancaster. Thus deprived of his power in

England, Gaunt left on an expedition to Portugal, during
which time his followers were persecuted.   In 1386, Chaucer
lost one after the other his two offices of comptroller.   All
that was left to him of past royal favours was his pension
and that of his wife, the latter however failing him in the
following year, probably through Philippa's death.   In
these reduced circumstances Chaucer was forced to borrow
on his pension, and even to have it transferred to a pressing
creditor.   All that remained to him was the pension of
£10 per annum, which the Duke of Lancaster had been
paying to him ever since 1374.

We do not know whether it was before or after the loss
of his offices, that Chaucer first conceived the idea of
writing the *Canterbury Tales*.   The critics are agreed that
he must have begun them either in 1385 or in 1386.   But
there is little doubt that his compulsory estrangement
from public affairs was all to the advantage of the great
poem, which grew apace during these years of enforced
leisure.   Chaucer had given up his house in Aldgate in
1386, and it is surmised that he went and lived in the
country, at Greenwich, on the pilgrims' road from London
to Canterbury, where there is proof that he was still living
seven years later.   This penurious retreat, however, was
not to his taste.   His private reverses caused him anxiously
to watch events at court, and opened his eyes to the evils
from which the country suffered, although he does not
seem to have heeded them much until then.   Like many
others, he hoped great things of the day when Richard,
a minor no longer, would throw off Gloucester's tyrannical
tutelage, and take the reins of state into his own hands.
Suddenly, on the 3rd May 1389, Richard made up his
mind to this.   Chaucer encouraged or congratulated him
(we do not know which) in an undated ballad, where the

sufferings of England are ascribed to instability. In the
envoy he made a direct appeal to Richard—

> Shew forth thy swerd of castigacioun,
> Dred God, do law, love truthe and worthinesse,
> And wed thy folk agein to stedfastnesse.
>
> *Lak of Stedfastnesse.*

Richard, for the space of a few years, proved true to the
hopes centred in him. Fortune smiled again on the poet.
Gloucester was set aside; Lancaster returned to England,
and as early as July, Chaucer was appointed clerk of the
king's works, which implied the superintendence of some
of the king's palaces and manors, a post moreover which
he was allowed to fill by deputy. And, to top the medley
of offices held by the poet during his life, the Earl of March
appointed him, in 1391, sub-forester of the Forest of North
Petherton, in the county of Somerset.

But " stedfastnesse " alas! was the thing which England
was destined most to lack during the reign of Richard II.,
and Chaucer's private career was bound to be affected
by the royal caprice and extravagance. In the summer of
1391, he lost, without any apparent cause, his superintendence of the king's manors, and found himself once
more in straitened circumstances. He got his friend,
the poet Scogan, to solicit the king on his behalf, and
obtained, on February 28th, 1394, a pension of £20 per
annum for life. But the finances of England were in a
lamentable state, and the annuity was not paid regularly.
We see the poet forced to borrow constantly from the
exchequer, sometimes even insignificant sums. His
financial difficulties continued to increase. Twice in 1398
writs were issued against him by a certain Isabella Buckholt,
and twice he failed to appear. The wary poet had secured
from the king letters of protection against his creditors,

which explains the sheriff's placid " non inventus." Just
about this time, his great patron John of Gaunt died, and
Chaucer was thus left without resources. But the usurpation of the throne by the son of John of Gaunt, Henry of
Lancaster, in October 1399, saved him. He tendered to
the new sovereign a *Compleint to his Empty Purse*, where
he entreated " the conquerour of Brutes Albioun " . . .
" verray king," " by lyne and free eleccioun " . . . to
" have mind upon his supplicacioun! " In answer,
Henry IV. assured him a pension of £26, over and above
the £20 which Edward III. had once granted him. The
old poet then rented a house situated in the garden of
the Chapel of St. Mary, near Westminster Abbey. But
he had no time to enjoy his revenues or his new dwelling.
He died on the 25th October 1400, and was buried in the
neighbouring abbey, the first to occupy " the poet's
corner " in that great national Pantheon.

This rapid summary of the last fourteen years of
Chaucer's life, exclusively based on the official documents
where his financial vicissitudes are recorded, runs the risk
of making this part of his career appear more sombre
than it really was. His greatest work, the one most
replete with joy, was written during that time, and the
satisfaction of having found his true genius at last, the
frankly comical turn of many of the stories in which his
fancy delighted, consoled him no doubt for many reverses.
Poetry is a great comforter, and Chaucer had undoubtedly
a rich supply of practical philosophy. Even in the pieces
where he complains loudly of his poverty, he slips in
a joke which allays our anxieties. Even in those where
he declares that, disappointed with this life, his spirit
henceforth will only look heavenward, he threads together

popular images and quaint sayings, which prove that the source of joviality was not dried up in him.[1]

Moreover, he does not seem to have had a lonely old age. His wife was dead, but his children remained, although we do not know how many they were nor anything about them. Perhaps the Thomas Chaucer who had such a brilliant career under the Lancasters, and died full of wealth and honours in 1434, was one of them. In any case, we can name with certainty that " little Lowis his sone," aged eleven in 1391, and for whose education Chaucer wrote his astronomical Treatise of the *Astrolabe*. Further, if Chaucer had fewer friends at court, he had more admirers and disciples around him, who treated him both as a master and as a father. " Moral John Gower " alone, on account of his age and the bulk of his work, associated with Chaucer on equal terms, and professed for him a friendship disturbed at times, it is true, by some literary disagreements and perhaps a little jealousy. But Henry Scogan, John Clanvowe, Thomas Usk, the author of the *Testament of Love* (*c.* 1387), hailed respectfully the ageing poet. Lydgate and Occleve, the two young men who were destined to make a bid for his poetical inheritance, approached him with pious reverence, and doubtless anticipated by sundry signs of admiration, the many laudatory verses, with which they were soon to honour his memory. John Shirley kept his ears wide open, and collected all those particulars concerning the poet's work, which enrich the copy that he made of them in the following century. From that time on, it was understood that Chaucer was Venus's " owne clerk " (Gower), " the noble philosophical poete in Englissh," who " in goodnes of gentyl manlyche speche . . . in wytte and in good reason

[1] *Truth.*

of sentence . . . passeth al other makers " (Thomas Usk).
His fame, no longer insular, had reached even France,
whose metres he had so clearly imitated in his early poetry.
At a date as yet unsettled, but probably in 1386, Eustache
Deschamps, although he only knew Chaucer as the " grand
translateur," addressed him a pompous ballad, where he
praised the one who had " illumined the kingdom of Æneas,"
i.e. England. We should remember these tributes of
praise (not the most touching, nor the most enthusiastic
he was to receive), because, being the earliest to be proffered
him, they must have cheered and comforted the old poet
during the closing years of his life, when he was often in
want and may be in bad health.

II

Before passing from such a dry biographical sketch to the
study of the poet's work, one would like to outline his
character. But the documents which have reached us are
so few and contain so little information, that unfortunately
our description of him can only be conjectural.

The known facts tend to show that he lived a busy
and varied life, being in turn a page, a squire, a diplomat,
a government official (and what widely differing offices
he held—customs, roads, buildings, forests!). He mixed
with soldiers, with the citizens and merchants of the city;
he had dealings with foreigners in Flanders, in France, and
in Italy. He must have been a clever negotiator, to judge
by the frequent missions entrusted to him. A clever
courtier as well, for the sole merit of his verse could hardly
explain the enduring favour, which he enjoyed at court.

His good fortune was envied later by his disciple Lydgate
in less favoured times: he marvelled at the " prudent "
Chaucer, who, not less favoured than Virgil in Rome, or
Petrarch in Florence, owed to the liberalities of the great,
" vertuous suffysance." [1]   Prudence, or tact if one prefers
it, must indeed have had something to do with his prosperity.   Chaucer succeeded in winning for himself and in
keeping all his life, the protection, one might almost say
the friendship, of John of Gaunt.   The old king Edward III.
appreciated and loved him.   Capricious Richard II. gave
him as constant a patronage as he was capable of, and,
notwithstanding, the usurper Henry IV. took him into
favour from the time of his accession.   Women, naturally
partial to the poet of love, seem to have been particularly
kind to him.   There is every likelihood that the Duchess
Blanche of Lancaster and Queen Anne of Bohemia were
instrumental in obtaining many of the privileges he enjoyed.

It seems pretty evident moreover, that the success of
his courtly career was in no wise impeded by excessive
scruples.   In the dissolute courts where he spent most of
his life, he easily accommodated himself to the prevailing
atmosphere of gallantry.   We cannot say if it was in earnest
or only to follow out a poetical convention like Machaut,
that, forgetting his own wife, he made love to some irre-
sponsible beauty.[2]   And, no doubt, we cannot infer anything from that enigmatic document which represents a
certain Cecilia Champaigne as withdrawing, on the 1st
May 1380, a complaint lodged by her against Chaucer
" de raptu suo."   It is quite unnecessary to imagine here
one of those offences tried *in camera*.   The abduction of

---

[1] *Fall of Princes*, quoted in *Five Hundred Years of Chaucer Criticism
and Allusion* (in the press), by C. Spurgeon, p. 41.
[2] *Compleynte unto Pite.*

minors, in order to secure the administration of their estate, or to force them into a desired marriage, was common in those days. But there is no doubt of Chaucer's readiness to praise, according to the need of the moment, love that was virtuous or love that was not; we find him one day writing a prayer to the Virgin, at the request of the good Duchess Blanche of Lancaster, and the next praising some princely sinner, whose infringement of the marriage law had caused a scandal. That illicit love was the subject of his *Compleynt of Mars* seems evident, and equally obvious is the sympathy evinced in this poem for Mars and Venus at the expense of Vulcan. A plausible tradition, preserved by Shirley, who is usually well informed, reveals the facts of the case. This poem is said by him to have been written " at the comandement of the renomed and excellent Prynce my lord the Duc John of Lancastre," the accomplices being the Duchess of York and the Count of Huntingdon. Now, the duchess was the sister-in-law and Huntingdon was to become the son-in-law of John of Gaunt. The poem thus explained, shows absolute cynicism on the part of John of Gaunt, and extreme complaisance or moral indifference on the part of the poet. We have already seen how easily Chaucer could, at the bidding of Queen Anne, pass from the *Romaunt of the Rose* or the perfidy of Criseyde to a legend in honour of good women. In a word, the subject and tone of his verse often exhibit a clever adaptation to the reigning taste. He was quick to sin and quick to repent. His aim was to please and not to edify.

Moreover, he never claimed a more exalted role, and there was never in him the slightest trace of the pharisee. He was an easy-going man, the recipient of many pensions and lucrative posts, who, for a long time, lived a varied

and somewhat improvident life. He makes no pretence
about it, and is the first to confess that his " abstinence is
lyte." [1]   And yet many of his poems reflect a warm and
apparently sincere piety. This incongruity is to be met
with often enough, and we need not wonder at it.   Indeed
he need be a clever analyst who would exactly gauge
Chaucer's religious feelings, for they probably kept changing
from year to year and almost from hour to hour.   There
were varying moments in the day when he made fun of the
Mendicant Friars, when he prayed with fervour, by preference to the Virgin Mary, when his sly humour did not
spare even the gospels, or when he felt sick of the world
and looked heavenward.   It is probable that he was about
as much of a free-thinker as was possible in his day, living
without restraint, but not without remorse, lingering for
many years in the primrose path, and after a contrite old
age reaching the pious end to which his disciples have
testified.

   In order to get a glimpse of his features, we must collect
all the personal notations scattered through his work.
But we must be careful at the same time not to take too
seriously revelations, which sometimes smack of literary
convention, and sometimes are largely humorous.   To
start with, it should be noticed that he only began speaking
about himself when he was in mature age.   We have no
safe indication of what he was like in his youth.   When
writing to his friend Scogan in 1393, he points humorously
to his hoar head and round shape, as likely indeed to assure
him quick success in love! [2]   A few years earlier, when he
was nearing fifty, he causes himself to be unceremoniously
addressed by the pilgrims' guide, the innkeeper Master
Harry Bailly, who scoffed both at his corpulence and at

[1] *House of Fame*, l. 660.   [2] *Lenvoy de Chaucer a Scogan.*

his gloomy looks. The host is looking for a new teller of tales—

> And than at erst he loked upon me,
> And seyde thus: " What man artow? " quod he;
> " Thou lokest as thou woldest finde an hare,
> For ever upon the ground I see thee stare.
>
> Approche neer, and loke up merily.
> Now war yow, sirs, and lat this man have place;
> He in the waast is shape as wel as I;
> This were a popet in an arm t'enbrace
> For any womman, smal and fair of face.
> He semeth elvish by his contenaunce,
> For unto no wight dooth he daliaunce." [1]

Thus, Master Harry Bailly's first impression of the poet is that he is unfit for love. But what strikes him and surprises us, is that the poet had a vacant and abstracted look, from which one could apparently expect no kind of drollery. When at last he allows him to speak, the host expresses his fears in a few ironical words—

> " Now shul we here
> Som deyntee thing, me thinketh by his chere." [2]

The creator of the Wife of Bath must therefore have had in everyday life some resemblance to Molière, who was inclined to be silent and melancholy.

Elsewhere, Chaucer lays emphasis on his silent disposition and taste for solitude. He has said that when he came out of his office at the Customs, after finishing his accounts, he hurried home without talking to any one, not even inquiring after his nearest neighbours, and shut himself up with his books, so that he might well have been taken for a hermit.[3] He says in another place that reading was a passion with him; he loved and revered books, the

---

[1] *C. T.* (B. ll. 1884-1894).　　[2] *Ibid.* ll. 1900-1901.
[3] *H. of F.* ll. 652-660.

only witnesses we have of things gone by. It was only on holidays, and more especially in May, when flowers renew their bloom, that he could tear himself away from his books. Then the love of nature would fill his heart, and he would remain for hours, stretched on the grass, gazing at the daisy, which opens in the morning and shuts up again at sunset.

> And, as for me, though that my wit be lyte,
> On bokes for to rede I me delyte
> And in myn herte have hem in reverence;
> And to hem yeve swich lust and swich credence,
> That ther is wel unethe game noon
> That from my bokes make me to goon,
> But hit be other upon the haly-day,
> Or elles in the Ioly tyme of May;
> Whan that I here the smale foules singe,
> And that the floures ginne for to springe,
> Farwel my studie, as lasting that sesoun!
>
> *The Legend of Good Women*, ll. 29-40.

This lover of solitude does not seem to tally with the clever and adaptable court-poet. Can the man with vacant eyes, meditative tastes and reserved manner, be the same as the one who made his way so well amongst the great? There is at any rate, in those parts of his works where he speaks of himself, one recurring trait, which might throw some light on his worldly success. He was one of those who turn their own wit against themselves, who forestall disdain and mockery by representing themselves as small, insignificant, and even a trifle ridiculous. He is so modest in his pretensions, so given to self-effacement that no one takes umbrage at him. It requires some penetration to see through this modesty and to realise the subtle mockery at work behind it, aimed sometimes at the person he is speaking to, and sometimes at

human conceit in general. Those who do not see beyond
his humility, praise him for it and are inclined to patronise
this naive and inoffensive being. The others, who are
wiser, enjoy his subtle humour and are disarmed by his
charm. In any case, Chaucer invariably painted himself
in this way, which was not quite novel, since many instances
of it can be found in Machaut, his master, and in most of
the *trouvères*, for it had come down from a time when
the peaceful narrator, being a man of low birth, was forced
to propitiate rough and haughty patrons. It was necessary
to efface one's self in proportion to the praise one gave
them. Chaucer represents himself as slow-witted, easily
frightened, having little desire for knowledge or power.
Naturally enough, he is to be found amongst ill-treated and
unsuccessful, nay amongst bashful lovers. If he woos
Cupid, he is treated with disdain, and he gives as his
reason for not waiting on the god, that he is too old and
too heavy. He knows nothing of love except through his
books, and he sings of it without having experienced it.
Neglected by the god of Love, all that is left to him is to
plead for more fortunate gallants. He has been married
certainly, but has suffered so much that he is not likely
to be caught again. If he writes a poem, it is to order
and as a penance. Moreover, he is but a small poet and
knows it. Others have gathered the harvest and reaped
the grain; he can but glean after them. And so Chaucer
goes on in this half-mocking spirit, from the beginning to
the end of his writings, and what was at first perhaps
but a traditional literary attitude, seems to have become
in the end a part of his very nature.

Of his faults, he spoke at length himself, but we must
go to others if we want to hear of his virtues, for he had
some. His goodness and indulgence were great. If his

disciples, Occleve and Lydgate, exalted the poet, they also, in the course of their copious and common-place verses, lamented the man in terms of unmistakable sincerity. Their admiration was not a kind of official and distant worship.   A real affection bound the pupils to the " maister deere, and fadir reverent." [1]   It is touching to see Occleve representing himself as the thick-headed pupil of an excellent master:

> My dere maistir—god his soule quyte!
> And fadir, Chaucer, fayn wolde han me taght;
> But I was dul, and lerned lite or naght.[2]

Lydgate depicts him as the tolerant corrector of the verse submitted to him—

> For he that was gronde of wel seying
> In al hys lyf hyndred no making,
> My maister Chaucer that founde ful many spot
> Hym liste not pinche nor gruche at every blot
> Nor meue hymsilf to perturbe his *reste*,
> I haue herde telle, but saide alweie the best
> Suffring goodly of his gentilnes
> Ful many thing embracid with rudness.[3] . . .

These conversations had a spice of humour in them.   If his disciples expressed regret that the *Legend of Good Women* should be left unfinished, Chaucer would say to them (his answer suggests itself through Lydgate's explanations) that he would have liked to have found nineteen women perfect in goodness and beauty,

> But for his labour and his lesynesse
> Was inportable his wittes to encoumbre,
> In al this world to fynde so great noumbre.[4]

[1] Hoccleve, *The Regement of Princes*, quoted by Miss Spurgeon, *op. cit.* p. 21.   [2] *Ibid.*

[3] Lydgate, *The hystorye, Sege, and dystruccyon of Troye, v.* Spurgeon, *op. cit.* p. 25.

[4] Lydgate, *Fall of Princes, v.* Spurgeon, *op. cit.* p. 39.

Lydgate treasured the memory of these indications of sly mischief and humour. Occleve remembered only his goodness, and little by little Chaucer became transformed in his mind into a philosopher full of wisdom, a pious poet, almost into a saint. He still retained this impression when, twelve years after his master's death, he had the margin of his copy of *The Regement of Princes* illuminated with the only authentic portrait of Chaucer which we possess. The image of the master, he said, was still fresh and present to his mind, and he wished to fix it for the benefit of those who might have forgotten it. There he stands before us, a grave and venerable old man; it is Chaucer towards the close of his days, during the short period of piety which seems to have marked the end of his life, the Chaucer who wrote the *Balade of Truth* and compiled the *Persones Tale*. He is clad in black robes and wears a hood; his left hand holds a rosary and his quill-case hangs on his chest. The right arm and forefinger are stretched out, as if he were teaching. The hair, moustache, and two tufts of beard give a white setting to a face, the weary sadness of which is its outstanding feature, mingled with an air of timidity and good nature. Yet, there can be seen (it is not imaginary and due to the remembrance of his verse) in the half-closed eye and in the somewhat strained line of the mouth, just a touch of half-extinguished mischievous humour.

It must be confessed that by thus collecting together these scattered traits of the man's character, we are forced to piece together some which seem not only opposed, but almost irreconcilable. There are so few precise data to go upon, that one despairs of discovering amongst these different Chaucers, the courtier, the poet, the philosopher, the pious, the profane, the astute, the clumsy, the venerable

—which was the real one. But we must first of all take into account that some of these discrepancies are due to the fact that he is presented to us at widely differing periods of his life. Moreover, he who surveys his work as a whole, will see that these contradictions were probably the man himself, for this work, which after all is based on his very nature, is precisely made up of the same oppositions. Does not the chief originality of his tales consist in the alternation of poetry and realism, gravity and jolliness, just as doubtless they alternated in his life and in his character?

III

Before leaving his biography, there is one last question to be asked, for the answer may serve to throw a little more light upon his character. What traces has the history of his time left in his work? The events amongst which he lived seem at a distance, to have been diverse and tragic enough, for us to expect to find them abundantly commemorated in his verse.

The sixty years of Chaucer's life, between 1340 and 1400, cover two periods of English history of almost equal length, and different from each other as black from white. In his youth, he witnessed an uninterrupted series of victories and conquests, together with a patriotic exaltation such as his country had never before experienced. He was born, so to speak, to the sound of the bells which rang out the naval victory of Sluyce. As a child, he must have been told the story of Crécy and Nevil's Cross, when France and Scotland, the two great enemies of England, were together trodden under foot by the mighty Edward III.

He was a mere youth, on the eve of taking arms himself, when the Black Prince triumphed at Poitiers, and through many a long year he must have seen the splendid captivity in London of King Jean le Bon, who had been taken prisoner in that battle. All these wars, the vicissitudes of which fill the *Chronicles of Froissart*, and in which the valour and martial discipline of the English made their name dreaded throughout France, took place whilst he was growing up from youth to manhood.

But from 1369 onwards, the picture changes rapidly. The formidable Edward III. is but a senile monarch, the doting slave of the rapacious Alice Ferrers. His heir presumptive, that great and fierce captain, the Black Prince, is slowly sinking into a premature grave. In the course of eight years, from the breaking of the treaty of Bretigny to the truce of Bruges (1369-1378), almost the whole of France was freed from the English yoke. This rapid loss of such brilliant conquests showed plainly the vanity of the exploits which preceded them. Edward III. died in 1377, and after him things became even worse. His surviving sons quarrelled amongst themselves for the guardianship of the child of twelve who held the crown. Disorder and exactions reached such a point that formidable risings occurred, similar to the French *Jacquerie*, less brutal perhaps, but all the more dangerous. This upheaval of the down-trodden peasantry threatened the government of the land, imperilled all property, and even, it would seem, civilisation itself. At the same time, a religious schism divided the country: the preaching of the Lollards was weakening the discipline of the church, but the new movement was not strong enough yet to set up in its place a new organisation. England, who but a while before was mistress of the sea and of part of the Continent, was now paralysed; her coasts were attacked and her territory violated by foreign raiders. When the young Richard II., in 1389, took in his own hands the reins of power, the evil seemed checked for a few years, but it broke out afresh in an aggravated form. Capricious, wasteful, tyrannical, Richard ruined his kingdom, and by degrees turned the whole nation against him. Finally, plunder and outrages reached such a point that the feelings of loyalty died out: the legitimate king was deposed and shortly after put to death. The crown passed to his cousin Henry of Lancaster, and under his firm rule the wounds of the stricken kingdom were to be healed. But Chaucer went down to his grave immediately after Henry's accession and only saw of his reign the crime from which it started.

Chaucer was not only a witness of these troubled times, he also played an active if modest part in the military and diplomatic events. He was closely attached to some of those who were then making history. His worldly interests and his sympathies as a man forced him to watch politics closely. The rare documents, which persevering inquiries have gathered concerning his life, show us plainly how intimately his personal history was bound up with that of his country and of those who directed its destinies. Now what strikes one first, when passing from the poet's biography to the study of his works, is the scantiness of the allusions the latter contain to the events which he witnessed or took part in. Chaucer must have had a close view of what seems to us at a distance the essential history of his times. But curiously enough, he hardly says anything about it. There is no reference made to it not only in his romantic verse, but also in that which is most strikingly realistic.

To start with, there is not a single patriotic line in his work, which is all the more surprising at a time when this feeling was beginning to rise with some force in English hearts, in turn buoyed up by victories and chastened by misfortunes. It had expressed itself in a mixture of bombast and insult directed against England's enemies, Scotland and France, in the warlike songs of *Laurence Minot*, written in Chaucer's early youth. This alliterating *Tyrtæus* had celebrated in stirring terms practically every success of Edward III. In his opinion, the French and the Scotch were hateful and ridiculous beings, only capable of treachery and cowardice. He hurled at them his weighty sarcasms. His verse, with its robust rhythm and rhyme, must have run from mouth to mouth. Nothing of the kind is to be discovered in Chaucer. And yet he might have found it useful, in order to ingratiate himself at court, to sing in his turn the victorious king. But no; the sole allusion he has to the battlefields of the great national war, is contained in one line describing the young pilgrim squire, who

> had been somtyme in chivachye,
> In Flaundres, in Artoys, and Picardye,
> And born him wel, as of so litel space,
> In hope to stonden in his lady grace.
> Prologue to the *Canterbury Tales*, ll. 85-88.

By the side of this squire, we do see a yeoman, his servant, described as a perfect bowman, but without a word being said as to the part he played in the famous combats, where the English archers distinguished themselves.

As for France, is it remarkable that Chaucer never speaks of her as of a country at war with his own? He has for her but words which testify to his poetical relationship; he loves and translates or imitates her writers, and does not mind acknowledging his debt on occasion. Wars had little interest for him, and if he represents a soldier of his day, he makes him fight far away, in eastern countries, either because the names of those regions are stranger and more suggestive to the imagination, or because he prefers to the national warrior a denationalised hero, less English than Christian. This is the case of the Knight in his Tales, who is a worthy rival of John of Bohemia or of Pierre de Lusignan, both celebrated by Machaut. There are few known countries he has not visited. He seems to have been fighting for some forty years already when Chaucer introduces him to us, but we do not see clearly whether he was at Crécy or at Poitiers. Chaucer's silence is all the more significant in that French poetry, at that time, was becoming rather aggressive: Deschamps' eulo- gistic ballad was addressed to Chaucer between two utterances of anger against the English.

Chaucer did not show much more interest in the reverses and internal troubles of his country, than he did in her triumphs. Of the terrible plagues that desolated her during his life-time, he only speaks incidentally and in no serious way: the physician, who appears amongst his pilgrims, made his money, he says, during one of them; in the *Pardoner's Tale* it is simply stated that death killed thousands of people at the time of the previous epidemic, and moreover the scene is laid in Flanders. But nowhere is there the least semblance to that powerful picture of the pestilence, painted by Boccaccio at the beginning of the *Decameron*, not even to the rhymed account of a con- temporary plague, given by Machaut in his *Jugement du Roi de Navarre*.

The peasant rising made no impression on him either. Not to mention the too widely different Langland, the poet

Gower, Chaucer's friend and rival, devoted a whole Latin poem to an allegory of this fierce revolt, and expressed in it the terrors he had experienced. Chaucer only makes a jocose allusion to Jack Straw and his hordes and to the shrill cries they uttered when they were about to kill a Fleming, and this by way of an illustration to help us to understand the hue and cry raised in a farmyard after a thieving fox.

IV

But if we collect together and scrutinise the rare contemporary allusions to be found in Chaucer's works, and if we note at the same time what subjects he avoids, we feel growing within us the conviction that both silences and allusions might in some way have been caused by a desire to please his patron John of Gaunt. The great lord and the poet his client, were partners in the same game. It is of course impossible to say in what measure the poet's attitude was dictated by his wish to ingratiate himself, or reflected the sincere feelings of a supporter who had no need to be convinced. In any case, one vaguely feels that if it were possible to realise the duke's policy and make out his character, one would at once better understand Chaucer, whose fortune at all times rose and fell with that of his patron.

Unfortunately John of Gaunt remains an enigma. His actions are well enough known, but it is the interpretation to be put upon them which leaves room for endless argument. Despite very conscientious researches, Mr. Armitage Smith, his most recent biographer,[1] has failed to make him

John of Gaunt, by S. Armitage Smith.   Constable, 1904.

out.   There was too much contradiction from the first
in his character.   According to the chroniclers one reads,
he appears as a gallant and wise prince, or as a scheming
traitor.   On the one hand, there is evoked the figure of a
very noble lord, the eloquent mouthpiece of reason and
patriotism, as afterwards represented by Shakespeare in
Richard II.; he it is on whose lips he puts the redundant
panegyric of England—

> this sceptred isle,
> This earth of Majesty, this seat of Mars,
> This other Eden, demi-paradise;
> This fortress, built by nature for herself,
> Against infection and the hand of war;
> This happy breed of men, this little world;
> This precious stone set in the silver sea. . . .
>
> *King Richard II.* Act ii. Sc. 1.

On the other hand, and very early, he is painted as a great
criminal, rapacious and double-faced, plotting against the
life of his nephew, the young king, in order to seize the
throne, ruining England in order to aggrandise his house,
and in addition sunk in vice and debauchery.   Sometimes,
the contradiction comes from the fact that the chronicler
is for or against the Lancastrian dynasty.   But the chief
reason is to be found in the relations of John of Gaunt
with the religious reformer Wyclif, whom he took under
his protection.   The later Reformation will be partial
to " the first protestant," and this partiality will naturally
lead to the Shakespearian glorification.   The orthodox, on
the contrary, will look upon him as an emissary of Satan,
and the " odium theologicum " will pour down on him
in the *Chronicle of the Monk of St. Albans.*   So that one
does not know exactly where apotheosis and where
calumny begin.

His moral personality escapes us between such excesses

of honour and of obloquy. We have only his actions to judge him by, and they themselves are deceptive, often contradictory. His whole life was equivocal: he was divided between his egotism as a powerful feudal lord, the master of huge landed estates, and the part he had to play for many years as acting head of the English government. More than once his patriotism was in conflict with his interests. It is probable that he unconsciously directed royal politics along the lines which his personal ambitions favoured. Without being aware that he was betraying his mandate, he used the English forces to further his designs and to conquer either for himself or for his daughters the kingdoms of Castile and Portugal. If, after conducting personally some plundering but fruitless expeditions in France, he became after 1374 the staunch supporter of a reconciliation with her, it was perhaps both in order to put an end to a hopeless war, and to have his hands free, that he might carry on his wars in Spain and Portugal.

His government at home was likewise a mixture of good and evil. He was no doubt the most unpopular man of his day, up to the time when the follies and despotism of Richard diverted public anger from John of Gaunt to the king himself. He haughtily rejected the demands of parliament for administrative reforms. When the men of Kent made a rush on London and the court, it was John of Gaunt whom they made responsible for all the evil; he whom Wat Tyler and his followers singled out for vengeance, and their fury was only satisfied when they had, not looted, but utterly destroyed the duke's magnificent palace, the Savoy. It is nevertheless to the influence of this same enemy of the public good that we must attribute, so it seems, the few happy years of Richard's personal government, which ended with Gaunt's disgrace.

Was he loyal to his nephew? The royal child was but
eleven when he became his chief guardian. Time and
again he was suspected of plotting against his life for the
sake of his crown. The accusation, sometimes only whispered, sometimes cried aloud, was continually renewed.
John of Gaunt always succeeded in clearing himself and
in regaining the confidence of the sovereign. When he
died, he had seemingly conquered this suspicion, but he
was hardly in his grave, when his own son justified all
the calumnies by dethroning and putting to death the
legitimate king.

His attitude in religious matters is just as puzzling. He
was Wyclif's great protector, used him as a weapon against
the bishops who aspired to political predominance, and
was looked upon as the scourge of orthodoxy, the sworn
adversary of the established clergy. Yet he never had
at any time the least sympathy with the doctrinal reform
of Wyclif. What is more, he himself never carried out
any of the disciplinary innovations urged by Wyclif. He
maintained plurality of livings in his own domains; he
was surrounded by friar-confessors; he had masses said
for souls in Purgatory; he protected monks and endowed
abbeys; he founded chantries; he had his enemies excom-
municated whenever he could; he dictated with a perfectly
clear mind the most traditionally orthodox will, giving
instructions that ten large candles should be lighted round
his body, in commemoration of the ten commandments
which he had broken; above these ten candles, were to
be placed seven more, in memory of the seven works of
charity and the seven capital sins; above these again, five
candles in honour of the five wounds of Jesus and of his
five senses; and " tout amont " three more " en l'honneur
de la benoite Trinité." Finally, this so-called Lollard

founded a line of fiercely orthodox princes, who persecuted the Lollards to the point of complete extermination.

In his private life assuredly there was no trace of the moral purity, practised and taught by the Lollards. Chaucer, it is true, bears an unimpeachable testimony to the great affection of John of Gaunt for his first wife, and to his violent grief at her death. But he was no sooner a widower, than he made a mistress of one of the ladies of honour of the late duchess, and to further his ambitions, he at the same time married Constance, daughter of Peter the Cruel. When later Constance died, he scandalised his country by marrying his mistress and making his bastards legitimate. Is the persistent calumny of his enemies responsible for the report that, in a corrupt court, his morals were such as to mark him out as a debauchee? At his death, astounding rumours were in circulation. His body, ruined by excesses, had rapidly decayed, and this was caused " per exercitum copulæ cardinalis cum mulieribus. . . . Magnus enim fornicator fuit."

Apart from his dissolute life, of which there seems to be pretty ample proof, we know nothing of his character, except what is revealed by two very similar expressions of Froissart and Chaucer. They refer to his mind rather than to his heart. Froissart, who is not generally prone to praise him, calls him " sage et imaginatif," that is to say, " resourceful." Chaucer, a more partial but surely a shrewd judge, shows him in the midst of a passionate grief

so tretable,
Right wonder skilful and resonable.[1]

It seems probable, indeed, that the father of the prudent and politic Bolingbroke had a good fund of skill and sense.

[1] *B. of the Duchesse*, ll. 553-554.

Contemporary writers were struck by the contrast between
the reserve of John of Gaunt and the impetuous and brutal
nature of his younger brother, Gloucester. On the other
hand, if he did not possess the military genius of the Black
Prince, he never had his fits of savage cruelty. If there
was ambiguity in his nature, there was also balance.

To sum up, a policy of peace and even of alliance with
France by royal marriage, a stubborn opposition to the
popular claims, protection granted to Wyclif less from
religious conviction than a policy, and as a consequence
hostility from the advocates of war, the lower classes, and
the clergy, these are indubitable facts in his career, and
they explain well enough the reticences and disclosures
of Chaucer. We understand better now why the poet was
silent concerning the French war, why he was loth to
mention the great rising of 1381, not wishing to displease
his patron, and perhaps unable fully to approve his conduct
on this occasion. We see also why his satire was chiefly
directed against the clergy, thus endorsing certain of the
accusations of the Lollards, without however going over
to their doctrine. Even small details reveal his association
with the Duke of Lancaster. That Pierre de Lusignan,
for instance, who haunted the poet's thoughts with his
far-away exploits and his tragic death, he may well have
been seen by Chaucer, the court page, in 1361, at the
Savoy Palace, where John of Gaunt entertained the King
of Cyprus with lavish hospitality. If, on one occasion,
Chaucer inveighed against Duguesclin, it was not because
of some episode in the French wars, but because of the part
taken by the French hero in the murder of Pierre le Cruel,
the father of the Duchess Constance and father-in-law
to John of Gaunt. And finally, we shall see presently that
if Chaucer one day broke his habitual reserve and went

so far as to give the king some very bold advice, he did it
probably in order to serve the interests of his patron.

During the parliamentary session, held at Salisbury in
May 1384, John of Gaunt was denounced by a Carmelite
brother as a traitor to the king and as having plotted his
assassination. The scene took place in the room of one
of the king's favourites, the Earl of Oxford, who is suspected of having engineered the accusation. Richard
flew into a passion; without inquiring any further, he
ordered that his uncle should be seized and taken to the
gallows. When he was asked to look more closely into
the matter, he behaved like a lunatic, took off his hat and
shoes and flung them out of the window, and they had
great difficulty in calming him. John of Gaunt succeeded
in clearing himself, but all the same the friar's denunciation
left a sting in the king's mind. A similar accusation was
brought against Gaunt in the council itself, in February
1385, and Richard's mother, the Princess Jeanne (" the
pretty maid of Kent "), needed all her influence to reconcile
uncle and nephew. In the summer of the same year, the
king, with John of Gaunt, went on an expedition into
Scotland, and when John expressed different views from
his on the plan of the campaign, Richard burst into reproaches and accused his uncle of treason. Throughout
the whole of this period, we see the young favourites who
surrounded the young king—he was only nineteen—
doing their best to undermine the credit of the Duke of
Lancaster.

If then, knowing these facts, we read the Prologue of
the *Legend of Good Women*, which Chaucer is generally
thought to have written in 1385, we can see they are translated into a transparent allegory. The poet makes the
Queen Alcestis give some wise counsel to the young god

of love, who personifies Richard.   She warns him against
the bursts of passion to which he is liable, and points out
to him the unfairness of passing a sentence without giving
the culprit a hearing:

> A god ne sholde nat be thus agreved,
> But of his deitee he shal be stable,
>
> .   .   .   .   .
>
> He shall nat rightfully his yre wreke
> Or he have herd the tother party speke.
>
> Prologue A, ll. 321-325.

She dwells on the danger of lending an ear to insinuations.

> Al ne is nat gospel that is to yow pleyned;
> The god of love herth many a tale y-feyned.
> For in your court is many a losengeour,
> And many a queynte totelere accusour,
> That tabouren in your eres many a thing
> For hate, or for Ielous imagining,
> And for to han with you some daliaunce.
> Envye (I prey to God yeve hir mischaunce!)
> Is lavender in the grete court alway.
> For she ne parteth, neither night ne day,
> Out of the hous of Cesar; thus seith Dante;
> Who-so that goth, alwey she moot [nat] wante.
>
> Prologue A, ll. 325-341.

She adjures the god,

> nat be lyk tiraunts of Lumbardye,
> That usen wilfulhed and tyrannye.
>
> Prologue A, ll. 335-336.

Then she describes the duties of a good king: he must
listen to the complaints and petitions of his people, and
rule his lieges with justice.   But she here adds a parenthesis
which, being quite outside the main drift, betrays Chaucer's
real purpose.   Whilst the accused brought before the king
of love is a humble and puny person, the poet himself,

Alcestis insists on the duties of a king towards the lords of his realm:

> And for to kepe his lordes hir degree,
> As hit is right and skilful that they be
> Enhaunced and honoured, and most dere—
> For they ben half-goddes in this world here.
>
> Prologue A, ll. 370-373.

Finally she returns at the end to the offence committed by a prince, who condemns a man without giving him a chance of speaking a single word.

That Chaucer should thus dare to dictate rules of conduct to the king, shows plainly enough that he must have been impelled by a desire to serve his protector, whilst feeling at the same time that he was shielded by him. Moreover, he ranged on his side Queen Anne (represented by Alcestis), well knowing that he was safeguarded by Richard's impetuous affection for her. The allegory enabled him also to keep at a certain distance from actual facts; the serious advice and the daring reproaches which he put in the mouth of the young queen—she was then only seventeen—could hardly have been uttered by a girl of her age; they were much more likely to have come from Princess Jeanne, and to have been spoken with the authority and experience of a mother. In short, Chaucer could not fail to have congratulated himself upon the unique opportunity thus offered him, of prudently serving a cause to which his interest bound him, while at the same time voicing lessons of wisdom by which his country might benefit.

The same compound of pure motives and interested views reappears in all the other verse of Chaucer touching on public affairs. No doubt, under the wretched reign of Richard, he was moved by the country's misfortunes; he

regretted, as we saw, the instability of affairs in England;
he grieved to see that virtue, pity, disinterestedness, were
no longer to be found in the world.   But, whilst adjuring
the monarch to " shew forth the swerd of castigatioun "
against the authors of these evils, it is undeniable that
he was encouraging him at the same time either to free
himself of his favourites or to overthrow Gloucester's
tutelage, all alike hostile to the Lancastrian party, and
consequently injurious to the poet's own interests.   Thus,
even in these discreet audacities, Chaucer remained the
courtier poet.   In the midst of the general misfortune,
he was anxious about the consequences which the mis-
management of public affairs might have on his own
pensions.   Appeals to the Treasury are prominent in his
later ballads (*Fortune*, *Lenvoy to Scogan*).   It was with
a request for money that he hailed the usurpation of the
throne by the son of his great patron.   Elsewhere, his
lament assumed such a general character as to be without
danger for him, but at the same time without possible
effect.   It became, with the help of Boethius, philosophical.
Chaucer took refuge from the moral miseries of the present
in the contemplation of the Golden Age (*The Former
Age*).   He realised that true nobility lies in virtue, when
he saw the vices and crimes which polluted the great
men of this world (*Gentilesse*).   And at the end, on his
death-bed, according to tradition, he invoked " Truth,"
which frees us from evil and consoles us in misfortune;
he turned to heaven and to the future life in order to
escape the bondage of the earth (*Truth*).   And this last
ballad no doubt expresses the inmost wisdom of the court
poet, who found himself forced to keep unbroken silence,
although a spectator of scenes which wounded alike his
moral sense and his good sense.

In short, either because his tastes led him elsewhere, or at the dictates of prudence, Chaucer is almost wholly silent in his poems about what we should call politics.   He avoided the subject, sometimes for artistic reasons, sometimes in order to get a more direct hold of the realities of life, on the humble plane where most of his countrymen spent their days and waged their battles, without troubling themselves overmuch about either kings or governments.

CHAPTER II

I. State of the English Language about 1360. II. Chaucer at the school of the French *trouvères*. III. His lyrical poetry.

I

CHAUCER'S first aim in writing verse, one may even say his sole aim, was poetry for its own sake. He had no wish to influence his contemporaries, nor to pass judgment on political events, nor to reform morals, nor to evolve a system of philosophy. He had set himself an artistic ideal, and knowing how crude were the attempts of his predecessors, he applied himself assiduously to the study of foreign masters. Somewhat late in life, he realised that he had a gift of observation, and straight away turned to the description of the men around him and their doings, not from any desire of bettering them, but simply because he found in life that which amused and interested him. He never had but one ambition, which was to write pretty or humorous verse. And because of that, he spent the greater part of his life in rendering pliable and mellow the rough English tongue, in hammering it into all kinds of metres, in learning the technique of his art. No one can realise the greatness of the task accomplished, who has not read the awkward poetry produced in England before him, or even the poetry of his own time.

It is impossible to exaggerate the importance of his role as the creator of English poetry, or at least of English

44

versification. Except for the octosyllabic verse, which
was already in use, he had to fashion for himself all the
other metres he used. He imported from France and
perfected under Italian influence the decasyllabic verse,
which was to become the heroic verse, the chosen metre
of the great poetry of England. He used it by turns in
stanza form and in couplets; he threw it into moulds
hitherto unknown in England—the rondeau, the virelai,
and the ballad. Of his numerous innovations two were
destined to prevail, the seven-line stanza (a b a b b c c),
to which his name was given, and the couplet. But what
a vast amount of preparatory work, what trials, what
hesitations, must have preceded the finished verses! We
can assume that the whole of his youth and part of his
middle age were spent at this task, the stages of which
we are unable to follow, owing to the loss of almost all his
earlier works.

The difficulty of the undertaking was quite out of
proportion to what it would be in a language already
adapted for poetry. There was nothing of the kind in
England in 1360. No dialect had as yet taken the lead
for literary purposes; there was not even a common
literary language. Whilst the use of English was steadily
extending to all classes throughout the fourteenth century,
and making its way into the schools, the law-courts, and
the parliament, poets were still groping for a proper
medium. John Gower, the contemporary and friend of
Chaucer, bore witness to this uncertainty by writing the
first of his three great poems in French, the second in
Latin, and the third in English. But English was split
up into dialects differing sufficiently from each other to
hamper intercommunication; the differences in vocabulary
and syntax were such as to render a man barely intelligible

to those who did not speak his own dialect. Further, the poetical ear did not derive its enjoyment of verse from the same principles in all dialects; whilst people from Northumbria and the west of England preferred alliteration, whether combined or not with rhyme, those from the centre and south-west favoured and cultivated rhyme alone. The former used an exclusively accentual verse, the latter a verse which was both accentual and syllabic. The first were akin to the native poets before the Norman Conquest; the others followed closely the pattern of French versification. Chaucer, who was one of these latter, did not know how to make " rim, ram, ruf " like the harsh singers of the north, and was therefore divided by an insuperable gulf from the English poets of his time who possessed the most force and vigour. He may have known the fervent and turbid effusions of the author of *Piers Ploughman*, perhaps even the stanzas of the one who wrote the beautiful mystical vision of the *Pearl*, or of him who fashioned the robust descriptions of the *Green Knight*, but he was utterly out of touch with their technique. He was by birth and surroundings confined to the language spoken in the neighbourhood of London, which was then also the language of the court, the " King's English," and which was soon to become, owing largely to his own work, the sole literary language throughout the country.

Indeed, no previous poetical performance had seemed to destine this dialect to such fortune. None was poorer and more barren before Chaucer took it up. What little real poetry had appeared in English since Anglo-Saxon times, had been produced outside the limits of this dialect. Why wonder at it? Was it not in the vicinity of court and of the universities that English had the most humble and precarious existence, always subordinated to Latin

or French?   Kings, nobles, and clerks alike held it in scorn.
French, long the sole language of those who were above
the common herd, had held its own at court later than
elsewhere, as in its natural fortress.   An attempt to
breathe into this dialect a higher poetical life might well
seem foredoomed.   This, nevertheless, was Chaucer's aim
from the first, definite and unswerving.

His attitude, novel in every respect, was as follows.
The courtly poets of his district still wrote in French,
or rather in Anglo-Norman, in that patois into which
the language of the conquerors had degenerated, and
which made the Parisians smile; on the other hand,
popular poets in that same district only used English for
practical purposes and without any thought for beauty;
whereas Chaucer, for his part, deliberately chose this
common tongue, because it alone was really living and
because it had spread up to the higher classes of the people,
but he resolved at the same time to endow it with all the
grace and refinement, which instinct and knowledge enabled
him to appreciate in French poetry.   And, if we grant
him in this a clearer vision of his aims than he really had,
we cannot overrate the consequences of his choice.   He at
once became an accessory to the social forces, which made
London the political and commercial centre, and the
universities the intellectual nuclei of the country;   the
excellence of his writings and their fame helped alike
towards this result.   Undoubtedly, there had been during
the previous three centuries quite a number of poets writing
in the London dialect, but they had little talent; even in
Chaucer's life-time there were poets capable of force or
grace, but they belonged to counties where the dialect was
already archaic and they clung to obsolete poetical modes.
Chaucer had come at the psychological moment, and by

throwing the weight of his genius into the balance decided the future. He was the real " father " of English poetry, inasmuch as he founded the modern literary language of England.

To infuse into the native vocabulary the courtliness of France, was his first and most essential task. He cast the English words of a purely Teutonic origin, and the already acclimatised words of French origin, into the poetical moulds of France. He expressed in English all the graces and delicate shades of meaning which he found in French poetry. His severance from the literary past of England is as clear and as final as his resolve to stand by the particular English of his district. That is why all the primary sources of his poetic art must be looked for in France. They are to be found, not in Anglo-Norman poetry, unimaginative and formless, but in the pure specimens of proper French poetry, which he happened to know.

II

The time was not altogether propitious to his aim, it would seem, for French poetry was never more wretched and destitute than during the period extending from Rutebeuf to Villon, or, if it be preferred, from the *Roman de la Rose* to Charles d'Orléans. What a poor, thin, and yet pretentious garden it is, where we can discover little else to-day but artificial flowers growing between box-hedges of eccentric shapes. It is surprising to compare this lifeless poetry with the rich prose of the same period. Indeed, fourteenth-century French endures from a literary point of view solely through Froissart's *Chronicles*. Yet

it was to this artificial and sickly garden that Chaucer
came for seeds and cuttings.   And it so happened that at
the date when he came, he found at first the most effete
head-gardener.   The poetry of that century only escapes
absolute dullness through the somewhat childish grace of
Froissart's verse, or through the prosiness, occasionally
lively and racy, of Eustache Deschamps.   But Machaut,
their master as well as Chaucer's, is too often just purely
wearisome.   And it seems a strange destiny, which gave
as a pupil to the droning canon of Reims the mischievous
Chaucer, so prone to smile at long-winded affectation and
at stilted lyrical strains.

Lack of deep sentiment and absence of vigorous thought
render Machaut's " dits " insufferable to us—lengthy
debates where, around some point of amorous etiquette, are
woven descriptions in the manner of the *Roman de la Rose,*
and where a story is suggested by means of hackneyed
allegories.   The style is generally intricate, without nerve
or relief; the rhymes already exhibit a tendency, on the
part of the author, towards that false wealth of identical
sounds which ushered in the " conceits " of the " rhétori-
queurs."   Surely, in spite of the initial reverence inspired
by Machaut's past renown and the praise of great princes
and ladies, in spite of the romantic interest thrown over
his old age by the love-affair with pretty, forward, Péronne
d'Armentières, it is difficult nowadays for the reader of his
works, not to resent the drowsy numbness that creeps over
him, while pushing on through the interminable pages of
futile verse.

These are very great blemishes indeed.   But for all that,
Machaut presented an array of delicate qualities, which
would render him attractive and valuable to his foreign
disciple.   He was a musician as well as a poet, and had

a lasting concern for art and harmony. He was a sort
of virtuoso, always in quest of new groupings of verse and
fresh combinations of rhymes. Was he not foremost in
introducing and spreading poems of definite length and
structure, such as the sonnet, the ballad, the rondeau, and
the chant royal? He sought rare poetical forms, capable
of producing as such the emotions which his nature was
too poor to arouse. He could also take up a commonplace
image, develop and adorn it, put it in a pleasing light and
make a gem of it for all time. That is why there are in
his works small poems or passages of longer poems, which
are not lacking in prettiness or brilliancy, and can still please
for a moment. Take, for instance, the eighty-second rondeau
in the flamboyant style—

> Blanche com lys, plus que rose vermeille
> Resplendissant com rubis d'Oriant. . . .

But his mastery chiefly appears in soft and pretty verses
at the beginning of his rondeaus and ballads, which, with
their languishing love-themes, make one hope often to find
in them the equivalent of the contemporary sonnets of
Petrarch. They exhibit the same mannerism, but without
Petrarch's high and rare spirit, which keeps gathering force
until the end. A ballad, with its twenty-one lines, is too
large a thing for his inspiration. His rondeaus, being
shorter, are more uniformly happy. The following (cxxv.)
is a good example, and may be compared with Chaucer's
rondeau given below [1]—

> Faites mon cœur tout à un coup mourir,
> Très douce dame, en lieu de guerredon;
>
> Puis que de rien nel voulez réjouïr
> Faites mon cœur tout à un coup mourir;

[1] See p. 62.

Car il vaut mieux assez qu'ainsi languir
Sans espérer joië ne guérison.

Faites mon cœur tout à un coup mourir,
Très douce dame, en lieu de guerredon.

The first lines of his *Dit de la Marguerite* are particularly graceful, and Chaucer remembered them for the Prologue of his *Good Women*—

J'aime une fleur qui s'ouvre et qui s'incline
Vers le soleil, de jour quand il chemine:
Et quand il est couché sous sa courtine
    Par nuit obscure,
Elle se clost, ainsois que le jour fine.
Ses feuilles ont dessous couleur sanguine,
Blanches dessus plus que gente hermine
    Ne blancheur pure. . . .

In short, Machaut is a refined versifier, not a great artist, but nothing if not an artist. He was better suited than one would think to educate a foreigner, who already possessed deep poetic qualities, but who came to France to learn the technique of his art, just as to-day hundreds of foreign art-students throng the studios of the Paris painters to learn the rules of their craft. Chaucer moreover, soon rivalled the external dexterity of Machaut and cast in equally intricate forms a heartiness and wealth of human emotion, of which his master was not capable.

We cannot attempt here to make a list of the things for which Chaucer was indebted to Machaut, any more than of those he owed to the poets of his own generation, Froissart, Deschamps, Otto de Granson. This was partly done already by Sandras, as early as 1859, in his *Etude sur G. Chaucer considéré comme imitateur des trouvères*, and has been carried much further by later investigations. It can be safely said that each new contribution increases

Chaucer's debt, by bringing to light imitations of subject and form hitherto unsuspected, stories transcribed and lines translated, which heretofore had passed as original.[1] No doubt, when we possess the complete edition of Machaut's works (the first volume has just been published in the *Anciens Textes Français*), some hitherto unsuspected borrowings will be revealed. This one volume, where the *Lay de Plour* is printed for the first time, shows that the varied and difficult stanzas of this elegy probably incited Chaucer to similar experiments in his *Compleint of Anelida*, a fact as yet unsuspected. Moreover, a closer inquiry tends to prove that where Froissart for instance was thought to have copied Chaucer, it was the other way about. Until quite late in life Chaucer was interested in the poetic tourneys of France. He followed with a somewhat ironical interest the *tensons* on the comparative merits of the leaf and the flower. He associated himself with the symbolical worship of the " Marguerite " (or daisy), which in the latter half of the century, out of regard for some great ladies of that name, displaced that of the rose.

It is nevertheless to the *Roman de la Rose* that Chaucer was especially indebted for his poetical initiation. As a matter of fact, we do not know at what precise period of his life he wrote his translation of that famous work, nor if the fragments of the poetical English version which have come down to us are his, although most commentators incline to think that the first of these fragments, corresponding to the 1678 first lines of the original, is in his own hand

---

[1] Since these lines were written, they have received strong support from Mr. J. L. Lowes's contribution on *Chaucer and the Miroir de Mariage*, from which it appears that Chaucer made abundant use of Eustache Deschamps's poem for his most original creation, the Wife of Bath's Prologue. See *Modern Philology*, vol. viii. nos. 2 and 3.

and not the others. This translation generally follows the text very closely, line for line; most often it preserves the meaning and style of the model, and manages to retain much of the original neatness of expression and grace. No better exercise could be devised to train the versification and style of a young poet, writing in a language as yet incompletely formed. If the translation is less good than its model, it is because of its inferior rhymes. The rhymes of Guillaume de Lorris are both correct and full, pleasant in sound and fresh in tone. Hampered in his difficult task of translator who wishes to be accurate, Chaucer did not equal the charming style effects of Lorris. His rhyme is still a little dull in sound and colour. Compare these two sets of verses—

Avis m'iere qu'il estoit mains,	That it was May me thoughte tho,
Il a jà bien cincq ans, au mains;	It is fyve yere or more ago;
En Mai estoie, ce songeoie,	That it was May, thus dremed me
El tems amoreus plain de joie,	In tyme of love and jolitee,
El tems où tote riens s'esgaie,	That al thing ginneth waxen gay,
Que l'on ne voit boisson ne haie	For there is neither busk nor hay
Qui en Mai parer ne se voille	In May, that it nil shrouded been,
Et covrir de novelle foille. . . .	And it with newe leves wreen. . . .
Roman de la Rose, ll. 45-52.	*The Romaunt of the Rose*, ll. 49-56.

The bright rosy tints of the original have faded in the process.

Chaucer, with his usual modesty, did not hesitate to acknowledge his inferiority in the matter of rhyme. Even when he had in his turn become a master and performed some rhyming feats of his own, he still complained of his inability to vie with French masters in this respect. In 1393, when writing a line for line translation of Otto de Granson's stanzas, he craved mercy for his verse on account of his great age, and also because of the difficulties which made this translation a true penance for him—

And eek to me hit is a greet penaunce,
Sith rym in English hath swich scarsitee,
To folowe word by word the curiositee
Of Graunson, flour of hem that make in Fraunce.
                              The Compleynt of Venus, ll. 79-82.

It was in this case excess of deference, but what is worth remembering is the artistic concern which inspired the complaint.

The influence which the *Roman de la Rose* had on Chaucer should certainly not be reduced to a mere stylistic training. This romance, which was the great poetical well from which the fourteenth century drew inspiration, was really the one poem which had the most constant hold on Chaucer. Its double character, due to the difference, nay to the contrast between the two poets who wrote it, far from shocking Chaucer, because it spoilt the unity of the poem, increased the attraction which this sort of poetic Bible had for him.   According to the mood he was in, and more especially according to his age, he drew inspiration from Guillaume de Lorris or from Jean de Meung.   To the first he went in his youth.   Later, the abundance of ideas, satires and classical reminiscences which pervade Jean de Meung's work, suited better his need for more substantial and more humorous reading matter.   Jean de Meung became then, and remained till the end, his principal instructor, as can be seen in a hundred passages borrowed from him, even in Chaucer's final masterpiece.   But perhaps one ought not to represent as successive influences those which were often simultaneous.   It was the alternation of grace and force, of pure poetry and ironical philosophy, of airy charm and rough energy, of pretty fancy and coarseness—it was the very inconsistency of the whole poem, which made him select it as a favourite. There, he found food for his twofold inclination.   Did not this duality exist in his very nature? When, in his tales, he mingled delicate and farcical stories, grace and irony, the beautiful and the coarse, the serious and the funny, he embodied in a living work of genius the antithesis between the two parts of the *Roman de la Rose*.

But if the *Roman de la Rose* helped him at first to train his feeling for form, it hindered nevertheless his genius in a way. It led him to adopt and to retain for many years the allegorical style. Such was his regard for this poem that it checked the appearance of his dramatic talent, and it needed a journey to Italy to help him to discover it. We might the more regret this long restraint, had Chaucer not produced in allegorical form some works which are full of charm; and also, if we did not feel that it was of value for him to cultivate and enrich his art by exercises which smack a little of the workshop, before venturing on that difficult task—often so disastrous to formal beauty of painting life at first hand and without intermediary.

Did Chaucer explore French poetry beyond the *Roman de la Rose*? Very little, it seems, although for his *Troilus*, beside Boccaccio, he very probably made use of the *Roman de Troie* by Benoît de Sainte-More, and had elsewhere possible reminiscences of Marie de France. But he does not appear to have been acquainted with the best of the French *trouvères*. By this time, the primitive *chansons de geste* had passed out of fashion, as well as the oldest lives of the saints, which were also the noblest. People no longer sang the lovely *chansons de toile*, and hardly ever the sprightly *pastourelles*, which had been replaced by poems of definite length and structure. He did not even know the best verse romances, for there is nothing to warrant the supposition that he had read Chrestien de Troyes. On the other hand, he was familiar with the degenerate romances of chivalry which were then popular, and also with the adventures of *Renart* and with the licentious *fabliaux*. But people read them for the subject alone, and it is doubtful whether they had any influence at all over his art. It is even possible that most of the latter compositions only reached him through English versions; it was certainly the case with certain romances which he parodied in his *Sir Thopas*. In any case, most of those poems exhibited such a lack of artistic sense that one does not see what he could have learnt from them.

This survey of Chaucer's French reading should not lead us into the belief that we have as yet ascertained the extent of his debt. In making a minute inventory of the things borrowed by Chaucer from French poets, commentators only point out the outward signs of an influence which went much deeper. It is surely significant to read in the notes of a learned edition, such as the one by Professor Skeat, the innumerable comparisons with French poets, which Chaucer's text suggests. Almost at every page, his well stored mind remembered a line read in one of them, a remark, a description, a phrase, a humorous saying. But all that means very little, and much can be said in favour of those who state the facts as to these borrowings, and at once put them aside as negligible quantities. They rightly proclaim, in order to safeguard Chaucer's originality, that in borrowing so largely, he only did what the other writers of his day had done, what a Shakespeare, a Molière, or a La Fontaine would do later. If Chaucer's debt were limited to these details, we could indeed make light of it, but he owes another debt, far greater and more diffused, indefinable and yet quite certain. It does not consist in some special bounty conferred on him: it is a legacy which he enjoyed. Or rather, it should not be looked for amongst the gifts of fortune, but in his very nature. His mind was French, like his name. He was a direct descendant of the French *trouvères* and he had all that was theirs, save the language. It is precisely in his efforts to render the English language literary and poetical, that the fact is most easily detected. Not that Chaucer gallicised grammar and vocabulary more than did his contemporaries, but, the first great literary artist in his country, he tried to express, and did express, in his own language, the poetical beauty which he felt in French verse, and which happened to be that which instinctively he most desired. We may add that he expressed no other, if style alone be considered. Absolutely nothing of the Anglo-Saxon literary past subsisted in his verse, although it was being revived around him, very little modified as to form and spirit. Now, there is something which appears very characteristic to one who has read the forcible and sombre, fervent and often turbid, effusions of the old English poetry before the Norman conquest, and that is that in passing from these to Chaucer, we experience exactly the same sense of surprise at the absolute difference, the same impression of change in the air and sky, of a voice tuned to another key, which come to us when we leave these same productions to read the early French *trouvères*. And we find that precisely the same terms are needed to characterise alike the atmosphere of old French verse or of Chaucerian poetry.

How are we to define those characteristics which make him French in essentials? For those who are familiar with the *trouvères* (I allude to the best of these only, the others do not count), no such explanation is needed. But no reader gets so strong and clear an impression as the one who encounters them on coming out of that long darkness, seamed by lightning and strange glimmerings, which corresponds to Anglo-Saxon poetry. It is above all a sensation of daylight regained: it is an incipient clarity, but not that one, as has been too often implied, which is a purely abstract quality, made up of instinctive logic; or negative and due to an absence of subtle and rare symbolism. It is that, no doubt, and coupled with what it carries with it, the gift of story-telling and the instinct for clear, abundant, and well-ordained detail. But it is infinitely more. It is a light as real as that of dawn, flooding all things and gladdening men's eyes. The word " clair," one of those gems of the French language, which expresses this sensation, is, if one looks into it, the favourite expression of the old French poets, constantly met with in the *Chanson de Roland*, to which it gives its lucid atmosphere. It is curious to see how eagerly Chaucer picked it up and used it to render the same effects in so many of his finest passages. He hung it at the end of the most lovely line of his prayer to the Virgin Mary—

> Continue on us thy piteous eyen *clere*.
>
> *An A B C*, l. 88.

He used it most effectively at the beginning of his ballad to the beauties of yester-year—

> Hyd, Absolon, thy gilte tresses *clere*.
>
> *Legend of Good Women*, Prologue A, l. 203.

He applied it to sounds with no less felicitousness, when he spoke of the bells on the monk's bridle, which could be heard

> Ginglen in a whistling wind as *clere*,
> And eek as loude as dooth the chapel-belle.
>
> *Canterbury Tales*, Prologue, l. 170.

The light which pervades Chaucer's work, fine and white, rarely touching the higher colouring of southern poetry, is precisely of the same quality as that of the Ile-de-France. Nothing is better calculated to give us the impression that with him we have not changed climate. As in the case of the French *trouvères*, there runs through his work a joyousness born of the pleasure of living, and which shows itself in a partiality to sunny scenes, a constant reminiscence of spring time, may-bushes, flowers, birds, and music. There is a line in which he sums up the description of the squire's youthfulness, and which might be used to define his whole poetry (what else is the brilliant essay by the American writer Lowell but a commentary on this line?)—

He was as fresh as is the month of May.
Canterbury Tales, Prologue, l. 92.

Now, though this line may never be found in Chaucer's predecessors, it is quite French: it is, as it were, the essence of early French poetry: it falls back into a French decasyllable as into its natural mould—

Il était frais comme le mois de mai.

The sound of Chaucer's voice is like our *trouvères'*, neither too high nor too low. The tone of it, like theirs, is pure and a little thin. It never swells, for he would rather muffle it. It is an even voice tuned to relate without fatigue or jar a long story, not rich nor full enough perhaps for the highest lyrical strains, but kept up to the medium pitch, whereby meaning is most clearly and correctly conveyed to the mind. Again, his charm is derived from an easy simplicity, from a perfect correspondence of words to thought—his best lines being simply notations of facts, external details, or traits of sentiment. He exhibits a constant restraint in emotion and satire alike, which debars screams and sobs, which softens irony into sly mischief, and provokes a quiet smile rather than uproarious laughter. There is everywhere an impression of sober sense, which implies a watchful intelligence rather than wild passion, and which a final analysis shows to proceed from a perfect balance of mind and temper.

These qualities belong to the old French poets and to Chaucer alike. We see his literary origin confirmed by the fact that he has them all and does not go beyond them, except on rare occasions and under Italian influence, when he soars simultaneously, one feels, above the usual virtues of the French mind and of his own. Whenever he goes outside France, he also goes, in some measure, outside his own nature.

It should be added that together with the virtues of the French *trouvères*, he exhibits those defects which are to be found even in the best of them. Like them, he is often oblivious of the art of condensation; like them, he chatters often with charm, but it must be allowed that it is chattering. On occasion he lacks vigour and spirit; he loiters where he ought to quicken his pace; he walks where he ought to fly. His poetry, when restrained, borders on prose; it is at times clumsy, slow and even commonplace; it pads many a line with expletives which are not the less superfluous for being unassuming. And to make the resemblance complete, these obvious defects are cleverly turned into account, thanks to an air of simplicity and artlessness, and they are used sometimes to convey his most subtle humour.

These characteristics are not confined to his youth alone, but remain permanent throughout his career. It is wrong to speak of the French period of Chaucer's development. He is always French, but as a French writer might also do, he drew treasures from other lands, he saw and marvelled

at the beauty of antiquity or of Italy. Thus, to a ground-
work which never disappeared, he added some Italian and
Latin variations, and in the end again, it was in his French
style and manner that he painted contemporary society
in England.

III

He seems to have begun with lyric poetry, making known
to his countrymen the learned new forms—ballad, virelai,
rondeau—which Machaut had just brought into fashion
in France. If nothing remains of these first attempts,
nothing at least which can be identified with certainty, his
later work offers a sufficient number of specimens of his
skill in this style. It is in truth but a tiny stream of lyric
which skirts the large fields of his narrative productions,
and it is not by any means the most characteristic, nor
curiously enough the most personal part of his work. But
it is here we catch the artist in his studio. Whether it
treats of love or piety or morals, his lyric poetry is always
an imitation as regards form, and nearly always as regards
subject. He uses it less to express his feelings than to
train his style and versification. That is why it should be
studied, without any consideration of date, before passing
to other forms, in which he left a deeper personal mark.

The natural conclusion of what has been said is that he
lacked almost wholly that passion and fire, that airy fancy,
which are characteristic of truly lyric poets. We find in
him none of those " translunary things," or of that " fine
frenzy," upon which the English Renaissance poets were
later to pride themselves. We find with him no trace of
those spontaneous songs in free rhythm, which form the

delicious undergrowth, as it were, of Elizabethan poetry. He is more attracted to story-telling than to singing. He has more tranquillity than enthusiasm. He is little given to flights of fancy in his verse. Hence, he is never loth to imprison his feelings in the most rigid frames devised by French poets.

He soon proved as successful at this exercise as the cleverest of them. His *virelais* are lost, but we still have a triple rondel on a " Merciles Beaute," for whom the poet sings at first his unrequited passion. It is mere amorous convention without a quiver of the voice. But any *trouvère* might have been happy to put his name to this trifle, the first part of which we quote here, as it is the best—

> Your yën two wol slee me sodenly,
> I may the beautè of hem not sustene,
> So woundeth hit through-out my herte kene.
>
> And but your word wol helen hastily
> My hertes wounde, whyl that hit is grene,
> Your yën two wol slee me sodenly,
> I may the beautè of hem not sustene.
>
> Upon my trouthe I sey yow feithfully,
> That ye ben of my lyf and deeth the quene;
> For with my deeth the trouthe shal be sene.
> Your yën two wol slee me sodenly,
> I may the beautè of hem not sustene,
> So woundeth hit through-out my herte kene.
>
> *Merciles Beaute*, I. Captivity.[1]

The workman's skill is here as evident as the depth of the passion remains doubtful. Should the reader be prone

[1] Mr. J. L. Lowes, who has done more than any single critic to show Chaucer's indebtedness to his French contemporaries, has pointed out, as the probable models of this " triple roundel," two short poems of Eustache Deschamps. (See *The Modern Language Review*, January 1910.)

to sympathise with the dying lover, he will soon be
undeceived. The last of the three rondels will reduce the
whole thing to a mere joke. In it Chaucer seems to scoff
at the very style he has just employed—

> Sin I fro Love escaped am so fat,
> I never thenk to ben in his prison lene;
> Sin I am free, I counte him not a bene.
>
> *Merciles Beaute*, III. Escape.

But Chaucer was decidedly susceptible to the kind of
emotion which comes chiefly through the ear and which
a pleasant rhythm can arouse, albeit the heart may have
been but little stirred at first. A good proof of it is supplied by his prayer to the Virgin, his "A B C." The
learned critic Ten Brink, basing his opinion on this prayer
as well as on some other effusions addressed to the Virgin
Mary, which are to be found in Chaucer's work, concluded
that he must have passed through a period of intense
devotion, more especially towards the Virgin Mary. That
is possible. But we are told on the other hand that the
"A B C" was written by command, to please the Duchess
Blanche, and we also know that this prayer, like the other
pieces dedicated to Mary, is an almost literal translation.
It is a version of a passage in the *Pèlerinage de la vie
humaine*, written about 1330 by Guillaume de Deguileville,
a monk of the abbey of Chalis. The passage in point is
a puerile devotional composition, a sort of rosary in honour
of Our Lady, of which the first letter of each of the twenty-
three stanzas corresponds to one of the letters of the
alphabet, taken in order. Chaucer followed Deguileville
stanza after stanza, preserving the meaning, without,
however, being too much at pains to reproduce it exactly.
It seems as if the subject mattered little to him; he does
not always understand the French very well and he does

not care. What he aimed at was the artistic effect. He rejected the original French stanza of twelve octosyllables on two rhymes, which was flat, monotonous, and dull, very little superior to those lines in which are taught the commandments of God and the church. Instead, he used the more ample dissyllabic verse and the eight-line stanza of the French courtly ballad, with its delicate interlaced rhymes. He introduced also cleverly devised pauses to express or imitate emotion. What a contrast if we compare the results! Deguileville prayed to the Virgin in this wise to save him from sin—

> Temple saint où Dieu habite
> Dont privé sont li herite
> Et à tous jours deshérité,
> A toy vieng, de toy me herite,
> Reçoif moi par ta mérite,
> Car de toi n'ai point hésité.
> El si je me suis hérité
> Des espines d'iniquité
> Par quoy terre fu maudite,
> Las m'en clain en vérité,
> Car à ce fait m'a excité
> L'âme qui n'en est pas quite.

And here is what Chaucer made out of this poor material—

> Temple devout, ther God hath his woninge,
> Fro which these misbileved pryved been,
> To you my soule penitent I bringe.
> Receyve me! I can no ferther fleen!
> With thornes venimous, O hevene queen,
> For which the erthe acursed was ful yore,
> I am so wounded, as ye may wel seen,
> That I am lost almost;—it smert so sore.

An A B C, ll. 145-152.

By means of an improved stanza, a more ample rhythm and a more dramatic tone, especially at the end, Chaucer attains a fervour of which his model was incapable. Let who will examine the two prayers as a whole and he will find that Chaucer's, which is essentially artistic—I feel it is so and crave Ten Brink's pardon—is also the most moving, and the more spontaneous prayer of the pious Cistercian monk seems cold beside it.

Chaucer was no less sensitive to the sound and attractiveness of words than he was to rhythm. He knew the charm inherent in a list of proper names rightly chosen. French poetry was already groping after the " ballade des neiges d'antan," and took a melancholy pleasure in enumerating the beautiful ladies of yester-year. There existed a ballad on this subject before Chaucer, rather prettily turned—

> Hester, Judith, Penelopë, Helaine,
> Sarre, Tisbë, Rebequë et Sairy,
> Lucresse, Yseult, Genèvre, chastelaine
> La très loial nomméë de Vergy,
> Rachel et la dame de Fayel
> Onc ne furent si précieux jouel
> D'honneur, bonté, senz, beauté et valour
> Con est ma très doulce dame d'onnour.
>
> Si d' Absalon la grant beauté humaine . . .
> *Tristan*, ed. Francisque Michel, vol. i. p. 38.

The rest of the ballad is in praise of the valorous and the wise. Chaucer read this ballad and closely imitated it in the one which he put in the centre of his prologue to the *Legend of Good Women*. He is also graceful, and might appear more so if one could read his song without remembering Villon's, vibrating with regret for the things which are no more. It is remarkable that he is again more con cerned about fine lines than about the meaning; he retains two masculine names, Absalom and Jonathan, amongst feminine beauties, who alone ought to be named in his poem, and does so because he cannot bring himself to sacrifice the first line which pleases his ear—

> Hyd, Absolon, thy gilte tresses clere.
> *Legend of Good Women*, Prologue A, l. 203.

And it is precisely through this feeling for the sound of words, that Chaucer attained the verbal lyrical qualities into which he initiated his countrymen.

He displays a similar dexterity here and there in his original verse. On two or three occasions even, it is animated by a warmth which makes him a real singer. He is this certainly in the first two stanzas of his *Compleynt of Mars*, where a bird hails the dawn of Saint Valentine's day—

> " Gladeth, ye foules, of the morow gray,
> Lo! Venus risen among yon rowes rede!
> And floures fresshe, honoureth ye this day;
> For when the sonne uprist, then wol ye sprede.
> But ye lovers, that lye in any drede,
> Fleëth, lest wikked tonges yow espye;
> Lo! yond the sonne, the candel of Ielosye!
>
> With teres blewe, and with a wounded herte
> Taketh you leve; and, with seynt Iohn to borow,
> Apeseth somwhat of your sorowes smerte,
> Tyme cometh eft, that cese shal your sorow;
> The glade night is worth an hevy morow! "—
> (Saynt Valentyne! a foul thus herde I singe
> Upon thy day, er sonne gan up-springe).
> *The Compleynt of Mars*, The Proem, ll. 1-14.

This is a really charming dawn song. But the skylark soon comes back to earth, and the jog-trot of prose follows closely on the flight of song. Chaucer has sustained better and more often the elegiac note. His complaint of Anelida to Arcite, who had forsaken her, is a beautiful thing, despite its monotonous length. Here the tender soul of the poet, easily moved by human woes, especially if they be feminine, successfully expresses in a

variety of complicated and marvellously difficult rhythms,
the sincere effusions of a bruised heart, still amorous and
ready to forgive in the height of its undeserved sorrow.
As regards subject and as a *tour de force* in rhyme, it is a
match for Machaut's *Lay de Plour*. Chaucer prepared
himself for this elegy by several trial poems which have
survived, and which testify to his artistic care. But here
art does not kill pathos. He can impart the ring of
truth to Anelida's voice and make her express the most
touching thoughts, while submitting himself to the most
exacting verse-scheme—

> Alas! wher is become your gentilesse!
> Your wordes ful of plesaunce and humblesse?
> Your observaunces in so low manere,
> And your awayting and your besinesse
> Upon me, that ye calden your maistresse,
> Your sovereyn lady in this worlde here?
> Alas! and is ther nother word ne chere
> Ye vouchesauf upon myn hevinesse?
> Alas! your love, I bye hit al to dere.
>
> *Anelida and Arcite*, ll. 247-255.

The metrical artifice is still heightened in the following
stanza, without however hampering the easy flow of
emotion. Nay, the emotion is even increased by the
number of pauses and the brevity of those rhymed fragments which seem punctuated with sighs—

My swete foo,	why do ye so,	for shame?
And thenke ye	that furthered be	your name,
To love a newe,	and been untrew-e?	nay!
And putte yow	in sclaunder now	and blame,
And do to me	adversitee	and grame,
That love you most,	god, wel thou wost!	alway?
Yet turn ayeyn,	and be al pleyn	som day,
And than shal this	that now is mis	be game,
And al for-yive,	whyl that I liv-e	may.

Anelida and Arcite, ll. 272-280.

The sustained pathos of the complaint of Anelida was never repeated in Chaucer's lyrical work. The measured tone of the story-teller, which was customary with him, spread gradually to all his productions. Nevertheless, up to the end, he practised on occasions those exercises in lyrical form which had been his first concern. Several later ballads have been preserved, but they are either moral or humoristic.

The distinguishing features of the moral ballads are their dominant gravity and unusual compactness. There is nothing new in the thoughts expressed by the poet. Chaucer generally borrowed them from the philosophical treatises of his beloved Boethius, and discreetly adapted them to his own times. These ballads were of course inspired by the misfortunes and the vices which met his eye, but he preserved in them all a certain vagueness of allusion. The one called *Truth*, which is perhaps the last he wrote, and also the most beautiful and noble, is an appeal to men to flee from the world and turn their minds to God. Composed of a number of maxims, it is full and vigorous. But one is surprised to find that even in such a short composition Chaucer cannot keep up the exalted tone. Interspersed between purely religious stanzas, to one's astonishment one reads a stanza full of practical and worldly advice, of utilitarian and even egoistic wisdom, written in a popular, homely style—

> Tempest thee noght al croked to redresse,
> In trust of hir that turneth as a bal:
> Gret reste stant in litel besinesse;
> And eek be war to sporne ageyn an al;
> Stryve noght, as doth the crokke with the wal.
> Daunte thy-self, that dauntest otheres dede;
> And trouthe shal delivere, hit is no drede.
>
> *Truth*, ll. 8-14.

This irresistible tendency to familiarity is a characteristic common to all the more personal ballads of the poet.   They are really familiar epistles, similar to many of those written at that time by Deschamps, but marked by Chaucer's peculiar playfulness: the *Compleint to his purse*, which Marot might have signed; *Lenvoy to Bukton*, where Chaucer dissuades his friend from marrying, and, in order to convince him, sends him his *Wyf of Bathe ; Lenvoy a Scogan*, where he declares himself too old a bird to write love-verses again.   In proportion as he breaks away from imitation and expresses his true nature, he relinquishes the lyrical heights for the comic plane, and the only thing he retains of that particular style, is the difficult and complex arrangement of verse and rhyme.   It is no accident therefore that he should have composed in a mocking tone the most vivid and artistic of his ballads— the one with which the clerk of the pilgrimage concludes his story of Griselida, ironically entreating women not to imitate the excessive patience of which Griselida was once guilty.

On the whole, apart from a few lively or moving passages, Chaucer is but rarely and weakly lyrical.   It cannot be said that in this style he rises much above his French contemporaries, and it is impossible to place him on the same rank with Petrarch.   But it was important that he did aim at lyrical poetry and at times hit the mark.   These moments were so many flights towards verbal beauty and sonorous verse.   If Chaucer had not fashioned his style by cultivating the ballad, rondeau, and other delicate stanzas, he could not very well have become the poet he was in the narrative style, towards which his natural genius led him, and which easily becomes prosy.   We should not have had the burning stanzas of *Troilus and*

Criseyde, where he vies with Boccaccio in passion, nor the *Prioress's Tale*, where he brings into play all the resources of a highly-trained style in order to suggest a suave art-lessness. Who knows even if he would have been capable of the energy and vividness which characterise the couplet of his *Knightes Tale ?* One can go further and ask whether, verging so closely on vulgarity, he could have asserted himself as a poet even in the licentious tales of the Miller, the Reeve, and the Somnour. His comic verse, lusty and racy, with its strong regular rhythm and yet suppleness enough to render the inflexions of the speaking voice, is partly the outcome of the fine lyrical exercises by which he trained himself.

Finally, this lyrical preamble should not be isolated from the rest of his productions. It is but part of a whole, it is the summit and the crown of his work. It is the most elevated of the diverse styles practised by Chaucer. The poet's varied powers would appear to us impoverished and lessened, if his voice had not been capable here and there of some vocal triumphs. One aspect would be missing in a work whose chief excellence lies perhaps in the variety and contrasts of its aspects.

CHAPTER III

THE ALLEGORICAL POEMS

I. *The Book of the Duchesse.* II. *The Parlement of Foules.*
III. *The Hous of Fame.* IV. *The Legend of Good Women.*

APART from this narrow fringe of lyrical verse, Chaucer's
work appears as purely narrative, and falls into two clearly
defined groups. In the first part of his literary career, he
submitted to the restrictions of a style which had been
popularised by the *Roman de la Rose*; in the second part he
freed himself from them. If the chronology of his works,
as established by patient inquirers, tends to show that
during a few years of his life he cultivated both styles at
once, we must remember that this chronology often rests
on slender presumptions, and refrain from too strict an
acceptance of it.[1] In any case, it seems preferable to be
guided in the study of the work by this clear idea of progress
towards freedom. The other divisions which have been
suggested are all faulty in some way or other. The one
for instance which classes the poems according to three
successive periods, French, Italian, and English, risks the
implication of an error. As we said, there is not a single
moment at which Chaucer was not under French influence;
it is no less evident in the *Canterbury Tales* than it is in the
Book of the Duchesse. If, on the other hand, it is certain
that in his allegorical poems, ever after the *Parlement*

[1] Since this was written, the arguments of Mr. Lowes, tending to
prove that *Troilus* was written after the *Hous of Fame*, have further
increased the conformity of the chronology to the artistic development.

of Foules, Chaucer borrowed from the Italians, these imitations are like ornaments arranged on a permanent background. They may be temporarily disregarded, in order not to obscure the dominant fact that Chaucer, in the first period of his maturity, obeys the artistic formula set down in the *Roman de la Rose*. This characteristic is common to all the poems which will be studied in this chapter.

I

The first of Chaucer's poems, and almost the only one which can be dated with any certainty, is that which he wrote towards his thirtieth year on the occasion of the death of the Duchess Blanche of Lancaster, which occurred in 1369. The " good duchess " was mourned by more than one. Froissart wrote a few graceful lines about her in his *Joli buisson de Jeunesse*—

> Elle morut jone et jolie
> Environ de vingt et deus ans,
> Gaie, lie, friche, esbatans,
> Douce, simple, d'umble samblance;
> La bonne dame ot a nom Blanche.

The duke's sorrow was no doubt as violent as it was quickly assuaged. Chaucer, who may have experienced some personal regret over this premature end, desired to please John of Gaunt by praising the virtues of the spouse and the grief of the survivor. He called into play all his erudition and all his art, without scrupling to embody in his long elegy verses previously written, such as the story of Ceyx and Alcyone, in which he had imitated Ovid and to an extent the *Dit de la Fontaine Amoureuse* by Machaut. The result of this great effort was a voluminous and composite funeral monument, which surprises us to-day by its arti-

ficially rather than ingeniously complicated plan, but
where Chaucer's nature nevertheless peeps out in places,
in the shape of fresh and dainty flowers, which grow in
abundance between the stones of this elaborate piece of
flamboyant architecture.

The framework of the poem is purely conventional.
First there is a proem, where Chaucer complains of not
being able to sleep. This insomnia, of which he does not
know the cause, deprives him of all joy. He has been
suffering from this complaint for eight years; one doctor
alone could cure him (understand some " merciless beauty "),
but he will not say any more on this subject. Now, a few
nights ago, as sleep persistently fled from him, he had a
romance brought to him, the *Metamorphoses of Ovid*. The
story he read was that of Ceyx and Alcyone.

King Ceyx was shipwrecked and drowned. His wife
Alcyone awaited him in sorrow, and then had a search made
for him in vain. Her grief breaks the poet's heart, as he
reads about her misfortune. Alcyone prayed to Juno and
begged her to give her back her husband, or at least to let
her know in a dream what had become of him. Juno
thereupon dispatched a messenger to Morpheus, the god
of dreams, ordering him to cause the shade of Ceyx to
appear before Alcyone. Ceyx informed Alcyone of his
death, and asked that burial be given him. But Alcyone
woke up broken-hearted and died on the third day.

Here Chaucer stops reading, without going as far as the
metamorphoses of the pair into halcyons. He has now
learnt what he wanted to know, to wit, the existence of a
God who governs sleep. Heretofore, he only knew one
God. He takes a vow to give Morpheus rich offerings,
a feather bed and pure white doves, and sleep is granted
him. In his sleep there comes to him such a marvellous

dream that neither Joseph nor Macrobius could explain it. This dream is the poem itself.

Like most of the poems of the time, Chaucer's dream begins with the vision of a beautiful May morning. What his scheme lacks in originality, Chaucer makes up for by the wealth and charm of detail. Far back beyond Machaut and Guillaume de Lorris, he joins hands here with Chrestien de Troyes, whom he did not know, and recalls the latter's prettiest decorative pictures.

He fancies that he has been awakened by the singing of a multitude of birds. He looks out of the window and finds them sitting on the tiles of his chamber-roof, singing

> The most solempne servyse
> By note, that ever man . . .
> Had herd; for some of hem song lowe,
> Some hye, and al of oon acorde.
>
> *The Book of the Duchesse*, ll. 302-305.

The place where he stands is not unworthy of this heavenly melody—

> And, soth to seyn, my chambre was
> Ful wel depeynted, and with glas
> Were al the windowes wel y-glased,
> Ful clere, and nat an hole y-crased,
> That to beholde hit was grete Ioye.
> For hoolly al the storie of Troye
> Was in the glasing y-wroght thus,
> Of Ector and King Priamus,
> Of Achilles and Lamedon,
> Of Medea and of Iason,
> Of Paris, Eleyne, and Lavyne.
> And alle the walles with colours fyne
> Were peynted, bothe text and glose,
> [Of] al the Romaunce of the Rose.
> My windowes weren shet echon,
> And through the glas the sunne shon
> Upon my bed with brighte bemes,
> With many glade gilden stremes,

And eek the welken was so fair,
Blew, bright, clere was the air,
And ful atempre, for sothe, hit was;
For nother cold nor hoot hit nas,
Ne in al the welken was a cloude.

The Book of the Duchesse, ll. 321-343.

Suddenly, he hears the sound of a hunting horn under his window, and sees a troup of huntsmen go past. He mounts his horse and joins them. He learns from one of the riders that they form the hunting party of the Emperor Octavian. After a long chase, the stag they had started puts the dogs off the scent. The poet is walking away from the tree where he has been stationed, when a whelp comes to him and fawns on him. He tries to catch it, but it escapes and leads him down a path of flowery grass, a delight-ful avenue planted with tall trees ten feet apart, and full of deer, roe and fawns, which run away on seeing him. There he espies a man in black, leaning with his back against an oak. He is a tall fine-looking knight of about four and twenty. (As a matter of fact John of Gaunt was then twenty-nine.) Approaching unnoticed, Chaucer hears him lamenting, the while he hangs his head down. He listens and finds that the knight is reciting in the most sorrowful voice a complaint of some ten or twelve verses, the subject of which is the death of a peerless lady. The knight has hardly uttered it when the blood rushes back to his heart and he turns as pale as death. He seems about to faint. The poet goes up to him and with difficulty makes his presence known. After exchang-ing a few courteous words, he remarks that the hunt seems at an end, to which the knight replies that he has no thought of the hunt. Begged by the poet to communicate to him the cause of his sorrow and thereby make it lighter to bear, he answers that there is no possible alleviation for his woe, and bursts out into a sort of antithetic complaint. His delight has been turned into despair. In a bold figure of speech, which anticipates the rhetoric of Shakespeare's Constance, he exclaims—

> I am sorwe and sorwe is I.
>> *The Book of the Duchesse*, l. 597.

He accuses perfidious Fortune, who has taken his queen away at chess and checkmated him. The poet does not understand the simile, and upbraids the stranger for entertaining a sorrow which is out of proportion with the cause. Thereupon the knight decides to speak without metaphor. From his early youth, he said, he had been Love's tributary, but his passion had no definite object. He was like an unsullied tablet, ready to receive all that the hand might wish to portray or paint. Now, one day, he came upon a company of ladies playing and dancing, and noticed one among them who surpassed all in beauty

> as the somere's sonne bright
> Is fairer, clerer, and hath more light
> Than any planete [is] in heven,
> The mone, or the sterres seven. . . .
>> *The Book of the Duchesse*, ll. 821-824.

He said to himself that it would be better to love this one in vain than to win all the others. Her look was frank; it drew and held yours. She was all harmony and balance, neither too serious nor too glad. She knew nothing of love as yet, and entertained for all good people the feelings of a sister. The beauty of her face was such that to attempt to describe it seems to him useless, but

> be hit never so derke
> Me thinketh I see her ever-mo.
>> *The Book of the Duchesse*, ll. 912-913.

Her speech was soft, eloquent, free from scorn, incapable of harming any one, and frank

> her simple recorde
> Was founde as trewe as any bonde,
> Or trouthe of any mannes honde.
> *The Book of the Duchesse*, ll. 933-936.

Her neck was

> whyt, smothe, streght, and flat,
> Withouten hole . . .
> *The Book of the Duchesse*, ll. 942-943.

Her throat

> Semed a round tour of yvoire.
> *The Book of the Duchesse*, l. 946.

Her name was Whyte (Blanche). He could never tire of describing the beauty of her body. Among ten thousand, she would have proved the outstanding ornament of a company—

> Me thoght the felawship as naked
> Withouten her, that saw I ones,
> As a coroune withoute stones.
> *The Book of the Duchesse*, ll. 978-980.

Her virtue equalled her charm. Her goodness, moderation, and reason could not be told. And a last trait, she did not like setting those who loved her, distant and dangerous enterprises.

Her accomplishments were so great and so varied that the poet can hardly believe them: he insinuates that this is an ideal portrait, drawn by a lover. But the knight swears that it is not so. After an ostentatious display of his knowledge of ancient history, he declares that had he been the foremost amongst the heroes of those glorious times, he would none the less have held her for a woman of surpassing merit. Then he gives an account of their first meetings, at which everything took place according to the rules of courteous love. For a long time the young man had no other desire than to see his lady, for in her presence all his sufferings vanished. But after a while he felt that the time had come to declare his love or to die—

> With sorweful herte, and woundes dede,
> Softe and quaking for pure drede
> And shame, and stinting in my tale
> For ferde, and myn hewe al pale,
> Ful ofte I wex bothe pale and reed;
> Bowing to her, I heng the heed;
> I durste nat ones loke her on,
> For wit, manere, and al was gon.
> I seyde " mercy! " and no more;
>
> *The Book of the Duchesse*, ll. 1211-1219.

He plucked up heart, however, spoke and swore to her love and devotion eternal. But she answered " No," and he, more unhappy than Cassandra, went away without daring to say another word. He lived for a whole year in great despondency, and then boldness came back to him and he once more declared his love. This time the lady understood that his devotion was real, and that he could not live without her.

> So whan my lady knew al this,
> My lady yaf me al hoolly
> The noble yift of her mercy.
>
> *The Book of the Duchesse*, ll. 1768-1770.

This seemed to the lover like coming back to life. They married, and he says how sweet their union had been, undisturbed till the end—

> Therwith she was alway so trewe,
> Our Ioye was ever y-liche newe;
> Our hertes wern so even a payre,
> That never nas that oon contrayre
> To that other for no wo.
> For sothe, y-liche they suffred tho

Oo blisse and eek oo sorwe bothe;
Y-liche they were bothe gladde and wrothe;
Al was us oon, withoute were.
And thus we lived ful many a yere
So wel, I can nat telle how.[1]

The Book of the Duchesse, ll. 1287-1297.

" Where is she now? " asks Chaucer, who requires a detailed explanation in order to understand.   " It is she that I have lost," replies the knight, " she is dead."—" Nay! "—" Yis, by my trouthe! "—" Is that your loss? By God! hit is routhe! "

The poet had no time to say more, for the hunt was over and the huntsmen returned suddenly.   King Octavian rode back to his palace, and as he got there a bell struck twelve. The sound awoke the poet, who found himself lying in his bed, still holding in his hand the book where he had read the story of Ceyx and Alcyone. Whereupon he resolved to turn this dream into verse.

As a matter of fact, he composed 1334 octosyllabics about it, which seems a good deal. The work contains some accessories which obviously burden it, and which might be suppressed to advantage. The proem has charm, but forms a story almost complete in itself. Half the effusions of the doleful knight are marred by trivial antithesis, and exhibit a pedantry which spoils his pathetic complaint. Everywhere we find a sort of loose verbosity, the matter is too often diluted, and there are many repetitions.

French poets are often put under contribution, even in places where the elegy seems most personal and the descriptions most life-like. The description of the flowery path into which the little dog leads the poet, is made up

---

[1] This is a close translation of some pretty lines in Machaut's poem, *Jugement du bon roi de Behaigne.*

of lines and fragments of lines taken from the *Roman de la Rose*. The Duchess surely owes to Nature some of her charms of body and soul; but some are also derived from the *Dit du Vergier*, the *Fontaine Amoureuse*, the *Remède de Fortune*, and the *Jugement du bon roi de Behaigne* by Machaut. Yet, in spite of these reservations, the *Book of the Duchesse* is a remarkable work, delightful in parts, and exhibiting an original talent which shows through imitation itself. Moreover, we must not forget the time and place at which it was written. It is the first poem in English where art attains at times the level of excellence. This must be said without any restrictions. The six following lines may be quoted for instance as being equal for simple pathos, for the harmonious adaptation of metre to meaning and sentiment, for the music of the rhyme, to the most delicate productions of Tennyson himself. This first instance of perfect beauty in English poetry is worth remembering. It is the passage relating the death of Alcyone, and the first three lines contain the farewell addressed to her by the shade of Ceyx—

> " And far-wel, swete, my worldes blisse!
> I praye god your sorwe lisse;
> To litel whyl our blisse lasteth! "
> With that her eyen up she casteth,
> And saw noght; " [A]! " quod she for sorwe,
> And deyed within the thridde morwe.
>
> *The Book of the Duchesse*, ll. 209-214.

There are to be found throughout the whole poem other exquisite touches, which seem all the more remarkable that the poetic language was only just out of its infancy. We notice here and there lines to which the felicitous association of the most ordinary words imparts a distinct character—

> She usëd gladly to do well.   1013

And these well-shaped lines, strangely enough, are found
next to slack expletives and shameless stop-gaps—

> Hir throte, *as I have now memoire,*
> Semed a round tour of yvoire.—ll. 945-946.

Thus, we are able to see, almost at one glance, the starting
and the culminating point of Chaucerian art.

At the same time, he introduced into the most factitious
of all poetic styles a sense of reality and a dramatic
force, which brought life and colour to the conventions
he dealt with.   Instinctively, and thanks to the natural
and easy swing of the dialogue, Chaucer rediscovered and
brought to the allegory qualities which were to be found
in the old verse romances.   Under what proves here to be
the beneficial influence of Machaut's *dits*, he substituted
human beings for the personified abstractions of the
Roman de la Rose.   But he went much further than
Machaut in the way of realism.   It is a conversation, on
the whole brisk and natural, which takes place between
him and the unknown knight.   Moreover, the dramatic
tone of the narrative, it should be noticed, counteracts
defects which are even turned to account and which add
to likelihood.   The verbosity of the bereaved knight, his
repetitions, the desultory way in which he enumerates the
virtues of his mistress, are certainly in keeping in a spontaneous effusion like his.   Thanks to these, the narrative
loses its stilted and didactic character.   The very fact
that his confidence is so prolific and disconnected, imparts
to it a certain pathos.   Moreover, in the attitude of the
confidant, who is none other than the poet himself, we can
already detect the Chaucerian humour.   For the first time
he describes himself as the man " of little wit," slow of
understanding, who marvels at a great passion, the lyrical
elevation of which is beyond him.   So that nearly all the

characteristics of Chaucerian poetry can be found indicated
here in this still somewhat clumsy poem, which closes the
period of his youth.

II

Thirteen years later Chaucer turned once more to allegory, when in 1382 he wished to celebrate the betrothal of
Richard II. to Anne of Bohemia. Anne, the daughter of
the Emperor Charles IV., had been affianced in turn to a
Bavarian prince and to a margrave of Missenia; but after
some negotiations which, according to Froissart, lasted a
whole year, her hand was finally given to the young King
of England. It is not at all certain, but it is probable,
that this betrothal was the event commemorated by
Chaucer in his *Parlement of Foules*. He had been one of the
negotiators who discussed and rejected a proposal of
marriage between Richard and one of the daughters of
the King of France. It was therefore only natural that,
after acting the diplomatist in the matter, he should have
seized the opportunity of playing the poet's part. His
reading had widened considerably since writing the *Book
of the Duchesse*. He had gained closer intimacy with the
ancients, and he had become acquainted with Italian poets,
without however losing touch with his French models. In
consequence, his poem is a curious mixture of imitations of
all sorts. The title and part of the subject were suggested
to him by a *lai* of Marie de France, *Li Parlemens des
oiseaux pour faire Roi*. Alain de l'Isle, in his *Planctus
Naturæ*, supplied the picture of nature on whose garment
the various species of birds are represented. The *Dream
of Scipio* by Cicero, with the commentary by Macrobius,
served him for prologue. In order to describe the ideal

garden where the scene takes place, he turned to the
Roman de la Rose, to Claudianus' *Raptus Proserpinæ*, and
to Boccaccio's *Theseide*. Here and there are to be found
a few borrowings from the *Divina Commedia*. This increased wealth burdens the work, but it does not prevent
its remaining true to the type of fashionable contemporary
allegories, in the French style. Where Chaucer, under
Italian influence—and more especially that of Boccaccio—
really separates himself from his first masters, is in the use
of a decasyllabic stanza instead of the monotonous octosyllabic couplet. This renders his touch at once broader
and more vigorous, but still an impression of conven-
tionality and artificiality remains, if indeed it is not
increased.

After reading an old book by "Tullius," relating how the
African appeared to Scipio in his sleep, and revealed to
him the happy place where virtuous men dwell after their
death, the poet falls asleep. The African then appears to
him also and leads him to the gate of a palace, on each
half of which is written a different inscription, one inviting,
the other threatening; the latter reminds one faintly
(without the awe-inspiring effect, it is true) of the famous
line, read by Dante at the entrance of the Inferno. Like
a piece of iron between two loadstones, the poet hesitates.
His guide reassures him promptly, by telling him that the
inscriptions were meant for Love's servants, of which he is
no longer one. He could go in without fear and be an
interested spectator in a contest, in which he was not
called upon to take part. Thereupon, Chaucer enters the
marvellous garden. He describes the trees, the flowers,
the singing of the innumerable birds, the ravishing sounds
of musical instruments, the soft whispering of the winds,
the clear and temperate air. Soon, he discovers Cupid

sharpening his arrows, and around him are Plesaunce, Aray, Lust, Curteseye, Craft, and a host of others. He reaches a building with great jasper-pillars, the Temple of Venus, around which dance dishevelled women, and on the roof of which sit hundreds of doves; before the door are Dame Pees and Dame Pacience. Within, stands the god Priapus, being crowned with garlands of flowers, and far beyond, in a dim recess, is Venus herself.

Coming out of the temple, the poet next sees in the Park Nature, " the noble emperesse, ful of grace, the vicaires of thalmyghty lorde." It is Seynt Valentyne's day—February the 14th—when every bird comes to choose his mate. Nature bids the birds take their place according to their kind, and here they are formed into groups, birds of prey, small birds that feed on worms, water-fowls, and those that live on seeds. Nature, who holds in her hand a female eagle of great beauty, tells them all to declare their choice: each is to speak according to his rank, and female birds remain free to give or to withhold their consent.

Three eagles speak first; they choose the female eagle which Nature holds in her hand, and they express themselves like true knights in a court of love, whilst the damsel blushes suitably. They declare that they would die without her, and plead their love with both passion and respect; their speech lasts from dawn until sundown. The rank and file of the fowls noisily protest. The order of the ceremony is disturbed, and it becomes impossible to hear any one; whereupon Nature asks each species of birds to elect a representative. This is done, and in turn are heard the male falcon, chosen by the " foules of ravyne "; the goose speaking for the water-fowls; the turtle-dove selected by the seed-fowls, and the cuckoo representing the worm-eaters. The subject of the debate is the manner in which a lover should pay his court, and each bird, according to his kind, reveals himself either chivalrous or coarse or tender or selfish. After all these declarations, constantly interrupted by protestations from various parts of the assembly, Nature delivers judgment: the lady is to have her free choice, but Nature advises her to choose the royal eagle. In a trembling voice, the female bird begs Nature to grant her a year's respite. This is agreed to and the eagles will wait until then. The other birds, however, choose their mates and take them away at once, and, as they go, all sing a rondel to a French tune: " Qui bien aime a tard oublie." The noise of their singing awakens the poet and brings his dream to a close.

We have here a strange mixture: allegory and mythology, Nature and Venus, Scipio the Elder conjured up into a *fabliau*. But it is precisely in this incongruity that Chaucer's budding originality is best shown. The *Parlement of Foules* is undoubtedly remarkable in the first place as a poetic exercise where he rivals the best masters known to him, but its chief interest lies in this, that it enables us to appreciate, through the thick veil of convention, the true nature of the poet. If in the first part Chaucer is only learning the practice of his art, by turning Cicero into verse and by reproducing the rich descriptive stanzas of Boccaccio, he shows his hand in the second in a certain vivacity of narrative, which is all his own, and in the clever blending of sentimental poetry and comedy. We have already here some of that variety of tone, that dramatic briskness, that air of gaiety mingled with romance, which will be the chief glory of the *Canterbury Tales*. And in this aristocracy of birds made fun of by the lower classes and repaying it with scorn; in these beings with prosaic instincts who scoff at exalted sentiments, have we not the same kind of antithesis which will be met with constantly in the Tales? Replace the royal eagle by the Knight, the goose by the Miller, the cuckoo by the Monk, and the turtle-dove by Griselidis; tear up the fable and draw away the thin veil of allegory, and you have all the principal elements of the great poem.[1] This is a scene of the great human comedy, exhibiting almost full fledged the impartiality of the *conteur*, who no doubt prefers noble sentiments, but who deems it his duty to give a place to the others. Whilst snubbing material minds, he reveals their innate common-sense, and uses them to expose the affectation inherent in the refinements of courtly love.

III

We know that the *Hous of Fame* was written while Chaucer held the comptrollership of the customs, but we have no means of fixing more exactly the date of its composition. Upon the whole, however, recent research tends to prove that it was earlier than was formerly conjectured, perhaps earlier than that of the *Parlement of Foules* and of *Troilus and Criseyde*. The use of the short couplet and the lighter style of the whole piece favour an early date. On the other hand, the overloading which was so noticeable in the two previous poems, is even greater here, as if the poet had extended his reading to yet further and more diverse fields. He took the main idea from Ovid, that of the House of Fame; his portrait of the goddess from Virgil—the *Æneid* was quite fresh to his mind, especially the episode of Dido's

[1] Read in this connection the debate between the birds (ll. 561-617).

love for Æneas; he was saturated with Boethius, whom he was busy translating, and who supplied him with his natural philosophy. At the same time, it seems as if a recent perusal of the *Divina Commedia* had flooded and somewhat disturbed his mind. All this reading was like newly acquired wealth to him; it dazzled him, and he had not yet assimilated it properly. He thought he would be able to use all this, without interfering with the ordinary allegorical setting. At heart, he remained the faithful disciple of the *Roman de la Rose*, whose machinery he retained, and whose short line he once more borrowed. And so he went on at his own easy pace, half bewildered and half mischievous, through the beautiful palaces he had just discovered.

The origin and object of this poem cannot easily be explained. It is the most disinterested Chaucer ever wrote, one might say it is the most fanciful, for he does not appear to have written it for any special occasion. It was not a task imposed upon him, nor was it the natural and irresistible outlet of stored up impressions.

Considering the light and playful tone of the work, it does not seem possible to admit with Ten Brink that the misunderstood poet, the official, debarred by his daily work from attaining the fame he coveted, here gave expression to his melancholy. It is much simpler to imagine that the poet, conscious of his growing powers, wished to emulate the *Roman de la Rose*, and its well-nigh innumerable progeny of so-called visions,[1] and to raise an allegorical structure of equal amplitude. In order to compete better with the famous poem, he made use of all his learning, either by going straight to the Latin writers

[1] *See* Sypherd, *Studies in The House of Fame,* 1907 (Chaucer Society).

already known to Lorris and Jean de Meung, or by imitating
the great Italian poems which they could not have known.
But in tone and inspiration, he is still very near to the
French. The episodes of Virgil or Dante, when retold in
Chaucer's somewhat thin *trouvère's* voice, seem to shrink
and dwindle. It is also curious to see how he endeavours
to drape all his borrowings, as well as his own inventions,
in the robes of the then fashionable allegory.

But allegory is not the best thing about the poem. The
structure as a whole is rather queer than beautiful, and
very different indeed from the first plan of the *Roman
de la Rose*, which is neat, clear cut, and almost grand in
the simplicity of its lines. Chaucer has no definite aim
at first, and lingers over details which delay his progress
unduly. Sometimes one is even tempted to ask whether
he has any aim in view. He is incapable of the sustained
purpose, the careful artifice, which are the chief conditions
of a good allegory. Reality has too many attractions
for him, and he cannot be the slave of fancy very long.
He mischievously pricks the bubble which he himself has
blown. He left the work unfinished, and the structure of
it is so strange that it is difficult to conjecture how it would
have ended. Through lack of plan, the subject of the poem
surprises more than it interests, and the work as a whole
is not pleasing. It is not in the general conception that
we find Chaucer at his best, but in the occasional ingenious
working out of the different parts, and in the detail, which
is often intimate and charming. Above all, one is pleased
to discover in this book, the most self-revealing he ever
wrote, passages where he gives us an idea of his daily life,
of the books he read, of his character and turn of mind.

We may dispense with a minute analysis of this long
poem. The slow working up of the allegory, which was

a feature of the previous poems, is here again noticeable, and this time even more complicated. We have a discussion on the origin and veracity of dreams, an invocation to the God of Sleep, and then the dream itself. The poet is in the temple of Venus, where he beholds, painted on the walls, the whole story of Æneas, more particularly of his love affairs. Still marvelling at this sight, he comes out of the temple and finds himself alone in a sandy desert. At that moment a golden eagle swoops down on him and carries him off, in a dizzy flight, to the Palace of Fame, situate in the heavens, in such a way as to overhear every sound on the earth. He visits this palace where he beholds the goddess with the thousand eyes surrounded by the Muses; on the pillars of the big hall stand the famous poets and historians. This gives Chaucer an opportunity of enumerating the writers he most admires. It is a curious company, among whom figure pell-mell Iosephus the Ebrayk, who told the gestes of the Jews; the " toulousain " Stace, who related the Theban war; the great Homer, and close to him Titus (Dictys?) and Lollius, by whom perhaps is meant Boccaccio; Guido de Colonna, who also related the siege of Troy; Gaufride, that is to say Geoffrey of Monmouth, who wrote the history of the Bretons descended from the Trojans; Virgil, who sang Pius Eneas; Ovid, the clerk of Venus; Dan Lucan, the great poet who conferred enduring fame on Cæsar and Pompey; Dan Claudian, who told the rape of Proserpine.

Whilst Chaucer was admiring the place, he saw various groups of men entering the hall, who had come to make requests of fame. The goddess appeared to him erratic in the way she bestowed her favour, granting glory right and left, sometimes against all reason, sometimes with great fairness. Æolus published her answer by blowing his trumpet. But Chaucer had come purposely to learn how new tidings were made. Accordingly, he leaves the Palace of Fame for the House of Rumour, which is ever whirling around its axis and is full of deafening noises. The place is filled with a countless multitude of people, who whisper in each other's ears contradictory rumours, real or false. Messengers, courtiers, pilgrims, seamen, pardoners, throng the house and bring tidings. Thence all these tidings escape to the House of Fame, where the goddess gives each a name and grants it duration or bids it die. . . . And the poem ends here abruptly.

The fiction is often cleverly handled where the game of allegory requires only mental ingenuity. Take for instance this little scene, which symbolises the mixture of truth and falsehood of which most tidings are made—

> And somtyme saugh I tho, at ones,   2088
> A lesing and a sad soth-sawe,
> That gonne of aventure drawe
> Out at a windowe for to pace;
> And, when they metten in that place,
> They were a-chekked bothe two,
> And neither of hem moste out go;
> For other so they gonne croude,
> Til eche of hem gan cryen loude,
> " Lat me go first! "   " Nay, but lat me!
> And here I wol ensuren thee
> With the nones that thou wolt do so,
> That I shal never fro thee go,
> But be thyn owne sworen brother!
> We wil medle us ech with other,
> That no man, be he never so wrothe,
> Shal han that oon [of] two, but bothe
> At ones, al beside his leve,
> Come we a-morwe or on eve,
> Bewel cryed or stille y-rouned."
> Thus saugh I fals and sooth compouned
> Togeder flee for oo tydinge.

This is epigrammatic and witty, but it lacks the personal
stamp.   In this poem, the accessories are more interesting
than the parts belonging to the logical development of the
story.   For good or ill they give us an insight into Chaucer's
personality.   Nowhere is the distance which separates him
from the ancients so well marked as in the first book,
where he relates the *Æneid* in his own way.   His transcription of Virgil's sonorous hexameters into short lines
looks to us like parody.   It is the breath of a child blowing
through the heroic trumpet—

> " I wol now singe, if that I can,   143
> The armes, and al-so the man,
> That first cam, through his destinee,
> Fugitif of Troye contree,
> In Itaile, with ful moche pyne,
> Unto the strondes of Lavyne ! "

The liberties he took with proper nouns and titles, constantly
remind us that Chaucer saw the ancients with the eyes of
a *trouvère* and not of a humanist.   Priam and his son
" Polites " are killed by " Dan Pirrus."   " Dan Eneas " is
in the company of " the knight Achates," when he meets
Venus.   Here and there the poet introduces popular
sayings into the ancient tale; he advises ladies to be
warned by the example of Dido and to distrust strange
flatterers—

> Al this seye I by Eneas   286
> And Dido, and her nyce lest,
> That lovede al to sone a gest;
> Therfor I wol seye a proverbe,
> That " he that fully knoweth therbe
> May saufly leye hit to his yë; "
> Withoute dreed, this is no lye.

Such childish irreverence cannot but astonish us in a poet
who knew Petrarch.

But the original part of this unequal poem is the second
book, which describes Chaucer's impressions whilst he was
being carried away to the farthest heaven by the golden
eagle.   It has been supposed that the *Hous of Fame* was
the work of Chaucer referred to later by his disciple Lydgate,
under the name of " Dante in ynglyssh."   And there are
indeed in the general plan, in the invocations, in the
details even (not to mention one direct allusion to Dante),
enough obvious reminiscences of the *Divina Commedia* to
render this supposition plausible.   The eagle is next of
kin to the one who bore Dante up to the sphere of fire
(*Purgatorio*, canto ix. l. 19).   But it is Dante retold by a
humorist.   It is not exactly parody, but verse and tone
are set in a lower key.   We need not shrink from admitting
that Chaucer does not belong to the same race as Dante,
since he admitted it himself.   We may even enjoy the
roguish way, in which the citizen of London sets out in
his own way to emulate the great Florentine's journey
through space.   What is delightful is the accuracy with
which Chaucer describes himself, declaring that he is
unsuited for such exalted flights, consoling himself with
that easy scepticism which is natural to him, and confessing
that he prefers walking on solid earth.

This is not so much irony as a sort of cheerful, bantering
good-humour, and it should be noticed that although the
poet admits he is too small a man for lofty ambitions, he
is still capable of admiring them.

The beautiful eagle with golden feathers swooped down
on him with the swiftness of lightning, and seized him in its
powerful claws as it would have done a lark.   Then it
carried him so high that the poor man lost all consciousness
for some time.   He awoke when the eagle addressed him
with a human voice.   The bird tried to comfort him,

promising that no harm would come to him, and bidding
him look at the magnificent spectacle before him. The
poet, however, could not help feeling anxious—

> "O god," thoughte I, " that madest kinde,   584
> Shal I non other weyes dye?
> Wher Ioves wol me stellifye?
> I neither am Enok, ne Elye,
> Ne Romulus, ne Ganymede
> That was y-bore up, as men rede,
> To hevene with dan Iupiter,
> And maad the goddes boteler."

The eagle reassures him—

> Thou demest of thy-self amis;   596
> For Ioves is not ther-aboute—
> I dar wel putte thee out of doute—
> To make of thee as yet a sterre.

The God of Thunder only wishes to reward the poet, who
had served so long and so faithfully his nephew Cupid
and the goddess Venus without guerdon for himself, and
who, despite his feeble wit, had written books, songs and
ditties in reverence of Love and his servants, without
sharing in his bounties. Jupiter is grateful to the poet
for having so often made his head ache by his disinterested
labour, in the service of lovers, he himself not being one.
He considered also that his task as a poet had been rendered
more difficult by the daily duties appertaining to his office.

> Iupiter considereth this,   641
>
> .   .   .   .
> . . . that thou hast no tydinges
> Of Loves folk, if they be glade,
> Ne of noght elles that god made;
> And not only fro fer contree
> That ther no tyding comth to thee,
> But of thy verray neyhebores,
> That dwellen almost at thy dores,

Thou herest neither that ne this;
For whan thy labour doon al is,
And hast y-maad thy rekeninges,
In stede of reste and newe thinges,
Thou gost hoom to thy hous anoon;
And, also domb as any stoon,
Thout sittest at another boke,
Til fully daswed is thy loke,
And livest thus as an hermyte,
Although thyn abstinence is lyte.

That is why Jupiter wishes Chaucer to visit the House of Fame. He wants to give him pleasure and distraction, as a recompense for his labours and devotion to the ungrateful Cupid. He will learn more things in this house about love and lovers, their faith, their perfidy, their joys, their discords, their deceptions, than there are grains of sand on the seashore and grains of corn in the barns.

Chaucer at first refuses to believe that Fame could hear all this, even if she had all the magpies and spies of the realm in her service. But the eagle, who has read Boethius, explains the process in detail. The House of Fame stands just midway between heaven, earth and sea, so that all sounds must pass through it. He explains how all things behave according to their nature, the stone falling and smoke rising. Now, sound is nothing but broken air. Each word or sound behaves like a stone thrown in the water; it makes a ring, which produces another and so forth, until becoming wider and wider they at last reach the opposite bank. In this way, asserts the bird, all sounds reach the House of Fame. The eagle is delighted with his own explanation, and proud to be able to speak in unlearned fashion to an unlearned man in terms so palpable

that he may shake hem by the biles.   868

He insists on the poet giving his approval to his theory.
Chaucer is as wary in his answer as a Norman peasant.
He merely says that the system seems to him a plausible
and likely one.   The eagle promises to give him soon an
absolute proof, but meanwhile, after his arduous lesson,
he wishes him to have a little recreation—" By Seynt
Iame, now wil we speken al of game! " (885-886).   He
asks Chaucer to look down at the earth and see if he
can still recognise anything, town or house.   The poet
looks and beholds

feldes and plaines,   897
And now hilles, and now mountaines
Now valeys, and now forestes,
And now unethes, grete bestes;
Now riveres, now citees,
Now tounes, and now grete trees,
Now shippes sailinge in the see.

But the eagle does not stop there; he soars higher, so high
that the whole world, to the poet's eye,

No more semed than a prikke;   907

For they are beyond the point of space reached by
Alexander the Macedonian, or King Dan Scipio, or Dedalus,
or Icarus.   The eagle then bids the poet look upward and
see " the eyrish bestes " (932), that is to say, the signs of
the zodiac; he shows him the Milky Way, the Galaxy
" which some call Watlinge strete " (939).   Then he rises
higher still.   Chaucer sees now under him stars, clouds,
rains, snows, tempests.   His first feeling is one of admiration, but a doubt soon seizes him; is he there in body or in
spirit?   God knows, but not he, for God had not sent him
a clear enough understanding.   He reflects, however, that
Martianus and the Anticlaudianus had described with
truth these heavenly regions, and that they could be

trusted. But he is not one to enjoy these giddy heights for long.

> With that this egle gan to crye: 991
> " Lat be," quod he, " thy fantasye;
> Wilt thou lere of sterres aught? "
> " Nay, certeinly," quod I, " right naught;
> And why? for I am now to old."
> " Elles I wolde thee have told,"
> Quod he, " the sterres names, lo,
> And al the hevenes signes to,
> And which they been."   " No fors," quod I.

But the eagle again asks him if he would not like to see in their proper places in heaven all those beings, birds, beasts, women or men whom the gods have stellified: the Raven, the Bear, the fine harp of Arion, Castor and Pollux, the Dolphin, or the seven daughters of Atlas? Thus he would be able to test the truth of the accounts of the poets. But Chaucer is afraid lest their brightness should destroy his sight, and the eagle gives up trying to convince such a pedestrian mind. When he had carried him some distance further, he asks him if he did not hear a great sound: it was the rumbling noise coming from the House of Fame. The poet compares it to the booming of the sea against hollow rocks

> Whan tempest doth the shippes swalowe. 1036

They have reached their goal, and the flight is ended. But before allowing his guide to depart, Chaucer asks him if the noise which he heard came from the people who dwelt on the earth. The eagle says yes, but adds that each sound on entering the palace assumes the likeness of the person who had uttered it on earth:

> " And is not this a wonder thing? "
> " Yis," quod I tho, " by hevene king! "

It is significant that Chaucer's realism should have asserted itself for the first time so strongly in this excursion through an allegorical sky. Flying is not to his taste, and he frankly prefers walking; let him have feet, not wings. Just as Wordsworth, later, refused to accompany Coleridge on his aerial craft,[1] so Chaucer will not follow Dante into the regions where the earth is lost sight of. Solid ground suits him best. When travelling through the lofty Milky Way, he soon begins to regret the comfortable mud ruts, which scar the road from London to Canterbury.

His *Hous of Fame*, so characteristic despite its imperfections, is the journey of a sensible and playful mind through " the highest heaven of invention." It voices Chaucer's decided refusal to surrender himself completely to the sublime, or to believe deeply in the pure conceptions of the spirit.

IV

In the *Legend of Good Women*, the prologue alone is allegorical. But as this prologue is the only completed part, and is also the most original, the poem may rightly be classed with works of this kind.

At the time when Chaucer wrote it, probably about 1385, he had already composed, besides the poems we have just examined, his famous romance of *Troilus and Criseyde*. It seems as if this love-poem, together with his translation of the *Roman de la Rose*, had been the book which had served most to bring him fame. These two works had this in common, that they broke away from chivalrous poetry, and that instead of idealising woman, they repre-

[1] *See* Prologue to *Peter Bell.*

sented her in many cynical pages as sensuous, fickle, and dangerous. Against this disparagement of a sex accustomed to the incense of the poets, a protest was raised amongst the ladies of the court, denouncing the translator of Jean de Meung, the adapter of Boccaccio. His crime consisted in introducing into the domain of elevated and artistic poetry the malicious spirit of the *fabliaux*. The young Queen, Anne of Bohemia, anticipating the denunciations made later in France by the poetess Christine de Pisan, seems to have voiced these feminine remonstrances. The ostentatious chastity of her life, the almost idolatrous devotion of the young king her husband, made her resent all the more deeply the sarcasms uttered by the favourite poet of the court. She made known her grievance, and asked Chaucer, by way of penance, to sing, instead of faithless women, those illustrious lovers who had been true unto death, the pitiful victims of man's perfidy.

The prologue does not leave much doubt as to the conditions under which the subject of the *Legend* was suggested to, or rather forced upon, Chaucer. There he relates in a humorous and fanciful tone, under the transparent guise of an allegory, how he came to celebrate " the seyntes of Cupid." Nowhere else has he succeeded in bringing into a conventional allegory so much freshness and ease.

The beginning is delightful. He starts by telling us of his passion for books and for a certain flower, the daisy, which for him first symbolised the whole of nature. Then by and by the flower was transfigured and became his " lady sovereyne," which does not mean his mistress, but the Queen herself. No one would suspect that these flowing and apparently spontaneous lines are made up of reminiscences of Machaut, Froissart, Deschamps, from whom he borrowed the symbol of the daisy, even to the merest details. He most generously acknowledges his debt, and displays due modesty. Then the tone swells into a lyric, Boccaccio being now his inspiration. The whole of this beginning, as has been proved by Professor John Lowes,[1] is a veritable patchwork of imitations, and yet nothing could seem more natural or more personal. It has the charm of a rambling discourse, slightly derisive at first, but changing in tone by degrees, gaining in warmth, and finally reaching a sort of enthusiasm.

On the first morning in May,[2] the poet went out to kneel before his favourite flower:

> Upon the smale softe swote gras   118
> That was with floures swote enbrouded al.

The birds, having escaped the nets of the fowler, are glad with the tidings of spring; they warble on the branches and sing "blessed be seynt Valentyn!" Their beaks meet, and all render honour and obeisance to love. The poet is so moved by the charm of this day, that he thinks he might well have stayed there the whole month, without sleep, meat, or drink. He stretches himself on the grass, and, leaning on his elbow, remains there the livelong day, gazing at the "dayesye," or the eye of day, "the emperice and flour of floures alle." Nevertheless, it is far from his mind to praise the flower above the leaf, and he cares not for the quarrels of French poets about their respective merits; both are dear to him, and he cannot prefer one to the other.

At last, when evening has come and the daisy closes, the poet returns home to his house. He has his couch made in his "litel herber," and it is all strewn with

[1] *Pub. of the Mod. Lang. Assoc. of America,* vol. xix. no. 4.

[2] This analysis corresponds to Prologue B, the more harmonious version of the two that have come down to us.

flowers. Then, he falls asleep and dreams of what he had
seen and felt on that spring day. And in a meadow he sees,
coming from afar, the God of Love, clad in silk garments
embroidered with green leaves and petals of red roses.
His head is crowned with a sun which shines so brightly
that the poet can scarce look at it; in his hands he holds
two fiery darts as red as burning coals, and he has wings
like an angel. And he leads by the hand a noble queen
clothed all in green, with an ornament of gold in her hair
and above that a white crown with small *fleurons*, which
makes her look exactly like a daisy. She comes towards
him so benignly and so meekly that the poet at once breaks
into song, and composes a ballad in her praise, in which
he bids all the beautiful and virtuous ladies of history·bow
before her: Esther, Penelope, Marcia Cato, Isoude, Helen,
Lavinia, Lucretia of Rome, Polyxena, Cleopatra, Thisbe,
Hero, Dido, Laodamia, Phyllis, Canace, Hypsipyle,
Hypermnestra and Ariadne:

>   My lady cometh, that al this may disteyne.   255

Behind the God of Love follow nineteen ladies in royal
habits, and after these an endless crowd of women—the
poet could not have believed that since Adam there had been
born a third nor even a fourth part of the number he saw.

>   And trewe of love thise women were echoon.   290

When they see the daisy, they kneel down before her and
sing her praises. Then they all sit round in a circle, first
the God of Love and his Queen, and the rest according
to their station:

>   I kneling by this flour, in good entente   308
>   Abood, to knowen what this peple mente,
>   As stille as any stoon; til at the laste
>   The god of love on me his eyen caste,
>   And seyde, " Who kneleth ther? " and I answerde
>   Unto his asking, whan that I hit herde,

And seyde, " Sir, hit am I; " and com him neer,
And salued him.   Quod he, " What dostow heer
So nigh myn owne flour, so boldely?
For it were better worthy, trewely,
A worm to neghen neer my flour than thou."
" And why, sir," quod I, " and hit lyke yow? "
" Hit is my relik, digne and delytable,
And thou my fo, and al my folk werreyest
And of myn old servaunts thou misseyest,
And hindrest hem, with thy translacioun,
And lettest folk from hir devocioun
To serve me, and holdest hit folye
To serve Love.   Thou mayst hit nat denye;
For in pleyn text, with-outen nede of glose,
Thou hast translated the Romaunce of the Rose,
That is an heresye ageyns my lawe,
And makest wyse folk fro me withdrawe.
And of Criseyde thou hast seyd as thee liste,
That maketh men to wommen lasse triste,
That ben as trewe as ever was any steel."   334

And in conclusion the god threatens him " by seynt
Venus," his mother, with the most cruel punishment.
Fortunately, the gentle queen intercedes for the poet.
She reminds Love that a god should never give way to
anger, but that it behoves him to be gracious and merciful.
Who knows if the man was not falsely accused? The
court is full of flatterers.   Perhaps also he did wrong
without evil intent, and he may have been commanded to
write the two censured books.   In any case, to have
translated those libels was less grievous than if he had
invented them.   It would be just also to take into consideration all the books he had written in honour of love,
and the pious works he had helped to make known.   In
conclusion, she begs the god to hand the accused over to
her, promising to make him swear that he will offend no
more, but rather that he will sing the praise of women
who were true and faithful all their lives.   The god grants

the request of the merciful lady. Thereupon the poet
rises, thanks him, and begs to be told the name of his
rescuer. Then he tries to justify himself, and argues that
true lovers had nothing to fear from his exposure of the
faithless and the deceitful. As for him, he had only
wished to tell the truth and to put people on their guard
against falsehood. But the queen interrupts this special
pleading with " Lat be thyn arguinge! " and she tells him
that the only way to win her pardon is

> In making of a glorious Legende   483
> Of gode wommen, maidenes and wyves,
> That weren trewe in lovinge al hir lyves;
> And telle of false men that hem bitrayen.

When the book is finished, he is to bring it to the queen,
to her palace at Eltham or at Shene.

Then it is that Love tells the poet the name of the lady
to whom he owes the remittance of his sentence; she is the
good Queen Alcestis of Thrace. On hearing this, the poet
cannot repress his astonishment, for he well knows the
story of the wife who had died to save her husband, and
he pays an impassioned tribute to her virtues. The god
rebukes him for his great negligence in omitting her name
from his ballad " Hyd, Absolon, thy gilte tresses clere,"
knowing that Alcestis was the paragon of all loving wives,
and he enjoins him to insert her praise in the coming poem.
He further informs him that the nineteen ladies present
were those of his ballad, and instructs him to include them
in the same work: he will find their story in books. To
this he adds a few directions: the poet is free to select his
own metre, but he must begin with Cleopatra. Indeed, he
should not attempt to describe the many merits of these ladies,
but rather aim at being brief. Whereupon, Chaucer fetches
his books and sets to work at once on the first legend.

It seemed best to give this lengthy analysis of the Prologue, not only because of the particulars it contains about the poet's tastes, his attitude, and his relations with the court, but also because of the charm of his manner, the playful easy-going way in which he blends personal sentiments with the details of the allegory, and the lightness of touch which combines grace with humour. In the artificial style Chaucer never produced anything so happily wrought, nor apparently so personal.

Nevertheless, the mixture of common sense and play-fulness, which runs through the prologue, might appear out of place at the beginning of a poem of which the very subject seems to exact from the author a sort of chivalrous enthusiasm. Has he not undertaken to be devoutly partial to the heroines of love throughout, and to expose their deceitful lovers? Bias was here a necessity. The rules of the game demand that reality should be left on one side, or if one prefers to put it so, that the poet should lift himself above reality. What had to be done was to create a new humanity, composed of perfect women on the one hand, and of entirely faithless and heartless men on the other. No doubt such a poem is possible, one may even imagine it exquisite. But only a fearless idealist could undertake it: what is needed is that kind of imagination which boldly transforms the world to suit its own dreams. The great Spenser, so unreal and monotonous, could have done it. But few poets ever had a temperament less suited for lengthy litanies than Chaucer. He could describe the feelings of a woman's heart as well as any romantic poet, its meekness, its purity, its self-abnegation, its devotion, its anguish. But his nature was such that to see nothing but that, and to express nothing else, was quite impossible to him. Inevitably, while looking at one side, the reverse is ever present with him. His common sense renders him incapable of sustained enthusiasm. The irony which suffuses the prologue, sometimes spreads over the legends themselves, but it is always at the expense of the necessary idealisation. And, in all probability, it is to this antagonism between his nature and his subject that we must ascribe the non-completion of a book, undertaken with such manifest verve and care.

So long as the poet deals with a legend, in which he is really interested, all is well. The rape of Lucretia, the misfortunes of Philomela, fill him with genuine wrath against Tarquinius and Tereus, those cruel ravishers. He appeals to God against the latter, and his eloquent words, inspired by Boethius, ring with unmistakable gravity:

> Thou yiver of the formes, that hast wroght 2228
> The faire world, and bare hit in thy thoght
> Eternally, or thou thy werk began,
> Why madest thou, unto the slaundre of man,
> Or--al be that hit was not thy doing,
> As for that fyn to make swiche a thing—
> Why suffrest thou that Tereus was bore,
> That is in love so fals and so forswore,
> That, fro this world up to the firste hevene,
> Corrumpeth, whan that folk his name nevene?
> And, as to me, so grisly was his dede,
> That, whan that I his foule story rede,
> My eyen wexen foule and sore also. 2240

But in the case of Theseus or Iasoun, who were the Don Juans of ancient Greece, libertines rather than criminals, Chaucer finds it difficult to work himself up to his task of censor. His tone at times is a pitch higher than his feelings, so that one sees the humorist smile through the satirist, who is trying in vain to frown. Finally, a familiar touch tells us that his anger is quite spent. Hark at him apostrophising Iasoun:

Thou rote of false lovers, duk Iasoun!   1368
Thou sly devourer and confusioun
Of gentil-wommen, tender creatures,
Thou madest thy reclaiming and thy lures
To ladies of thy statly apparaunce,
And of thy wordes, farced with plesaunce,
And of thy feyned trouthe and thy manere,
With thyn obeisaunce and thy humble chere,
And with thy counterfeted peyne and wo,
Ther other falsen oon, thou falsest two!
O! ofte swore thou that thou woldest dye
For love, whan thou ne feltest maladye
Save foul delyt, which that thout callest love!
If that I live, thy name shal be shove
In English, that thy sleighte shal be knowe!
Have at thee, Iasoun! now thyn horn is blowe!
But certes, hit is bothe routhe and wo
That love with false loveres werketh so;
For they shul have well better love and chere
Than he that hath aboght his love ful dere,
Or had in armes many a blody box.
For ever as tendre a capoun et the fox,
Thogh he be fals and hath the foul betrayed,
As shal the good-man that ther-for hath payed.
Al have he to the capoun skille and right,
The false fox wol have his part at night.

In a still more familiar way, Chaucer takes to task the son
of Theseus, Demophon, who was as great a seducer as his
father:

And lyk his fader of face and of stature,   2446
And fals of love; hit com him of nature;
As doth the fox Renard, the foxes sone,
Of kinde he conde his olde faders wone
Withoute lore, as can a drake swimme,
Whan hit is caught and caried to the brimme.

It should be said on behalf of the poet, if there be any
need to plead his cause, that when he came to look more
closely at the lives of the nineteen good women, whose
virtues he had, at a little distance, so lightly praised, misled

by the titles of his Ovid or of the *De Claris Mulieribus*
of Boccaccio, he discovered, in the case of some of them,
certain traits which lessened somewhat his admiration for
them or mitigated his anger against their ravishers. He
must have wondered, in the light of later reading, what
had made him put on his list Cleopatra, the royal courtesan,
and Medea, the nefarious magician. His natural inclination
to sly humour could only increase under this disillusion-
ment. In almost every legend touches of comedy are
lurking. He has a flippant way of telling us that on
escaping from Troy Æneas lost his wife:

> And by the weye his wyf Creusa he lees.   945

When the tempest forces Dido and Æneas to take refuge
in a cave, he slyly adds:

> I noot, with hem if ther wente any mo;   1227
> The autour maketh of hit no mencioun.

In the *Legend of Hipsypile* he complacently expatiates on
all the nice things said about Jason by Hercules, who is in
the plot with the seducer. In the *Legend of Ariadne*, he
endows Theseus with a flowing eloquence, shows him to
be a glib talker, prodigal of oaths, and discloses at the
same time the weakness of Ariadne, who swallows his
flattery with avidity. If he comes across any miracles in
his text, he declares that you must believe in them if you
can,

> As of that scripture,   1144
> Be as be may, I make of hit no cure.[1]

Lastly, he ends the *Legend of Phillis* in the most frolicsome
mood:

> Be war, ye women, of your sotil fo,   2559
> Sin yit this day men may ensample see;
> And trusteth, as in love, no man but me.

[1] *See also* l. 1020.

Notwithstanding all this, the legends are full of noble
and impressive passages.   The most pathetic and the best
told, it is true, are those where Chaucer borrows from Ovid,
and where he attempts nothing more than to translate the
Latin poet.   This is the case with his Thisbe of Babylon,
his Lucretia, his Philomela, and his Hypermnestra, and
no doubt much of our admiration should go by rights to
the original.   Yet, however faithful Chaucer may wish to
be, he cannot translate without adding to the story a tone
and colour which are peculiarly his own.   He does not
possess the fine rhetoric of the model, and he is not making
use, as Ovid was, of a language already both rich and
supple.   The artlessness of his style and the awkwardness
of his as yet unmatured language, would suffice to differentiate him.   These drawbacks sometimes turn to his
advantage, for the familiar tone comes home to the reader,
the emotion is more direct and less encumbered with the
ornaments and refinements of style.   He often lacks the
relief and vigour of Ovid, but then he does not so often
distract the reader's attention, from the simple pathos of
the tale to the admiration of the writer's wit.

Chaucer is less fortunate when he selects other ancient
models.   Despite what he borrowed from Plutarch and
Florus for his Cleopatra, his treatment of the legend is not
convincing; in fact, it is one of the poorest in the whole
set.   Virgil does not suit him nearly so well as Ovid, as
can readily be seen from his *Legend of Dido*.   This little
poem amuses us to-day, for reasons which Chaucer very
likely did not foresee.   He has added more mediæval
colour to this antique subject than to any other.   The
hunt in which Æneas and Dido take part, the equipage of
both, above all, the courteous manner in which the hero
woos the queen, all this might have come out of the pages

of Benoît de Sainte-More or of Chrestien de Troyes. Dido's passion does not seem to have made a very strong appeal to Chaucer. The sentimentality of the *Heroides* was certainly more to his taste than the epic restraint of the fourth book of the *Æneid*.

After admitting the shortcomings of the poet, and acknowledging that he owed the best of his book to Ovid, it is only fair to add that his legends mark a very considerable progress in the direction of his masterpiece. It is after all of trifling importance that they should have been drawn from a remote mythology; they relate the eternal adventures of the heart, and, with the names changed, they become applicable to sorrows which are for ever renewed. Each one of them is a little drama of passion. The allegory has been done away with, and the poet can give free play to his simple and kindly humanity. He does this especially when he translates, but then, was he not the first to tell in melodious English verse many an imperishable story of love and despair? A translation which possesses as much feeling as he displays in the best passages, for instance in the lamentations of forsaken Ariadne, when, standing on the shore of the lonely island, she calls to her lover's fleeing barge to turn back, amounts to a creation. The poem enabled him also to discover in which direction his genius lay, for he had at last found, not only the form of narrative which suited him best, but even the metre which was to win for him such signal triumphs. The transition from the Legends to the *Canterbury Tales* merely meant giving up old times for new, replacing Greece by England, and finding a subject of his own choice, instead of the somewhat monotonous task prescribed for him by the good Queen Anne of Bohemia.

CHAPTER IV

I

THE poems examined in the previous chapter, enable us now to form a fairly accurate idea of the kind of art Chaucer practised, and the degree of excellence he could attain in serious poetry, in the school of his French masters. But, in composing the last three poems, he had already other models in view. With the exception of the *Book of the Duchesse*, they are very largely inspired by his Italian readings, and for the last of all, the *Legend of Good Women*, he drew direct from antiquity. This had the happy result, in the case of some of them at least, of adding breadth to his style and treatment. Whereas the *Book of the Duchesse* and the *Hous of Fame* were written in the short line, used almost exclusively by contemporary French writers outside lyrical poetry, in the *Parlement of Foules* and in the *Legend* he used the ten syllable line, as being nearer the hendecasyllabic verse or the hexameter. In the lengthening of the line lay the germ of an entire revolution. If we look closely, we see that these two extra syllables make room for an epithet, for the word which gives precision or colour. It alters at once the tone and movement of the line, and the poet, without sacrificing simplicity of style, can be lofty, grave, or forcible at will.

In these poems, moreover, Chaucer borrowed little details or even whole passages from ancient or modern Italian verse, and tried to reproduce in some measure the splendour which he had there discovered. But, however noticeable these influences may be in the poems mentioned, they were not sufficient to detach Chaucer's allegiance from his first masters. He remained a devotee of allegory with all its conventions; the new elements introduced were only given second place. As a matter of fact, Italy only really left her mark later on, in poems where she enabled him to free himself from personifications and symbols, where he was bold enough to tell a story in a direct way, and paint men and the passions of men without the help of abstractions or dreams. Her influence, in short, was really deep only when he drew from her both the substance and style of his poems. That is why we preferred to postpone the study of this influence until we came to *Palamon and Arcite*, and more especially to *Troilus and Criseyde*.

Chaucer doubtless came under the spell of Italy on the occasion of his first visit there in 1372, and he must have experienced it directly he set foot in the country. M. Jusserand has described admirably the wondrous spectacle, which must have been presented to an English traveller by fourteenth-century Italy, touched with the light of the early Renaissance. Before he had even opened a book, the freshly built churches and monuments revealed to him a new conception of art. Whilst in England the exaggerated Gothic arch was becoming flamboyant, Chaucer found in Italy a new kind of architecture, evolved through the abandonment of the pointed arch and the return to the plain semicircle. He could see antique columns, statues, and coins, being dug out of the ground, and the gods of Olympus coming to light, whose beautiful naked forms had already begun to inspire artists and to renovate art, whilst the walls of the churches were resplendent with the fresh beauty of the frescoes of Giotto and Orcagna.

Is there no echo in Chaucer's verse of the emotions which seized him on his arrival in Italy? One is tempted to ascribe to his naive admiration for the masterpieces of ancient and modern Italy, the cry of enthusiasm which. burst from his lips, when he beheld the stained windows of the glass temple, depicting the stories of the heroes of old:

> " Ah, Lord! " thoughte I, " that madest us,
> Yet saw I never swich noblesse
> Of images, ne swich richesse,
> As I saw graven in this chirche;
> But not woot I who dide hem wirche,
> Ne wher I am, ne in what contree.". . .
>
> *The Hous of Fame,* I. ll. 470-475.

But his sense of plastic beauty was too rudimentary and undeveloped for monuments, statues, and paintings to have left much trace in his work. It is possible, of course, to point out a few lines where he extols the beauty of the nude, describing Venus, for instance, " naked fletinge in a see " (*H. of Fame*, I. 133). But he owed this initiation to the poets, not to the painters and sculptors. The new splendour, which will now colour his style in places, has come to him through books. Moreover, it does not seem as if he owed this added richness as much to the Romans as to the Italians. The deferential admiration for the ancients which he displayed hereafter, was imitated rather than spontaneous. He went on translating Virgil, as we have seen, with the reed-like voice of a *trouvère*. He was more happy with Ovid, but only at the expense of making him more familiar. On the other hand, he reached at times the loftiness of some of the most beautiful fourteenth-century Italian poetry. Is it because he felt bolder when competing with contemporaries, and so was freed from the shackles of traditional respect, the nearness in time suggesting the idea of legitimate rivalry and of possible competition? I do not think so. It is rather because he never ceased to look at the ancients through the eyes of the Middle Ages, whereas he had a personal and direct impression of Italy. The same often occurred during the Renaissance, in the case of French and English poets. Spenser, for instance, owed much more to Ariosto and Tasso than to the ancients. And it is only when they draw from Italian sources that Chaucer and Spenser, otherwise so widely different, approach each other and even meet. Chaucer anticipates the poet of Una in a poem where, inspired by Boccaccio, he represents Ipolita on her chariot, so beautiful to see

> That al the ground about hir char she spradde
> With brightnesse of the beautee in hir face,
> Fulfild of largesse and of alle grace.
>
> *Anelida and Arcite*, ll. 40-42.

It is in the same poem and under the same influence that he finds the majestic line—an inspiration, not a translation— in which he hails Polymnia, the pensive Muse: O thou who

> Singest with vois memorial in the shade.
>
> *Anelida and Arcite*, l. 18.

Any one reading this quotation for the first time would surely believe it to be by Spenser, unless indeed he were to ascribe it to Milton.

These are heights to which Chaucer could but seldom attain, and only when impelled by the brilliance or the warmth of Italy. One thing is certain, there is about such lines a fullness and breadth which the French *trouvères* he knew, were scarcely capable of suggesting to him.

How then and by means of what reading was Chaucer thus initiated? He went straight to the great Italian poets. After the French writers, Dante, Petrarch, and Boccaccio became his masters, and they must have proved a strange and tremendous revelation to him, who had followed hitherto the decadent French allegorists of the fourteenth century. The influence brought to bear upon him by these three Italian poets, was of varying degrees.

Dante had been dead for half a century when Chaucer visited Italy, and he was already considered as belonging to a former age. His mysterious *Commedia* was reaping its full measure of admiration, but Boccaccio was just about to write for it a commentary, such as is written on a masterpiece of the past. There is no doubt that Chaucer was fully aware of the greatness of Dante, and that he himself felt it. He calls him " the grete poete of Itaille." [1] Now and then, he goes out of his way to borrow an image from him, either in translating Boccaccio or in transcribing the *Golden Legend*. He took from him his invocation to the Virgin, and set it in front of a life of Saint Cecilia. He remembered the awful inscription affixed by Dante on the gates of hell, and put a similar one at the entrance of a park, which he designed according to a plan of Boccaccio, changing, however, its fearful admonition into a pleasant sentence.

He had wept over the death of Ugolino in the tower of hunger, and he related it in his own way in his "tragedies," doing ample justice to the pathetic side of the story, although failing to reproduce its austere sublimity. He did not feel the full force of the lines where Ugolino, hearing the door of the tower being shut at the time when the gaoler was wont to bring their food, realises the designs of

[1] *The Monkes Tale*, l. 470.

his enemies. Silently he watches the faces of his sons; he does not weep, but feels as if his heart were being turned into stone. His sons cry, and little Anselm says

> " Thou lookest so! Father, what ails thee? "
>
> Cary's *Dante*.

In Chaucer's version we miss the father's awful silence and his tearless woe. He says indeed that Ugolino does not speak, but instantly contradicting himself, he makes him exclaim: " Allas! that I was wroght! " And he adds:

> Therwith the teres fillen from his yën.
>
> *The Canterbury Tales*, B. 1. 3619.

But, on the other hand, he puts some very touching words in the mouth of the youngest child:

> " Fader, why do ye wepe?
> Whan wol the gayler bringen our potage,
> Is ther no morsel breed that ye do kepe?
> I am so hungry that I may nat slepe.
> Now wolde god that I mighte slepen ever!
> Than sholde nat hunger in my wombe crepe;
> Ther is no thing, save breed, that me were lever."
>
> *The Canterbury Tales*, B. ll. 3622-3628.

And so the terrible story loses its grimness and becomes something more pitiful, but at the same time less powerful.

Chaucer did not, however, only find in Dante stories which contained too much concentrated energy to suit his taste, or which were too sublime for his powers. He was fully conscious of the beauty of his style and verse, and he has left a few curious attempts at *terza rima* inspired by the *Divina Commedia*. Above all, he loved in Dante those exquisitely tender passages where the tragic poet seems to unbend. He has himself written a few passages, which, for simple pathos, invite comparison with the great Florentine. I am not alluding only to lines like those

where his *Troilus* (bk. ii. l. 1261) borrows the fine hymn to
the Virgin, and turns it into an invocation to Love:

> Che qual vuol grazie, e a te non recorre.
>
> *Par.* xxxiii. 14.

But there are some lines quite his own, which, for sober
perfection, stand out from the other models he had before
his eyes, and which are superior, one might say, to his
usual manner. This applies to the five lines, so full of
pious fervour, which he added to his literal translation of
the death of Lucretia, as related by Ovid:

> I telle hit, for she was of love so trewe,
> Ne in her wille she chaungëd for no newe.
> And for the stable hertë, sad and kinde,
> That in these women men may alday finde;
> Ther as they caste her hertë, there hit dwelleth.

But it was only on rare occasions, and then not for long,
that Chaucer was able to touch the same key as Dante.
The difference was too great between the impassioned
and merciless Florentine, the fierce politician, the mystic
visionary, and the English story-teller, enamoured of life
and all things living, whose slight lyrical vein was ever held
in check by his sense of humour. And Chaucer felt this
himself, for we have seen him describing in an allegory his
vain efforts to follow the great poet on his upward career,
when the golden eagle bears him away to the highest
heaven, and he, bewildered, wants to return to solid earth,
thus asserting in this curious way his material nature. His
is not the spirit to descend into hell, nor to rise up into
Paradise.

In Petrarch, there was even less than in Dante that
Chaucer could assimilate into his own poetry. If Dante
represented the epic energy of an age already past,
Petrarch was too far ahead of his contemporaries in the

realisation of the Renaissance. His humanism was too refined, too close to the ancients, too much illuminated with philology, for Chaucer to understand it fully, or to follow in its wake, except from afar. He may, like Petrarch, experience a sort of devout enthusiasm when speaking of the Greeks or the Romans, but for all that he is not any nearer their real spirit. As to Petrarch the sonneteer, his excessive subtlety and fastidious idealism could not appeal to a nature so normal, so evenly balanced, as that of Chaucer, in whom joviality was ever the hand-maid of tenderness. Few minds were less capable of sustained Platonism than his.

And yet Chaucer understood the greatness of

> Frbaunceys Petrark, the laureat poete,
> . . . . whos rethoryke sweete
> Enlumined al Itaille of poetrye.
> *The Clerk's Prologue*, ll. 31-34.

We have seen that he may have known him personally when Petrarch was sixty-nine, that is to say, a year before the Italian's death. Chaucer later diluted into three seven-lined stanzas one of Petrarch's sonnets:

> S'amor non è, che dunque è quel ch'i sento?

and made it the first cry of passion of his *Troilus*. It was to Petrarch alone, a mere translator on the occasion, that Chaucer ascribed the touching tale of *Grisildis*.

Here, however, Petrarch was only the intermediary between Chaucer and Boccaccio, whom the English poet does not seem to have known under his real name. When one would expect Boccaccio's name in Chaucer's verse, one discovers instead the enigmatic name of Lollius. And yet it was Boccaccio who, towards the middle of Chaucer's career, influenced him most strongly. He it was who supplied him with some of his most remarkable stories, and almost without exception, with the pattern for those verses which, in the English poet, are most decorative or most passionate. Chaucer, it is true, seems to have been acquainted only with part of Boccaccio's enormous work; it is not likely that he had ever read the *Decamerone*, he who was to be looked upon by posterity as the rival story-teller to Boccaccio. We have just seen that the tale of *Grisildis*, the only story from the *Decamerone* which he translated, had come to him through a Latin version by Petrarch. Chaucer's contribution consisted only in a few delightful details, and in the happy innovation of the stanza instead of prose, a form which suits perfectly the picturesque and unreal legend. Other stories, already told in the *Decamerone*, before finding a place in the *Canterbury Tales*, present such differences in the working out of the plot, that one is justified in believing that the two authors borrowed their subject from separate versions, derived from a remote common original. The influence of Boccaccio is so apparent, whenever Chaucer had some definite work of his before him, that the English writer, had he known the stories of the *Decamerone*, never could have used any of them without betraying their origin. Undoubtedly, Chaucer did not derive the *Merchant's Tale* from the *Enchanted Pear-tree* (7th day, novel 9), nor the *Shipman's Tale* from the first two stories of the 8th day, nor the *Manciple's Tale* from the *Cradle* (9th day, novel 6), nor the *Franklin's Tale* from the *Enchanted Garden* (4th day, novel 5),[1] nor the Pardoner's predication from the

[1] The question of the indebtedness of Chaucer's *Tales* to the *Decamerone* has been so often discussed, and is still so unsettled, that I cannot resist the temptation of throwing in a word *en passant*. I find in the *Franklin's Tale* proof (which to me at least appears conclusive) that Chaucer, when he wrote it, did not know Boccaccio's *Enchanted Garden*. He introduces (vv. 515-527) a graphic descrip-

Cibolo's, which closes the 6th day. It is not a case of borrowing, but simply of analogy. In all probability, Boccaccio and Chaucer made use of *fabliaux*, mostly French, for their different versions of these tales. The great fame attained later by Boccaccio's *Decamerone*, and the comparative oblivion into which his verse fell, make it difficult to admit that Chaucer knew the second and not the first. But the *Decamerone* did not achieve immediate

tion of a frosty December, vivid and excellent in itself, but without any relation to his subject. It is thrust in at the very moment when the magician is at work to remove the rocks from the coast of Brittany.

Now, such a description would have been perfectly apposite, had Chaucer related the same prodigy as Boccaccio, *i.e.* a garden in full beauty of flowers and blossoms caused to appear in the depth of winter. In fact there were two different legends; Boccaccio used one and Chaucer the other. But Chaucer, somewhat careless of his plot as usual, must have followed a narrative in which some blundering clerk had somehow mixed up the two forms of enchantment. It is possible that even if he had known Boccaccio's novel, Chaucer might have preferred the other piece of magic. But it is scarcely credible that, the *Enchanted Garden* being present to his mind, he should not have detected at once the preposterousness of the winter-scene in the plot he had purposely selected in preference to the other. For he could not possibly read Boccaccio and remain indifferent. He could not choose to differ from him without having his own reasons, and thus becoming a conscious artist. In all probability he was unacquainted with Boccaccio's tale, and, the other legend being unknown to him, he paid no heed to the extraneous character of the passage. Cf., however, Rajna's article in *Romania*, 32, 244 ff., who believes that the *Franklin's Tale* was inspired by the *Decamerone*. Professor Morsbach (*Englische Studien*, xxxxii. pp. 43-82) ascribes the plan of the *Canterbury Tales* to Boccaccio's influence. Mr. Robert R. Root (*Englische Studien*, xxxiv. pp. 1-17) admits Morsbach's point of view as regards the general plan, but does not believe in an imitation of the *Tales*, in particular of the *Enchanted Garden*. Consult also Professor Schofield's learned article on Chaucer's *Franklin's Tale* (*Publ. of the Mod. Lang. Assoc. of America*, vol. xvi. no. 3).

glory; the book was too openly licentious, and Boccaccio himself had to make excuses for it rather than be proud of it.

Now Boccaccio's fame about the year 1372 rested chiefly on his claims as a humanist and as a poet. Chaucer's indebtedness to him, as an interpreter of ancient history and mythology, is not inconsiderable, for he owed him the idea, and even several passages of, those " tragedies " which compose his *Monk's Tale*. It was the *De Casibus Virum Illustrium* he used; from it he borrowed several of the " tragedies " related by Boccaccio in Latin prose—Adam, Samson, Balthazar, Zenobia, Nero, Crœsus—and turned them into short poems of eight line stanzas. But he retained and exercised the privilege of adding other unfortunate lives to those related by the Italian author.

Again, it was Boccaccio who suggested to him his *Legend of Good Women*. It was probably inspired by the *De Claris Mulieribus*, where Boccaccio had related briefly in Latin prose the adventures of 105 famous women. True, in this instance, Chaucer owed him but little as regards the matter, which was chiefly borrowed from Ovid. But for the plan of the book, the prologue, and the successive lives, he followed his favourite model, although he never refers to him explicitly.

But the youthful poems of the Italian writer especially attracted Chaucer, so that Boccaccio had the honour of evoking the first passionate verse in a literature as yet unknown, but which was to become one of the most illustrious in Europe. It was by translating and reshaping the *Teseide* and the *Filostrato*, that Chaucer first introduced into English poetry a richness and passion both characteristic of the great southern literature.

Out of the *Teseide*, condensed and abridged, he made, probably after several successive attempts, his *Knight's*

Tale, dealing with the amorous rivalry of Palamon and Arcite, the two young men who loved each other as brothers, their affection being further intensified by a common captivity, until the day when the love of the same girl led them to take up arms against each other. The *Teseide* was a sentimental novel, submerged in a sort of epic poem numbering about 10,000 lines. Chaucer preserved the essence of it for his *Knight's Tale*, took the description of the temple of Venus for his *Parlement of Foules*, further retaining a few external details for his unfinished poem of *Quene Anelida and fals Arcite*.

English commentators, naturally enough, prefer to lay stress on the skill showed by Chaucer in remodelling the *Teseide*. They justly praise the sober art displayed by their poet, in reducing the exuberant *Teseide* to about one-fifth of its original size. They rightly point out also that Chaucer showed great independence of spirit in rejecting Boccaccio's stanza for the couplet, less lyrical in form, but better suited to a narrative. Let us add that the never failing realism and familiarity of Chaucer appear in many additions to the speeches or scenes. Less conventional in tone, his Theseus indulges in outbursts of humour and many bantering remarks, which were not in Boccaccio. Chaucer enlarges upon and treats in a spirited manner the popular aspect of that great festive gathering of the Middle Ages, a tournament; he forsakes champions and knights to describe the bustling armourers and the hubbub of small people. But what are these changes, however fortunate, compared to the enormous indebtedness of the poet to his model?

The value of this poem, rather devoid of psychology after all is said, lies in the breadth and richness of a certain number of scenes, and here Chaucer wisely remained the faithful follower of the Italian poet. It was thanks to this fidelity even, that he not only wrote the finest lines of his tale, but also gave English poetry some graceful or rich paintings, the equivalent of which are not to be found again until Spenser. Such for instance is the charming scene where Palamon and Arcite, prisoners in the tower, see Emilia picking flowers in the garden. Such are also the series of pictures representing the great tournament between the knights who had come to join the rivals; the gorgeous description of the lists and of the amphitheatre erected for the spectators; the description of the three temples of Mars, Venus, and Diana, where Arcite, Palamon, and Emilia retire to pray respectively; such are also the incidents of the combat between the two rivals. There is no doubt, for one who reads the *Knight's Tale* without an eye to comparison, that these pages by far excel the rest of the poem: as a matter of fact, they are the rather close transcription of the corresponding passages in Boccaccio. Chaucer's principal merit, therefore, is to have taken poetry where he found it, and to have adapted it for the benefit of his countrymen. He was thus accomplishing the first and by no means the easiest part of his task. He enabled the as yet untrained English heroic verse, to vie with the brilliant and supple " endecasyllabo " of the European language, which had outstripped all others in poetic accomplishments.

II

We must now consider the most famous of the poems in which Chaucer revealed himself as a disciple of Boccaccio. And it behoves us here to go into more detail, because this poem is Chaucer's masterpiece, with the exception of the *Canterbury Tales*. Moreover, it stands so clearly apart from them that the renown they have attained in no wise diminishes its special merits. The poem in question is *Troilus and Criseyde*, partly translated and partly adapted from the *Filostrato* of Boccaccio.

The *Filostrato* is undoubtedly a masterpiece. It is the most beautiful of those poems, in which Boccaccio expressed the voluptuousness of his sojourn in Naples and his youthful passion for Maria d'Aquino, the natural daughter of King Robert, whom he sang under the name of La Fiammetta. She was the earthly Beatrice, the sensuous Laura, best suited to the future author of the *Decamerone*. She comes to us as a true woman, not idealised, whose charm, beauty, and fickleness were brought out by Boccaccio in various stories. At once a realist and a romantic, he was able, in the framework of an impersonal tale and in pseudo-homeric garb, to portray the vivid picture of a heart stricken by love. All he retained of the legend were a few names and incidents. His *Filostrato* is one of the most enthralling accounts of compelling passion, which mark out the road between the adventures of Tristram and those of the Chevalier des Grieux.

Benoît de Sainte-More, an Anglo-Norman *trouvère* attached to the court of Henry II., had related the noble deeds and sufferings of Troilus, son of Priamus, who loved Briseïda, and was betrayed by her. In his tale, enlarged from a few hints in the Greek novels of Dictys and Dares, Briseïda is the daughter of the Trojan soothsayer Calcas. The latter, foreseeing the fall of Troy, went over to the Greeks, and succeeded in getting Agamemnon to arrange that Briseïda, who had remained in Troy, should be claimed from the enemy and restored to him. But Troilus and Briseïda were in love; the separation broke their hearts,

and before parting they swore eternal fidelity. Alas for
eternal vows! Diomede, who had been sent to fetch the
maiden, did not lose a moment, and instantly pressed his
suit. He was wounded in a fight some time later, and
Briseïda, who nursed him, gave him her love. Troilus was
treacherously killed by Achilles, after expressing his bitter
contempt for the faithless Briseïda.

Benoît's characters are vigorously drawn: Troilus is a
proud knight with a stout heart and strong muscle, who
avenges himself by rough sarcasm and hard blows; Diomede,
lover and contemner of women, vain, bold, accustomed to
easy victories, is a sort of primitive Don Juan; Briseïda,
carefully portrayed already, is a type of sensual and inconstant woman, confessing her frailty and her remorse with
equal artlessness.

This story was put into Latin at the end of the thirteenth
century by the Sicilian doctor, Guido de Colonna, in his
Historia Trojana, where he gave a colourless summary of
Benoît's tale, and burdened it with lengthy denunciations
of women. Boccaccio used both Benoît's narrative and
this Latin version. He took the tale out of its Trojan
setting and made of it a separate romance, in which he
expressed his own feelings as a lover " felled by love "
(*Filostrato*). In his hands the novel, divested of its
marvellous element, became simply psychological, a poem
full of burning sentimentality or listless languor. This
was the first realistic picture of that Italian immorality,
of that abandonment to voluptuous love, which is in direct
antagonism to Dante's chastity and Petrarch's Platonism,
a literary tone which, with the decay of religious ideals,
was destined to become characteristic of the Italian genius,
and which, five centuries later, the French novelist Stendhal
rediscovered and loved.

Boccaccio centres the interest around three characters. Diomede is merely sketched. The heroine Gressida, however, is fully drawn in a few sharp, masterly, although rapid strokes. Boccaccio made her a young widow, less coarse in her ideas and feelings than Benoît's heroine, but more experienced and corrupt, capable of feigned resistance, but not of sincere remorse. Troïlo, in whom he painted himself, is the principal and also the most engrossing character. He is a youth who spurned love and mocked other young men until he met Gressida. All at once he is conquered and transformed. He ceases to care for martial glory and the duty he owes to his country. All his virtue has given way to passion; he neither acts nor thinks: he is in the hands of an irresistible force. And this love makes him a noble and touching figure, for in spite of his effeminacy, he is so sincere and absolute in his devotion that he compels our sympathy.

The character of young Pandaro, cousin to Gressida, is Boccaccio's own creation. This Pandaro is the devoted go-between of Troïlo and his cousin; he plays his part with nobility and has the author's full acquiescence. The purest friendship is the motive of all his actions. He is full of worldly wisdom, common sense, and disinterestedness. He expresses the morality of the poem, to wit, that all is beauty and virtue that waits upon love.

The tone of the poem is therefore immoral throughout, but this is what gives it artistic unity. Everything in it arises from a dominant disposition of the mind and heart. It breathes sentiment and voluptuousness. Two scenes stand out in greatest relief, the one in the temple where the eyes of Troïlo and Gressida meet for the first time; and especially the wonderful one where Troïlo, after the departure of his mistress, gives vent to his despair

whilst riding alone by the places which had witnessed
their love.

Such were the data upon which Chaucer built the first
great love-poem written in the English language, one
which had no equal until Shakespeare borrowed from
another Italian the story of Romeo and Juliet. What
Chaucer retained, what he altered, and what he added to
Boccaccio's version, are equally characteristic.

He preserved, almost without alterations, all the passionate descriptions, which means that he introduced
hardly any alterations in the character of Troilus, the
brave warrior enslaved by love. The novelty of his
handling consists in this that he emphasised the shyness
of the young man, from an irrepressible inclination towards
the humorous. For Boccaccio, Troilus was a lover mindful
of the laws of gallantry and observing absolute secrecy
when he was bid to do so. For Chaucer, he remains for
a long time a disappointed lover, timid and fearful when
action is needed, and likely therefore to provoke a smile.
But the two great scenes which best describe his personality,
the one of the first meeting in the temple and the one where
he expresses his despair after the departure of his mistress,
are, the former an imitation, the latter a literal translation
from Boccaccio. It is undeniable that both in the English
and Italian versions they are the passages of highest poetry.
A reading of stanzas 29 to 99 in Chaucer's fifth book, will
convince any one of their superiority over the rest of the
work in style, passion, and pathos: they are at once the
essential part of the story and its richest ornament.
Chaucer's stanza flows there with an abundance and force,
which shows plainly the influence of the more passionate
Italian on the English writer, whose narrative is usually
thinner in texture and slower in movement.

But Chaucer does not always imitate. He also alters and adds: *Il Filostrato* numbers 5700 lines, *Troilus and Criseyde* 8240. It has been reckoned that Chaucer adopted 2600 lines of the original and modified or added 5640.

The changes are accounted for by the different moral outlook of the two poems. Chaucer is not by any means prudish; he is not much more so than Rabelais. There is nothing to shock him in the *fabliaux*. He does not mind plain speaking, nor shun indecent details, but his gallantry is Anglo-French, not Italian. He feels ill at ease in the intoxicating atmosphere of Boccaccio. The manners of the people around him are coarser perhaps, but not marked with the same enervating voluptuousness as those observed by Boccaccio. Chaucer cannot understand the southerner's conception of life, in which love is exalted and woman despised. He does not view actions and characters in the same light. This naturally led him to modify the parts of the mistress of Troilus and of his friend. He raised the one at the expense of the other: she becomes almost a victim whilst he is turned into a doubtful character, half-odious and half-comic.

The heroine in Chaucer is also a widow, whom he calls Criseyde, but he endows her with a freshness and innocence which are not to be found in Boccaccio. Although she falls in love with Troilus rather suddenly, she is genuinely virtuous and can resist her feelings. This provides Chaucer with some exquisite scenes, which he inserted at the beginning of the poem: they may not all be of his own invention, and be taken from other parts of Boccaccio,[1] but they assume a peculiar value from the way he uses them. Such is, for instance, the scene where Criseyde,

[1] *See* Karl Young, *The Origin and Development of the Story of Troilus and Cressida* (Chaucer Society, 1908).

after listening with becoming modesty to the entreaties of Pandarus, goes and plays with her nieces in the garden, where a passionate ballad sung by Antigone sets her dreaming of love. Later, at night, when she is alone in her chamber, love again comes to her in the trills of a nightingale, warbling in the moonlight on a cedar-tree, below her window. She falls asleep and dreams that an eagle with white feathers digs its claws into her breast, and, without causing her any pain, wrenches her heart out and puts his in its place. The poor woman is really torn between duty and love, between her desire for a virtuous life and the call of passion. The wiles of Pandarus contrive to bring about her fall, because her growing tenderness blinds her to his deceit. Her pity for Troilus, who is represented as dying for her, breaks down her resistance. Even in the last part of the poem, where Criseyde betrays Troilus for Diomede, the poet tries to minimise her guilt; he suffers with her, he will only half believe in it, and he puts on her inconstant lips the most touching words of remorse.

Unfortunately, the more modest Criseyde appears at the beginning of the poem, the more inexplicable is her treachery. The sensuous and fickle heroine of Boccaccio could, without any inconsistency, change her lover as often as she pleased. Chaucer's Criseyde can only do so by belying what is not affected modesty on her part, but her very nature, that fresh innocence with which the poet has endowed her. Not only has he failed to give her betrayal an appearance of truth, but he has bestowed on the young widow a maiden's candour, thus rendering the character at once charming and inconsistent.

And further, Criseyde being such a pure heroine, the character of Pandarus becomes necessarily more repulsive.

He is no longer content to be the accomplice of a wary coquette, but he is the corrupter of virtue. The character would indeed have been intolerable if Chaucer had not veiled its nastiness by ridicule.

Boccaccio's Pandaro was straightforward and determined; he went straight to his goal. He made no superfluous reflections, and his words were mocking and incisive. He always had plenty to say to Troïlo and Gressida, but there was not one word too much. He tried to rouse Troïlo from his indifference and to inspire him with the necessary boldness, or he besieged the weak defences of Gressida with sarcasm and pleasant cynicism. Chaucer's Pandarus is no longer the cousin, he is the uncle of the young widow. He entertains the same devoted friendship for Troilus, as in Boccaccio, but this friendship, considering his relationship to Criseyde, has a distinctly more unpleasant flavour. He is no longer a cynical young dandy, shrewd and sceptical; he has become a man, who indeed lacks neither experience nor discernment, but who is familiar in his speech, a scoffer, garrulous, a quoter of proverbs and maxims, in which he reminds us sometimes of Polonius and sometimes of Sancho Panza, whilst playing the part of Regnier's Macette. Chaucer never wearies of recording at length his discourses, his anecdotes, his equivocal remarks, his oratorical wiles, in short, all the devious ways of his hypocrisy. Here we find all the commonplaces of practical wisdom with which the poet's memory was so well stored. Maxims and sentences, examples and authorities, taken either from the *Roman de la Rose*, or from the *Consolations* of Boethius, are poured forth unceasingly. This garrulousness, although a curious and interesting trait of character, tends to render the action much slower. To it is largely due the addition by Chaucer of some 2000 or 3000 lines to Boccaccio's poem. However amused one may be at times, one cannot help remembering that Shakespeare was able to tell the loves of Troilus and Cressida, including Pandarus (and what unforgettable characters they are!), in 500 lines.

The verbosity of Pandarus is not his chief defect, from a literary point of view. In his remodelling, Chaucer included such diverse and incompatible traits that the character does not stand out clearly. His Pandarus is a compromise between the young knight of friendship as drawn by Boccaccio, full of zeal and discrimination in a peculiar part, and the Shakespearian Pandar, a corrupt uncle, the type of the benevolent go-between who brings young couples together out of senile depravity, a dotard and an obscene old man who makes no pretence to virtue, who sings a coarse song for the amusement of Paris and Helen, and who acts far less out of affection for Troilus than for love of his trade.

Half-way between the two, Chaucer's Pandarus is difficult to realise; he might seem unreal and impossible, if the poet had not succeeded in spite of everything in imparting life to him. He retains too much of Boccaccio's hero in his texture to be consistent with Chaucer's additional traits. He is not unsympathetic, being still the faithful one who sets morality aside to oblige a dear friend. He repeats word for word many sayings of the Italian model, but this ingenious wisdom does not tally with his unbridled garrulousness. Sometimes he appears clear-headed and thoughtful, sometimes diffuse and inclined to drollery. What age is he? We really do not know. The fact of his being Criseyde's uncle and his garrulity tend to make him appear old, but on the other hand, he is represented as young. He is himself capable of love; in vain he plays the wiseacre, thoughts of love disturb him as he lies abed one fine May morning, and he tosses on his couch with desire in his heart. In the company of Criseyde he is at times a much respected uncle, who gives debatable advice, and at other times a wag, a gay companion, who says such comic things that Criseyde holds her sides with laughter. He is so complex that we cannot give him our unqualified sympathy, nor think him altogether ridiculous. It is impossible to judge him, to realise the character as a whole, for we see two figures, one a young man with a gift of humour as in Boccaccio, and the other a grinning old man as in Shakespeare. Chaucer's Pandar in fact makes us see double.

Despite the indefinite outline and even incoherency of this Pandar, if we try to piece together the various traits of his physiognomy, we find that he has all the gestures and varied inflections of voice of a living creation. Moreover his function in the poem is obvious: it is he who invariably produces comical effects and impressions. See him at work: he changes the ardent sensuality of Boccaccio into jollity, and adds a comical note to the most passionate scenes. He is the chief agent in preparing the trap into which the chaste Criseyde falls, and Chaucer seems to commend him for having devised it so cleverly. Here Chaucer ceases to follow the *Filostrato*, not in order to invent, but to draw from another source, that of the tedious *Filocolo*, where Boccaccio curiously blended into the story of Flore and Blanchefleur many recollections drawn from his own life.[1] Chaucer found in this poem several of the expedients necessary to bring into each other's arms two lovers, one of whom was bashful and the other innocent.

[1] *See* Karl Young again, *op. cit.*

But Pandarus is there, who changes the sentimental scene of Flore and Blanchefleur into a real *fabliau*. The bewilderment of Pandarus gives a comic setting to a scene which otherwise would be one of unalloyed voluptuousness. However much he may have borrowed, Chaucer is this time entirely original in the use he makes of his material, and this is the part of his Troilus where his genius is strongest.

Pandarus had asked Criseyde and her attendants to dinner, declaring that Troilus was away. The elements become parties to his designs, for rain and thunder rage without, and it is impossible for Criseyde to think of returning home. Pandarus will therefore give her a little room for the night, and her servants will sleep in the common room. But Troilus is hidden all the while in a sort of loft, and a trap-door will enable Pandarus, and later the lover, to enter the room where Criseyde sleeps. With what eloquence Pandarus, first alone with her, describes to Criseyde the unexpected arrival of her knight, his pitiful condition and despair! Troilus is torn with jealousy and thinks himself sacrificed to a rival; he will die if she does not comfort him. Pandarus is so moving that Criseyde consents to receive the young man. But Troilus, by his feigned jealousy, brings tears into his lady's eyes, and is so overcome at the sight of her grief that he falls into a swoon. Pandarus has to restore him, to urge him on, and to rate him for his weakness. He only leaves the young people when he is sure of the success of his plot. But even after his departure something of his ribaldry remains behind, a sort of mocking echo which accompanies the passionate transports of the two lovers. It provides a delicate undercurrent of humour to a scene otherwise as ardent as Boccaccio himself could have painted it (*Troilus and*

Criseyde, Book iii. stanzas 172-178). Drollery is almost excluded from this passionate duologue, so full of sensuous ardour and poetry, save for two or three lines, which the poet could not repress.   But Pandarus had not gone very far after all, and his reappearance the next morning, after Troilus has been compelled to leave Criseyde, brings back the comic spirit which had been hushed for a while (*Troilus*, Book iii. stanzas 223-226).

Clearly, Pandarus represents humour grinning and capering by the side of sentiment. But for him the passion would be more engrossing; the mocking way in which he skips around the smouldering fire, which lights up his naughty face now and then, the satisfied air with which he warms his hands at it—all this distracts us from the long-drawn-out pathos. Side by side with those who give themselves up body and soul to love, we see those who only view it as a passing pleasure or as a relief for their feelings. Chaucer is not any more moral than Boccaccio, but he is less passionate. This Pandarus is Chaucer's real creation. He substituted a comic character for Boccaccio's ironical hero, and thus introduced comedy into tragedy. It is curious to note that Chaucer, in presence of an Italian book, behaved thus early in the same way as an English dramatist of 200 years later. He did precisely what Shakespeare did time after time. He adopted and retained almost intact the tragic theme and the sentimental beauty of the two lovers, but remodelled, transformed, or created the humorous characters. Thus Shakespeare related quite faithfully the love of Romeo and Juliet, but threw his chief originality into the treatment of the old nurse and of Capulet and into the creation of Mercutio. In the same way he reproduced the love-story of Viola and Olivia, and drew from his own imagination the frolics of Malvolio, of

the clown, of Sir Toby Belch, and of Sir Andrew Aguecheek.
For, no matter how powerful the tragic or sentimental
scenes presented by English dramatists, they seldom
constitute their most personal contribution. The comic is
their own special domain. And this humorous element,
thus introduced, imparts an air of vigorous realism, not
only to the particular scenes where it occurs, but to the
whole work. Chaucer acted instinctively in the same way
as Shakespeare more than 200 years before him.

It is therefore clear that Chaucer was not content merely
to translate Boccaccio. In one sense we may regret it,
for his innovations were not all pure gain. As is inevitable,
in every partial rehandling of a beautiful work, the harmony
of the Italian poem as a whole has suffered. Chaucer
retained too much compared to what he added, and kept
too close to his model. He hesitated too much between
imitation and independence. With all its merits, his poem
shows as little cohesion as would a picture, in which the
artist had painted the uncertain sky of a Kentish landscape
behind the luxurious vegetation of a Neapolitan foreground.
Out of this love-tale with its clear lines and exact proportions, without gaps or prolixity, he has made a slow-moving
and heavily weighted poem, where repetitions abound, and
which one cannot read without fatigue. The characters
he found in the model were all of a piece, and the true
relation between them and their actions was well preserved.
He thought he could widen a work perfect in itself
and still retain all its merits. Compared to Boccaccio's
deftness and sureness of touch, revealing both mastery
and national temperament, his inexperience seems a
little clumsy, one might almost say if one dared, a little
barbaric.

But it is far better that he should have proved unequal

to his task than that he should have been a servile imitator.
It was far better that he should have produced a work with
grave defects, but at the same time revealing a strong
originality and the working of a creative mind. Chaucer's
additions were detrimental to the harmonious whole, but in
themselves, they were most characteristic. They implied
a wider and more varied conception, in which, it is true,
the part played by imitation was too great to permit of a
happy fulfilment. Chaucer's aim was not like Boccaccio's,
to paint sentimentality alone, but to reflect life. In the
scent-laden atmosphere of the lady's bower where Boccaccio
would have kept us, Chaucer tried to let in a little fresh
air, as if a window had been suddenly opened. Moreover,
he did not care if together with the vivifying breath from
without, came the strains of ribald songs from the street
below. A healthful cleansing would not the less be secured
by that bold process. The important comic element
centring around Pandarus was introduced for this very
purpose. But as the method adopted by Chaucer was
chiefly to make Pandarus talk till he was out of breath,
the result was a long-drawn-out drollery, which moreover
lacked connection with any clearly drawn character in the
flesh suggestive of reality.

One hardly dares mention the word failure in connection
with a poem admirable in so many respects, one so carefully
worked out, and to which nothing that English literature
had as yet produced could be compared for style and
metrical ease. A glorious failure indeed, but nevertheless
the awkward and imperfectly realised conception of a man
of genius. Chaucer knew better than many of his future
critics, since he passed from *Troilus and Criseyde* to the
Canterbury Tales, and from Pandarus to the Wife of Bath.
Instead of an imitative exercise, where he enjoyed only

a semi-freedom, he looked for a subject which would be really his, for a frame-work wherein his genius could spread itself at ease, without endangering the serious and tragic side of the story. He had been half-Italian and half-English in his *Troilus ;* he would be solely English in his final work. The time was approaching, when he would get hold of a theme, which would enable him freely to use his own observations and to express his true nature.

CHAPTER V

I

Up to this point Chaucer, although he sought his inspiration in France or in Italy, nay, indeed, because of this very submission to foreign influences, is of interest chiefly to English readers. He deserves their admiration for having perfected his native poetic instrument, but his strength had so far been used almost wholly in translating and in adapting. He had not as yet produced a really new work, capable of supplying fresh material for the thought and imagination of any one already well acquainted with the French *trouvères* or the Italian poets. He had not as yet contributed anything notably novel to European literature either in matter or manner. It was only when he chose an English subject that he became a European poet. He became such by forcing his true nature from thraldom. When he had gained sufficient confidence in his own powers, he used his observations for the basis of his work; he told what he himself had seen, and expressed directly his personal vision of life and of men and women.

The date when he first conceived the idea of his *Canterbury Tales* is an important one in the general history of poetry. One would like to know the date with certainty, but above all to know how the conception arose in his mind, whether suddenly or little by little. Despite the many

136

powers he had already displayed, the appearance of this masterpiece has in it something half-miraculous. There is something unexpected in this late production. Nearly all the elements which went to compose it were already in his possession, but scattered and hidden under such a thick crust of conventions that it seemed almost impossible to rescue them. It is therefore surprising that the poem should have shot forth. It might so well have never been thought of! Chaucer had not as yet given any signs of a really original conception, and there was no reason to believe that any such power lay in him, was even suspected by him. It was still more improbable that the allegorist and romancer he had shown himself to be, would suddenly turn into a determined realist. He was in short " the grand translateur " praised by Deschamps, taking the word of course in its widest sense. He played the part of an interpreter between his own country and the Continent. What ground was there for expecting that at the age of nearly fifty, he should in his turn suddenly reveal himself as a master, a painter of English society on the one hand, and on the other, the creator of a work which, in the closing years of the fourteenth century, would far surpass the contemporary poetry of France, and even in some respects that of Italy?

And yet, for those who examine closely the development of the poet's talent up to the year 1385, and note its tendencies and its progress, as well as its failures, the *Canterbury Tales* no longer appear such an impossible achievement. We may even see in them the natural and almost inevitable fruition of all his past, if we admit the thought that Chaucer had already in him, before he composed them, the genius which was to be revealed in all its brilliance in the *Tales*. Then it is that his previous works appear like the successive forms through which his poetry passed, ever a little constrained and awkward, before it found its full realisation. He did not become an observer at forty-five; he had already seen and learnt much of life, but, being too modest a disciple, he had failed to find in his models an adequate mould wherein to cast his observations. Indeed, he already possessed that rich and diversified nature which could take in both the beautiful and the ugly, which was capable of both poetry and prose, which was made up of piety and scepticism, of grace and humour, but the literary styles which he had encountered could only accommodate the one or the other of these varied elements. He had been kept back by allegory or lyrical romance, when his genius unmistakably urged him towards a dramatic and realistic narrative, shot through with comedy and sentiment.

It is fairly certain that at this period of his life, he must have become conscious of the discrepancy between his nature and the work he had already accomplished, between himself and his models. Few poets have been endowed with so much soundness of judgment, so much self-knowledge, or so critical a spirit. He was quite capable of estimating what he had done, and of seeing clearly its faults and limitations. So far, he had only produced two complete works of any length, one a mere translation of the *Roman de la Rose*, and the other an adaptation of the *Filostrato*, the original harmony of which had been disturbed through his attempts at self-expression. He had begun two other important poems, but felt unable or unwilling to carry them to a close. Twice over, in the *Hous of Fame* and in the *Legend of Good Women*, he had realised so quickly how incompatible were the subjects with his natural genius, that he had given up the attempt ere the work was completed. In the first of these poems, he had tried to express, in the fashionable formula, the vanity of human judgments and the caprices of glory. The plan was ambitious and the beginning full of spirit, but he had stopped halfway, discouraged no doubt by the artificiality of the means put in his hand, so different from the free and vivid presentation towards which he felt impelled. He had humorously confessed his inability to confine himself to abstractions and dreams, and his lack of taste for flights in mid-air. The *Legend*, where he related the sufferings of neglected lovers, had brought him down to a less exalted plane. But another kind of lassitude had overtaken him, born of the monotony of a one-sided view; he had quickly wearied of pictures in which women were all faithful and martyrs, men all fickle and ruffians, where his humour, if indulged for a moment, sounded as profane and hollow as laughter in a temple. He must needs therefore write a poem which would be neither a translation, nor an adaptation, which would be free from allegory and indeed from excessive idealisation. He must discover a theme which would provide something better than a series of uniform pictures, one which would enable him to present real life with all its changes and contradictions.

Was he however on that account to throw aside everything that he had up to then translated or imagined and which had lain unpublisht? Amongst the shorter works stowed away in his chests, there were several which, considered singly, may have seemed to him somewhat narrow in scope, being the outcome of some special moment in his life; some pious in tone, others again sentimental, others frankly licentious. But if it were possible to combine them all, what a curious work they would form, of which monotony would certainly be the least defect. There was the story of patient Grisildis, a thorough panegyric of

feminine devotion and sustained sentimentality, but along
with it there was perhaps a monologue of a certain Wife
of Bath, which certainly provided a most striking contrast;[1]
all the good as well as all the bad that can be said of woman
was contained in these two antithetic poems.   Among the
same unused material was a pious homily in verse dealing
with the life of St. Cecilia, a moral tale in prose recounting
the virtues of the allegorical Dame Prudence, the wife of
Melibee, and together with these edifying productions, in
all probability, drafts of some coarse *fabliaux*.   There was
also a fine romance of chivalry, telling of the rivalry of
Palamon and Arcite, taken from Boccaccio's *Teseide*, and
a rhymed adaptation of an allegory by Nicolas Trivet,
reciting the tribulations of Dame Constance representing
Christianity.   And what else?   It is easier to conjecture
than to give a precise and complete list of the works which
stood finished or half completed in 1385.   In any case, he
felt himself able to add almost indefinitely to this series

[1] It is almost certain that this monologue was originally a separate
poem.   This is proved, not so much by the isolated reference made
to it by Chaucer in the *Envoy to Bukton*, as by the length of the
monologue and its abrupt beginning unconnected with the series.
Now it is difficult to admit that Chaucer wrote this confession after
the inception of the *Tales*, and did not think of including it from the
first.   It must therefore be anterior.   The only fact that seemed to
fight against this, was the supposed allusion to the expedition in
Frise in 1396, inferred from line 23 of the *Envoy*.   But Mr. Lowes
has recently shown that the mercilessness of the " Fresons " had
been proverbial for many years before (see *Modern Language Notes*
Feb. 1912).   It is true that Mr. Lowes as well as Mr. Tatlock ascribe
a late date to the *Wife of Bath's* confession, but they do not explain
the fact that her prologue, such as it is, is an independent work
thrust into the *Canterbury Tales*, not made for them.   Various
reasons, some of them peremptory, and which I cannot give in
detail here, favour the belief that several stories inserted in the
Tales were really written before Chaucer had thought of the work
as a whole.

of compositions in varying tones. If he could only find
the means of welding together these contrasting elements,
he would have attained for the first time that equilibrium
which his intellect demanded, and he would in this way
be able to give a true vision of human life with its contrasts
and continual change. What a new idea it would be to
have a great miscellany which would draw all these
extremes together in a natural way; a miscellany into
whose flexible texture the *fabliau* could easily find itself
close to the sentimental tale, the pious narrative next to
the romance of chivalry, the sermon by the side of the
satirical confession! How much better suited it would
be to the poet's nature, with its changing and unstable
humour, thus to elaborate this composite work, where he
could reveal himself by turns as a lyrical or epic poet, a
tender or licentious story-teller, full of imagination or
sentiment or humour or joviality.

And indeed the Middle Ages had produced, Chaucer knew
them well, long series of tales of eastern origin, such as the
Gesta Romanorum or the *Romance of the Seven Sages*. If
it is unlikely that he ever read that wonderful *Decamerone*,[1]
in which Boccaccio had recently revived this form, by giving
in his one hundred tales a vivid picture of Florentine society,
he must at least have known that close at hand his friend
Gower was writing his *Confessio Amantis*, wherein many
earlier compilations were put under contribution. But
in these collections, despite the number and range of
subjects, the stories themselves lacked variety of tone.
The learned Gower had imagined a lover confessing to
Genius, the priest of nature. Genius, in order to probe his
conscience, questions him about every conceivable sin, and,
the better to make himself understood, adds to the descrip-

---

[1] *See* note to Chap. iv. pp. 117, 118.

tion of each sin one or more stories illustrating it. The few readers of the *Confessio Amantis* know well enough how artificial is the link between the stories and the examples, and they have experienced the soporific power of the confessor's monotonous voice.

Infinitely more realistic and lively was Boccaccio's plan of presenting a gathering of society ladies and gallants, who, fleeing from Florence devastated by the plague, had taken refuge in a beautiful country house, where they charmed their solitude by telling stories in turn. If there is something painful in the levity of these people who can enjoy amusing anecdotes whilst the plague is raging, yet the theme is plausible and is carried out with marvellous dexterity and ease. But all the speakers belong to the same class, which makes them scarcely distinguishable, and they possess an even elegance of speech. It is impossible to form a clear image of any one of them. The tone remains inperturbably the same, although the tales range from the tragic to the comic, from the risky to the noble, from the tale of the *Enchanted Pear-tree* to the Romance of Grisildis. There is extreme variety in the subjects, there is none in the manner of handling them.

Indeed, nobody had thought as yet of breaking the inevitable monotony of a whole series of tales, however well told, which are either from the first to the last spoken by the poet himself, or which at the best reach us by way of unreal or identical characters, devoid of life. Chaucer decided to interpose between the reader and himself a variety of speakers, each one possessed of a marked individuality. Then it was that the simple but entirely novel idea occurred to him of devising a pilgrimage which would bring together all sorts and conditions of people. Ever since the spring of 1385 he had been living at his house in Greenwich, on the pilgrims' road to Canterbury, where they flocked from all the counties of England to the shrine of Thomas Becket.   He had had many opportunities of watching those motley cavalcades go by, in which men and women, knights and burgesses, artisans and clerks, commingled in temporary companionship. Perhaps he had himself once joined one of these parties, either from devotion or from sheer curiosity.   The idea once found, the rest was easy and went of itself: he had only to describe these pilgrims, each with the appurtenances of his rank and his individual traits, and then to put in each of their mouths appropriate tales.

II

The first condition necessary was to present clearly a whole band of speakers.   Nothing is more difficult, if we think of it, in any period; it is difficult to-day and it was even more so at a time when nothing of the kind had as yet been attempted.   It is surprising to see the simplicity of Chaucer's method, the complete absence of artifice in the *Tales*, the sureness of his touch in tracing the portraits which make up the Prologue. We shall deal later with their artistic merit.   What is of interest at the moment is, that his group of pilgrims constitutes a picture of the society of his time, which has no parallel in any country. Except for royalty and great nobles on the one hand, and the lowest ragamuffins on the other, two extremes unlikely to meet in the same company, he has painted in brief practically the whole English nation.

He sets before us a muster of about thirty people, belong-

ing to the most diverse professions. The Knight, with his
son, the Squire and the Yeoman or valet at arms personate
the warlike element. A Doctor, a Man of Law, an Oxford
Clerk, and the poet himself, give us a glimpse of the liberal
professions. Agriculture is represented by a Ploughman,
a Miller, the Reve or steward of a great lord, and a Franklin
or free holder; commerce by a Merchant and a Sailor;
industry and trade by a woman cloth merchant of Bath,
a Weaver, a Dyer, and a Tapicer; the provision trade by the
Manciple of a college of law, a Cook or tavern-keeper, and
by the host of the Tabard, the jovial and loud-voiced guide
of the band of pilgrims. From the ranks of the secular
clergy are drawn the good village Parson and the odious
Somnour or usher of an ecclesiastical court, who will be
joined on the road by a Canon devoted to alchemy.
The monastic orders are strikingly typified by a rich
Benedictine Monk and a Prioress with her Priest; and
not far from these is to be found a Pardoner of doubtful
honesty.

We see that Chaucer, in his endeavour to differentiate
the various speakers, availed himself first of the easiest and
most obvious of distinctions, the contrast in their professions. This gives the impression—and did then much
more so than to-day—of a pageant of costumes and colours
which strike the eye at once, of a number of habits and
tendencies easily grasped by the mind. By simply noting
the generic traits, the average characteristics of each trade,
he was sure to give some strongly drawn portraits,
between which confusion was impossible. Then all that
remained for him to do was to make each one talk according
to his condition and his nature.

How simple all this seems and apparently how idle to
make so much of it! Yet, it was an unprecedented inno-

vation (with the exception of some passages in the drama, as yet very primitive), and one which marks a turning point in European thought. In fact, it was more than a literary innovation, it was nothing less than a change of intellectual attitude. It was the tolerant and inquisitive spirit of science applied to the study of characters and customs. It was the first time that a writer proved himself clearly conscious of the relation between individuals and ideas. The latter cease to be an end unto themselves; they become a means of self-revelation for the one who expresses them, believes or takes pleasure in them.

They thus at once assume an unexpected value. The ideas hitherto given out by Chaucer had had in them but a small amount of originality. They were not so new, perhaps indeed not so strong, as those of Jean de Meung for instance. Indeed, it is from Jean de Meung rather than from Chaucer that one might have extracted some kind of a philosophy. But all of a sudden, and simply because these ideas become, as it were, the expression of a temperament, or the prejudice of a class, or the routine of a trade, they appear, although really little changed, rejuvenated, at times comic, at times penetrating, and even at times profound. The reason of this lies in the dramatic value set on them by the author. It does not matter what they are worth, separately and in the abstract. They are rich with meaning, from the fact of their being uttered by a definite character, who through them reveals or betrays himself.

To attain this object, the author naturally had to conceal his own personality, and there is no doubt that Chaucer was fully alive to the conditions of the realism to which he had bound himself. He claimed to be a mere interpreter or chronicler, who related, without change of wording or

tone, the stories he had heard. With his habitual smile,
he gave this very scrupulousness as an excuse for the
coarse or licentious passages to be found in his work:

> But first I pray you, of your curteisye,
> That ye n'arette it nat my vileinye,
> Thogh that I pleynly speke in this matere,
> To telle yow hir wordes and hir chere;
> Ne thogh I speke hir wordes properly.
> For this ye knowen al-so wel as I,
> Who-so shal telle a tale after a man,
> He moot reherce, as ny as ever he can,
> Everich a word, if it be in his charge,
> Al speke he never so rudeliche and large;
> Or elles he moot telle his tale untrewe,
> Or feyne thing, or finde wordes newe.
> He may nat spare, al-thogh he were his brother;
> He moot as wel seye o word as another.
> Crist spak him-self ful brode in holy writ,
> And wel ye woot, no vileinye is it.
> Eek Plato seith, who-so that can him rede,
> The wordes mote be cosin to the dede.
>
> *The Canterbury Tales*, Prologue, ll. 725-742.

Thus the characters are real, their thoughts such as they
were likely to have had, and their words precisely those
they used. But this gathering of characters, taken from
various callings on the one hand, and that impartiality
which allows each individual to express himself without
check on thought or word on the other, what is this but
the society of the time, painted body and soul with a
minute exactness ? And it is thus that Chaucer, who, as we
have said, kept himself aloof from history, becomes in his
turn an historian. He is just as truly the social chronicler
of England at the end of the fourteenth century as Froissart
is the military and political chronicler of the same period;
and all the more so in that he did not pretend to be writing
history or passing judgments or drawing moral conclusions.

What he has given is a direct transcription of daily life, taken in the very act, as it were, and in its most familiar aspects. Chaucer's work is the most precious document for whoever wishes to evoke a picture of life as it then was, precisely because he had no regard for the conventional hierarchy of men and events, because he went straight to the most commonplace among them and purposely selected these as being more comprehensively representative.

In their great allegories, Langland and Gower, besides replacing too often direct portrayal by a passionate recital of their own grievances and aspirations, in addition included any number of political allusions. That is why we do not get from them the same close presentation of life, such as it actually was for the thousands who move amongst so-called historical events, without suspecting in the very least that it is they who make history, or that history is being made all round them. Chaucer's pilgrims live their own lives, full of action or sentiment, loyalty or intrigue, as the case may be, and trouble themselves very little about the reigning sovereign or his favourite, about conquests or defeats abroad or troubles at home; theirs, in short, is the sort of existence which is the lot of the majority of men in all ages. What they care about is their purse, their love-affairs or their private feuds. They are more interested in their next-door neighbour than in the king, in their neighbour's wife than in the queen, in the district tax-collector than in the chancellor of the exchequer. For most of them the universe is bounded by their parish. And that is why we feel that they are in the poem such as they were in reality, why they are true to life and form the very back-bone of that history which they care so little about.

We have here the doings, thoughts, and sayings which

were like the daily bread of Englishmen about the year
1385, whilst beside or above them were enacted the
mirabilia, which we at a distance mistake for the realities
of the time: the wars with France, the Peasant Rising,
the quarrel of John of Gaunt with Gloucester, the rivalry
between the nobles and Richard II.'s favourites. Far
from being all similarly fascinated by these contemporary
upheavals, the pilgrims represent such a diversity of minds
as to be sometimes several centuries apart from each other,
which dispels the illusion of one soul and intelligence being
common to one given period. The devout Nun who recites
the miracle of St. Cecilia, might, so it seems, have lived
quite as well in the age of her heroine, and could without
much difficulty be found in a present day convent. The
Knight, brave, pious, and modest, would not have been
out of place, nay, he would have found himself in more
congenial company had he followed Saint Louis on his
crusades. The Oxford Clerk wanders homeless through
his own generation, an idealist whose eyes are set on some
sentimental dream, or who ponders in his mind the sayings
of Aristotle; it is but now and then and with a sort of
shock that he comes back to the present and is conscious
of treading solid earth. Several among them have no
precise date, unless one takes as an indication the cut or
the colour of their garb, for they are simply men practising
trades sometimes as old as the world, or whose persons
are made up of the elementary appetites of humanity.
Their characteristics are solely those of their sex, their age,
or their calling, the young Squire, the Wife of Bath, the
Merchant, the Shipman, the Doctor, and the Man of Law.

But there is nothing abstract in the surroundings amongst
which they live. Their meeting, the degrees of acquain-
tanceship into which they drift, the presence of certain

people who belong to a definite period, together with the minute description of their equipment, prevent their being lost in an atmosphere of vagueness. Fully typical of his country and times is the Yeoman with his " sheef of pecok-arwes brighte and kene " (Prologue, l. 104), carrying in his hand a " mighty bowe," the sight of which recalls the battles of Crécy and Poitiers, in which he and his fellows played such a prominent part. The Epicurean Franklin bears testimony to the growing prosperity of commoners, who were beginning to come to the fore, being some-times sheriffs and sometimes knights of their shires, that is representing their county in parliament. The wealth attained by certain corporations is exemplified in the apparel of those five members of a city guild riding together, each of whom would make a respectable alder-man. The importance which middle-class townsmen were gaining in their own estimation is shown in the bold manner of the host of the Tabard, who frankly tells each pilgrim, great or small, what he thinks of him. The Reve or steward, who made enough money out of his master to be able to make him a loan, shows how wealth was then changing hands.

But it is the clergy above all who help to date the poem. Not that Chaucer was by any means the first to point out the discrepancy between the duties and the actions of ecclesi-astics, or the corruption into which had fallen so many good works, started in a passionate impulse of faith and charity. For a long time back, writers of all shades, clerical or secular, pious or profane, had lashed with abuse the laxity of discipline and the shortcomings of individuals. We have only to remember Rutebeuf, Jean de Meung, the authors of the *fabliaux*, or the hermit and mystic Richard Rolle of Hampole, and it becomes at once obvious that

Chaucer came at the end, not at the beginning, of a long list of assailants. But the religious troubles which agitated England during his life-time have their echo in his poem, and make his sketches of clerics those of a definite date and place. He did not live in vain in the neighbourhood of William Langland, within earshot of Wyclif's predications against Rome, or in the midst of the rapidly increasing Lollards. His realistic genius, moreover, freed from the allegories which obscured the pictures of Jean de Meung or Langland, compelled him to draw from nature, whilst at the same time his natural moderation enabled him to be impartial where these others could not. Good or bad, his clerics are people whom he has seen with his own eyes. The picture is not a flattering one, but we know on reliable authority, through the complaints or invectives of the orthodox members of the community, or even from the popes themselves, that the great schism corresponded with extreme laxity of discipline and morals. The monastic orders had forgotten their primitive rule of poverty and labour; Chaucer's Benedictine Monk is a fat highly-fed individual, whose sole idea is hunting. The Franciscan Friar is but a clever and prosperous beggar, who uses his gift of fine language to ensure himself a merry life. The Prioress is a pleasant, tender-hearted, but rather affected person, who cares more about fine manners than about austerity; her chaplain is a lusty fellow who tells broad stories with zest. The Pardoner represents that cynical class of exploiters with doubtful qualifications, who speculates and lives richly on popular superstition. Ecclesiastical administration appears also in full force, from the bishop down to the archdeacon, and from him to that repulsive Somnour, who sells the powers conferred on him by the ecclesiastical courts, sacrificing poor wretches

and unwary lovers. The Canon, whom the pilgrims meet
on the way, has lost all sense of his spiritual duties: he is
a sort of learned person, an alchemist, whose thoughts are
bound up in the philosopher's stone, at once a dupe and a
duper, who extorts money from the credulous in order to
pursue his own foolish researches.

In strong contrast to these degenerates and parasites,
stands the figure of a true priest, who wins both respect
and love. He may not of himself redeem a faithless and
dishonest clergy, but he shows at least the attainable
beauty of true religion. The good village Parson is, with
his brother the Ploughman, the only Christ-like person
in the whole company. He is perfectly orthodox, but
nevertheless he owes much of his moral beauty to the
Lollards. It was their ardour for reform, their endeavour
to find in the Gospel a protection against an odious discipline and accumulated superstitions, which brought him
back to the primitive faith and to essential charity. He
would not have anything to do with Wyclif's attacks on
dogma, but he repudiated sternly the vices of ambition,
greed, laziness, hardness towards the poor, and servility
to the great, which, by bringing dishonour on the servants
of Christ, drove the Master out of the land. His virtue
rests chiefly in the contrast between himself and those
non-resident clerics who go to London to beg for chantries
and benefices.

All this belongs to the poet's own age; and so does the
peculiar mixture of devotion and cynicism, the mocking
attitude of the laymen towards the clergy, the easy manner
in which they introduce them, in their own hearing, into
doubtful stories. This lack of reverence has begun to be
tinged with incredulity: discreet and non-committal in
the Doctor, but finding a profane expression on the lips

of the Inn-keeper, and bearing a suspicious air of reverence
in the words of the poet himself, when he tries to justify
the discrepancy between his tale of Melibee and its original
by pointing out the discordance between the Gospels.
One feels that harmony has ceased to be perfect between
dogma and intelligence. The chasm is not grave enough
to call for an immediate revolution, but it is sufficient to
let scepticism into the temple. People are beginning to
have opinions of their own, to censure, to scoff; they often
laugh at scholasticism. The uncertain dawn of a renaissance or of a reformation, one does not know which, is
slowly breaking through the horizon.

Nothing brings out these discrepancies better than the
Canterbury Tales. Being neither a satire nor a work
written to edify, this poem gives us a convincing picture
of contemporary society, such as it must have appeared
to an acute and impartial observer.

III

Did Chaucer then evade the common law and succeed in
producing an artistic work free from the arbitrariness
which is the condition of art? Are the *Canterbury Tales*
like a slice of the life of the day cut out without any pre-
conceived plan? No, Chaucer could not any more than
other poets quite keep his personality out of his book: he
had to choose with a view to effect, to group so as to bring
order into disorder and light into confusion. His poem only
appears to us so luminous because of the wholesale elimination of that which remained obscure even to his observant
eye and because he focuses our attention on a restricted
number of questions.

A close examination of the *Tales* will reveal the fact that this work, apparently so diverse and easy-going, is really centred around two principal themes, love and religion, or in other words the woman and the priest, or again the joys and sorrows of married life running parallel to the actions and morals of the clergy.   If we consider separately the fragments of the incomplete work, the groups of consecutive tales which stand between the gaps, we shall find one or other of these motives the dominant factor, or else they alternate sometimes with perfect symmetry. The picture of courtly love followed by that of a crudely sensual love makes up the first fragment.   The fourth group sets forth the matrimonial principles of the Wife of Bath and the dispute between the Limitour Friar and the Somnour.   The fifth group, after extolling feminine virtues in Grisildis, contains the indictment of feminine wiles spoken by the Merchant.   Similar pleas again hold a prominent part in the other groups, although not quite so markedly, as for instance in the second group with the *Shipman's Tale*, relating the story of the wife who deceives her husband and is in her turn cheated by her accomplice; with the exceeding perfection of Dame Prudence, wife of Melibee, and the matrimonial quarrels of Chanteclere and Dame Pertelote in the *Nonne Prestes Tale*.   The chief figure in the third group is the Pardoner; the fifth centres around the sweet picture of the perfect wife, Dorigine; the last is all taken up with the saintly words of the good village Parson.

There are very few characters or stories which do not fit into these two generalisations.   Moreover, they are so far apart as to appear like the recreation of the mind or its stations along a road pointing always in the same direction. Fortunately, the themes are so simple and comprehensive that they do not betray the hand of the author. He adopted and retained them, it seems, because they were the ordinary topics of conversation between people of all classes. The Middle Ages, in truth, were summed up in this double train of thought; it is not Chaucer who introduced it to his readers, nor thrust it upon them. In other words, this preoccupation was common to both the poet and his time, so that, by giving it a prominent place in his work, he could be at once a docile chronicler and a spirited poet.

What we have to consider now is whether Chaucer treated these two leading questions and those depending on them with that absolute impartiality which would be tantamount after all to complete indifference. Did he never listen to the promptings of his sense of humour, nor incline towards satire? It is so tempting to laugh at ridiculous people, so gratifying to chastise dupers and hypocrites. The description of evil and of hell offers, it is well known, more variety of scope than the painting of Paradise and of virtue. Although Chaucer did not neglect the latter, he was certainly partial to the former. In his little world, the proportion of vices and good qualities is at the rate of two or even three to one. Vice proper looms large in the *Canterbury Tales*. But it would be doing them an injustice to describe them as a satirical work. The narrowness of satire which slashes the general defects of humanity or of the time; the moral purpose, real or affected, which generally accompanies satire and directs its blows, all this is quite foreign to Chaucer. He is entirely patient with, nay he accepts with a smile the imperfections of humanity as well as some of its vices. He does not give one the impression that he would feel happier in a more virtuous world. Moreover, he has not pledged himself to look only at the mud on the road; he likes also to glance at the flowers that grow by the wayside and even from time to time to lift his eyes to the heavens above.

Undiluted satire is very rare with him. In fact, when met with, it strikes one as a discordant note which mars the harmonious whole. One would like for instance to leave out of the Pardoner's confession the few lines where the chronicler cedes the pen to the moralist. The transactions of this dealer in indulgences aroused in him an indignation, which at times takes the merriment out of his laughter and ruins the truth of his picture. Chaucer makes him cry out on his own rascality—

> Thus spitte I out my venim under hewe
> Of holynesse, to seme holy and trewe.
> *The Pardoner's Prologue*, ll. 421-422.

Such mistakes in dramatic conception are not usual with Chaucer. It is no longer the lively and artful companion who speaks thus, but one of those abstractions of vice whose cynical confessions he imitates. It is Wicked-Tongue or False-Semblant (*Romaunt of the Rose*).

Usually, Chaucer's satire resembles that of the great comic writers. It is simply an insight into the hidden feelings and unconscious motives of the human machine. Like Molière, he sees the selfish causes of a man's actions, and views them with an equanimity, a serenity of which Molière was not always capable.

But if we wish to discover a Chaucer anxious to teach his contemporaries a lesson, we must not go to his humorous pictures, in which there is little to betray the slightest deviation between the original and the portrait. It is when he is trying to paint the beautiful side of things, when he is idealising, that we must watch him. The virtues of his Knight, of his Clerk, of his Parson are in fact so many hidden sermons. The Knight with his purity of morals,

his piety, his modesty, his courtesy to all, might very well
be a pattern of primitive chivalry, set as a model for imitation by a degenerate age, where the order had drifted
towards ambition, luxury, and sensuality. The good Clerk,
wrapped up in his books, who had not got enough practical
sense to procure a living, must have been a very rare thing.
Above all, the village Parson, whose noble personality is
made up of negations or abstentions: he did *not* excom-
municate those who refused to pay him their tithe; *nothing*
could prevent him from visiting his poorest parishioners;
he did *not* do himself what he forbade others to do; he did
not forsake his flock in order to go to London, and so forth.
In these praises given to one man are contained reproaches
for hundreds of others.

These touches show us the moralist in Chaucer side by
side with the painter. His abstention was not complete.
He saw the worst and regretted the best, at times. The
movement of disciplinary reform started by Wyclif had
not left him unaffected, and his knowledge of ancient books
of chivalry made him sigh when he looked at the present.
But even when he idealises in this rather general way, he
is so careful to avoid rhetoric, he builds up his picture
with so many concrete and precise details that he still
retains his customary air of a chronicler.

Besides, so diverse are his touches and colours that they
preserve him from any suspicion of one-sidedness; for
there is nothing that betrays the satirical spirit so much as
uniformity. But there are so many delicate shades between
the brutal revelations made by the Pardoner, and the im-
perceptible irony which accompanies the enumeration of
the Parson's virtues, that reality itself could not boast of
greater variety. Thus it is that we lose sight of that
delicate process of elimination, which is the necessary

consequence of any satirical conception.   The poet appears
as a mere onlooker, and if at times we think we have almost
caught sight of an expression of bitterness on his face,
we find ourselves looking only at an amused and indulgent
smile.

IV

Chaucer's realism is therefore an established fact.   He
held up the mirror to his age, and presented to it the least
distorted image of itself.   His temperament and clear-
sightedness made for accuracy, and no historical document
gives us, as does his poem, the people of Richard II.'s time
" in their habit as they lived."

Now, whilst real life gave him the characters and frame-
work of his poem, the literature in which his contemporaries
found pleasure supplied him with his tales.   He was as
little inclined to invent his stories as to create his pilgrims.
The conception of the whole was so new in its strict adherence to reality, that there was no need of inventiveness
in the detail.   Better still, the individual stories, however
commonplace in substance, were bound to partake of the
originality of the whole.   Except in the Canon's Yeoman's
tale, where he seems to have related an actual occurrence,
Chaucer drew from well-known, and sometimes very well-
known, collections of tales.   And this, as it happens, is
yet another life-like touch, for the pilgrims are not supposed
to invent but to repeat these stories.   Further, this method
has another and more striking advantage, inasmuch as it
endows the tales with a variety of subjects and style, far
greater than if they had all been the original productions
of the same mind, thus sharing a sort of family likeness,
common to children of the same father.

It is interesting to watch them go in one by one into this kind of literary Noah's Ark, all the various forms and styles cultivated by the Middle Ages, and which appear there in their native garb; prose, stanza, or regular rhyme, just as distinct as the pilgrims themselves, not all wrapped up in the cloak of a common elegance, like the tales of the *Decamerone*. Let us review them and briefly describe the origin of each, for they come from the four corners of literature, and the reason for their being in this collection seems to be merely that they were already in existence. Let us give first place to the weightiest and most virtuous.

Here are two tales in prose, one of which, the Parson's, is simply a sermon translated, for the most part, from the *Somme des Vices et des Vertus* by Frère Laurens; the other, Chaucer's tale of Melibee, is a moral allegory, literally transcribed from the *Liber Consolationis* by Albertino de Brescia, through the medium of Jean de Meung's prose version.

Here are, also in the pious vein, five tales in stanzas: the life of St. Cecilia, taken from the *Légende Dorée ;* next the Prioress's tale, a devout story on the well-known theme of a Christian child murdered by Jews. Then comes a vast allegory recounting the troubles of the early Christian faith, symbolised by Dame Constance—related by the Man of Law and translated from the Anglo-Saxon chronicle of the Dominican Nicholas Trivet. Next in order, the "tragedies" told by the Monk, a series of illustrious misfortunes from sacred or profane sources, on the plan of Boccaccio's *De Casibus Virorum Illustrium*. Now we have a moral and sentimental tale, the story of Grisildis by the Clerk, taken from Petrarch's Latin prose version of the last tale in the *Decamerone*. And last of the series, with its short, lively stanzas in tailed rhyme, a parody of ballads of chivalry, *Sir Thopas*, in which Chaucer incorporated numberless details borrowed from the fashionable romances of the time.

Behind these come the other tales, all written in the heroic metre and regular couplet, whose uniform garb hides great diversity of character, some noble, others tender, many bold and cynical. First of all, the Knight's tale, a romance of chivalry which is an abridgment of Boccaccio's *Teseide;*—the Franklin's tale, a sentimental Breton lay with a supernatural element, the source of which is unknown, but which is similar to the *Enchanted Garden*, the fifth tale of the tenth day in the *Decamerone;*—the Squire's tale, clearly of oriental origin, full of the magical attributes familiar to readers of the *Arabian Nights ;*—the Pardoner's tale, a moral allegory also derived from the East, the counterpart of which is to be found in the *Cento Novelle Antiche ;*—the Wife of Bath's tale, a fairy story connected with the Arthurian cycle; it has many counterparts, the hero being sometimes called Gauvain and sometimes, as in Gower, Florent; the subject had won popular favour and was destined to keep it (Voltaire made use of it in *Ce qui plaît aux dames*);—the Physician's tale about Appius and Virginia, borrowed from Livy, through the *Roman de la Rose ;*—the Manciple's tale, which is really the fable of the Raven, taken from Ovid's *Metamorphoses ;*—the Nonne Preestes tale, which is only an extension of an episode in the *Roman de Renart.*

At the end come five *fabliaux*, pure and simple, the one told by the Miller, of which many analogues have been found, but not the original; the one told by the Reve, which is the same as the famous *Cradle* tale of Boccaccio and La Fontaine, but based on an old narrative by Jean de Boves, *De Gombert et des deux Clercs ;* the one related by

the Shipman, in all likelihood an imitation of a lost French
version, and which is similar to the first tale of the eighth
day in the *Decamerone ;* the one spoken by the Friar,
which makes use of an anecdote, partly farcical and partly
supernatural, the source of which is lost, but of which we
have similar versions in various Latin miscellanies; the
one told by the Somnour, derived from the *Dit de la
Vescie à Prestre*, by Jacques de Baisieux; the one related
by the Merchant which develops the *fabliau* called *The Pear-
tree*, well known to readers of Boccaccio and La Fontaine.

To these tales, strongly spiced with *gauloiserie*, must be
added the confessions, such as the Pardoner's or the Wife
of Bath's prologue, and one might even add the Canon's
Yeoman's tale. Although made up of compilations and
reminiscent of former productions—for instance Brother
Cibolo in the *Decamerone* or the discourses of Elde in
the *Roman de la Rose*—these confessions are amongst the
most original passages in the *Canterbury Tales*. What
we must note is that this style existed long before (cf.
Rutebeuf's *Dit de l'Herberie*), and was generally employed
for the satiric exposure of the malpractices of a profession.

We have only recorded here the more notable borrowings
made by Chaucer, in the matter of subject and style. But
within this frame he incessantly poured forth, as was ever
his wont, maxims and images, developments and learning
acquired in the course of his reading, particularly in the
two volumes which were his constant companions, the
Roman de la Rose and the *De Consolatione*. So that his
great poem seems to be a kind of reservoir filled by the
whole literature of the Middle Ages, and enriched from the
most diverse sources. Because of this, it runs the risk,
may be, of losing some of its interest for modern readers—
especially readers in France where most of his stories,

both as regards intrigue and *dénouement,* have long since been familiar. But this loss in popular curiosity is not of much account. Far greater is the peril it runs at the hands of scholars who concentrate all their attention on the differences of detail between the Chaucerian version and those which preceded or followed it. In this case, the true nature and original spirit of the whole collection will not be appreciated. Let us try for a while to realise in ourselves the artlessness, ignorance, and childishness of the Canterbury pilgrims. Let us accept as original the stories which we are going to hear, without troubling ourselves about their origin. Let us be capable of feeling simple emotion, when we are told how Virginia was killed by her father to save her from the lust of Appius, or of laughing outright, as if this was the first time we had heard of the tricks of Renard, or the farcical stories of *The Pear-tree* or *The Cradle.* Let us forget, during our perusal of this poem, the questions of sources or influences, and even suspend all considerations about the literary merits of the book, and pay attention only to the huge comedy unravelling itself before us, to the varied entertainment provided for us by the many stories, each rendered peculiarly interesting by the voice, mien, and turn of mind of the speaker. Such is the way in which we should read, once at least, the *Canterbury Tales,* if we want to realise their true spirit, to enjoy the freshness and vividness, which made the delight and won the applause of their contemporaries. It goes against the grain to turn that book of merriment, meant to be read in the open air on a sunny, bracing day of April, into a text for the class-room or the scholar's study.[1]

[1] Here followed in the French edition a long chapter wholly filled by an analysis of *The Canterbury Tales.* It has been thought that such a description was not needed by the English reader.

CHAPTER VI

THE " CANTERBURY TALES ": A LITERARY STUDY

I. The Portraits. II. The Pilgrims in action. III. Adjustment of the *Tales* to the Speakers. IV. Value of the *Tales*. V. Style.

I

WE must now draw nearer to the picture and examine it in detail. Although unfinished, the *Canterbury Tales* court and justify a close scrutiny, for delicacy of touch equals in them magnitude of conception. They not only deserve this literary inquiry, but what is more they prove very instructive to whoever tries to discover the relation between the means employed by the poet and the ends achieved. This will become apparent if we study the way in which Chaucer draws his portraits, how he sets his characters in motion, and tells his tales; finally we ought to consider his style or rather the various kinds of style in which he cast his conceptions.

The portraits of the pilgrims were gathered together by Chaucer in the Prologue, which is a veritable picture-gallery. These twenty-nine companions of the road are like so many pictures hung on a wall. It is impossible to imagine a more direct, nay, one may well say a more naive mode of presentation. The most primitive artist of to-day would not be satisfied with such a monotonous method, and the most expert would shun a repetition of such audaciously simple means. Out of their frames, set at equal distance from each other, hung on the same plane and at the same height, the pilgrims look at us in turn.

The only diversity is caused by two frames left unfilled (perhaps provisionally), with only the names written at the bottom, that of the Nun, chaplain to the Prioress, and that of the priest accompanying her; or again by the five city artisans, members of one guild, who appear together on the same canvas, for the poet did not think it necessary to make a portrait of each.

Chaucer proceeds in precisely the same way as the primitives, giving all his attention to the exact drawing of the features and the choice of emblems. He has further in common with them a certain well-meaning clumsiness, a sort of stiffness in the contours, a fondness for trifling details which causes one to smile at first, finally a preference for bright colours, applied in uniform tints with no half-tones. Details in the portraits seem to follow each other at haphazard: touches of dress or equipment alternate with notes referring to character; these lapse for a while and again reappear. If he is describing the morals of a pilgrim, he sometimes interrupts himself to add a little more colour to his face or to his cloak—delightful negligences which make us forget the writer's art and increase the impression of truthfulness.

On entering the gallery, the eye is at first drawn to the brilliant patches of colour conspicuous in some portraits. Such is for instance the gown worn by the young Squire, all embroidered

> as it were a mede
> Al ful of fresshe floures, whyte and rede
> (*Canterbury Tales*, Prologue, l. 89),

and next to him the Forester, who serves him " clad in cote and hood of grene." The row of beads, worn by the Prioress around her arm, stands out in strong relief against her robes. It was of coral and every tenth bead was green, and appended to the beads was a brooch of gold. What a contrast between the ruddy complexion of the Franklin and his beard, white " as is the dayesye "! We cannot take our eyes off the hose " of fyn scarlet reed," so tight and smooth, worn by the Wife of Bath, any more than we can help noticing the Pardoner's hair " as yellow as wex," hanging on his shoulders like a soft " strike of flex."

There are a few faces which, for vividness of colour, are just as remarkable as the garments: the pimply face of the Somnour, fiery-red like a cherub's, flaming under his dark eye-brows; the Miller's, with his reddish beard, and on his nose the famous wart surmounted by a tuft of hair, the two black holes of his nostrils and his mouth as big as a furnace.

But there are duller tints for the eye to rest on, which, by contrast, help further to throw into relief the bright colours by their side: the fustian doublet of the doughty and modest Knight, all soiled by his hauberk; the thread-bare cloak of the poor Clerk, the greyish coat of the grave Man of Law, the bluish grey "surcote" of the slender Reve, and what is most remarkable, the absence of all indication of costume and colour in the portrait of the good Parson, which we are free to imagine illumined only by the radiant evangelical light of his eyes.

Chaucer then was able to rival the art of the painter. His portraits are as good as illuminated miniatures, and on reading the Prologue we have no need to regret that the pilgrims were not reproduced on canvas by some con-temporary master. The poet, moreover, has resources unknown to the painter, for sounds are at his disposal as well as colours. Chaucer is equally fortunate in turning these to advantage. He listens with equal pleasure to the jingling of the bells on the Monk's palfrey, to the pretty snuffling speech of the Prioress, to the affected lisp of the Friar, to the Pardoner's voice " as smal as hath a goot," to the deep bass voice of the Somnour, garlic-laden and more deafening than any " trompe."

We would have to quote nearly the whole of the Prologue as an instance of these concrete details, which give so clear an impression of a person.   The essential moral traits are set forth with the same apparent simplicity, the same command over the means of expression which Chaucer displayed in depicting typical colours or garments.   Simple biographical notes, suggestive anecdotes, traits peculiar to the individual or to his trade, lines which sum up a character, all these unite on the canvas into a forcible whole, with clean and vigorous outlines, albeit a little stiff at times, bathed in a clear atmosphere, a picture never to be forgotten.   And our thoughts wander back to those primitive painters, whom we are inclined to consider at first with the patronising air of grown-ups for children, but whose art in the end reveals itself to us as so conscientious, so exact and soul-searching, that we wonder whether the progress since accomplished in painting does not merely consist in exterior cleverness and idle subtlety, designed to evade or to obscure that which is essential.

The greatest difficulty of all was to represent these thirty pilgrims distinct one from the other, and we saw that Chaucer attained his object by embodying in each of them the type of one profession.   But he used other means besides to avoid confusion.   He painted them all with equal conscientiousness, but not with the same depth.   Whilst some of the pilgrims—the Merchant, the Man of Law, the Doctor, for instance, are only presented with the characteristics of their profession, most of the others combine these with other traits which strengthen them or mitigate their stiffness. Although he never omits the peculiarities appertaining to the trade (and this is what renders the pilgrims truly representative), Chaucer sometimes restricts or directs them with a view either to idealisation or to satire.   If the Knight is a pattern of bravery, or the village Parson the model of good shepherds, or the Oxford Clerk the type of a disinterested love of learning— inversely the Monk, the Friar, the Somnour, the Pardoner, without being at any time caricatures, do combine in their character the least estimable traits of their tribe.   Sometimes also a different kind of generalisation is used to strengthen the first one: the Squire is at the same time youth, the Ploughman perfect charity in the poor; the Wife of Bath the very essence of satire against women.

But this is not all: he strengthens perfunctory or earlier generalisations by adding details supplied by direct observation.   He combines personal with generic traits, and even when he is painting a type he gives one the impression of painting a unique specimen discovered by chance.   This applies to the Miller, the Reve, most of the clerics, and above all to the Prioress and to the Wife of Bath.   The proportion of these different elements is variously graded with an infinite cleverness not always apparent.   More general traits would have turned the picture into a frozen symbol, an uninteresting abstraction;   more individual traits would have confused it by depriving the mind of obvious means of identification.

Thus English society, which appeared to a visionary like Langland a seething and confused mass, where man pressed against man in a sort of semi-darkness, becomes with Chaucer a well-defined and well-lit group, both limited and representative, of men who stop before us just long enough to enable us to form an idea of their personality.   Each lives his life independently of the others, and will always be easily recognised, but their reunion sums up almost the whole of contemporary society.

It seems about time that we should quote here, to prove our point, a few of these portraits.   The only difficulty consists in making a choice.

Here are, to begin with, two ecclesiastics standing in strong contrast, one touched with irony, the other turned to edification.

> A Frere ther was, a wantown and a meryë,
> A limitour, a ful solempne man.
> In alle the ordres foure is noon that can
> So muche of daliaunce and fair langage.
> He hadde maad ful many a mariage
> Of yonge wommen, at his owene cost.
> Un-to his ordre he was a noble post.
> Ful wel biloved and famulier was he
> With frankeleyns over-al in his contree,
> And eek with worthy wommen of the toun:
> For he had power of confessioun,
> As seyde him-self, more than a curát,
> For of his ordre he was licentiat.
> Ful swetely herde he confessioun,
> And plesaunt was his absolucioun;
> He was an esy man to yeve penáunce
> Ther as he wiste to han a good pitáunce;
> For unto a povre ordre for to yive
> Is signe that a man is wel y-shrive.
> For if he yaf, he dorste make avaunt,
> He wiste that a man was repentaunt.
> For many a man so hard is of his herte,
> He may nat wepe al-thogh him sore smerte.
> Therefore, in stede of weping and preyéres,
> Men moot yeve silver to the povre freres.
> His tipet was ay farsed ful of knyves
> And pinnes, for to yeven faire wyves.
> And certeinly he hadde a mery note;
> Wel coude he singe and pleyen on a rote.
> Of yeddinges he bar utterly the prys.

His nekke whyt was as the flour-de-lys;
Ther-to he strong was as a champioun.
He knew the tavernes wel in every toun,
And everich hostiler and tappestere
Bet than a lazar or a beggestere;
For un-to swich a worthy man as he
Acorded nat, as by his facultee,
To have with seke lazars aqueyntáunce.
It is nat honest, it may nat avaunce
For to delen with no swich poraille,
But al with riche and sellers of vitaille.
And over-al, ther as profit sholde aryse,
Curteys he was, and lowly of servyse;
Ther nas no man no-wher so vertuous.
He was the beste beggere in his hous;
And yaf a certeyn ferme for the graunt;
Noon of his bretheren cam ther in his haunt;
For thogh a widwe hadde noght a sho,
So plesaunt was his " *In principio*,"
Yet wolde he have a ferthing, er he wente.
His purchas was wel bettre than his rente.
And rage he coude, as it were right a whelpe.
In love-dayes ther coude he muchel helpe;
For there he was nat lyk a cloisterer,
With a thredbar cope, as is a povre scolér,
But he was lyk a maister or a pope.
Of double worsted was his semi-cope,
That rounded as a belle out of the presse.
Somwhat he lipsed, for his wantownesse,
To make his English swete up-on his tonge;
And in his harping, whan that he had songe,
His eyën twinkled in his heed aright,
As doon the sterres in the frosty night.

Prologue, ll. 208-269.

Beside the delicate and yet slashing irony which presided over this picture, what earnest piety in the portrait of the good village Parson, the prototype of Goldsmith's vicar of Auburn and even of the sublime vicar of Valneige.[1]   His kindly face rests us from the many rogues who travel with

[1] *See* Lamartine's *Jocelyn*.

him.   We should note, moreover, the absence of sentimentality in this firmly drawn and touching likeness:

> A good man was ther of religioun,
> And was a povre Persoun of a toun;
> But riche he was of holy thoght and werk.
> He was also a lerned man, a clerk,
> That Cristes gospel trewely wolde preche;
> His parisshens devoutly wolde he teche.
> Benigne he was, and wonder diligent,
> And in adversitee ful paciënt;
> And swich he was y-preved ofte sythes.
> Ful looth were him to cursen for his tythes,
> But rather wolde he yeven, out of doute,
> Un-to his povre parisshens aboute
> Of his offring, and eek of his substáunce.
> He coude in litel thing han suffisaunce.
> Wyd was his parisshe, and houses fer a-sonder,
> But he ne lafte nat, for reyn ne thonder,
> In siknes nor in meschief, to visyte
> The ferreste in his parisshe, muche and lyte,
> Up-on his feet, and in his hand a staf.
> This noble ensample to his sheep he yaf,
> That first he wroghte, and afterward he taughte;
> Out of the gospel he tho wordes caughte;
> And this figúre he added eek ther-to,
> That if gold ruste, what shal iren do?
> For if a preest be foul, on whom we truste,
> No wonder is a lewed man to ruste;
> And shame it is, if a preest take keep,
> A [dirty] shepherde and a clene sheep.
> Wel oghte a preest ensample for to yive,
> By his clennesse, how that his sheep shold live.
> He sette nat his benefice to hyre,
> And leet his sheep encombred in the myre,
> And ran to London, un-to sëynt Poules,
> To seken him a chaunterye for soules,
> Or with a bretherheed to been withholde;
> But dwelte at hoom, and kepte wel his folde,
> So that the wolf ne made it nat miscarie;
> He was a shepherde and no mercenarie.

And though he holy were, and vertuous,
He was to sinful man nat despitous,
Ne of his speche daungerous ne digne,
But in his teching discreet and benigne.
To drawen folk to heven by fairnesse
By good ensample, was his bisinesse:
But it were any person obstinat,
What-so he were, of heigh or lowe estat,
Him wolde he snibben sharply for the nones.
A bettre preest, I trowe that nowher noon is.
He wayted after no pompe and reverence,
Ne maked him a spyced conscience,
But Cristes lore, and his apostles twelve,
He taughte, and first he folwed it him-selve.

Prologue, ll. 477-528.

The two other portraits are distinct from the preceding ones in this, that the poet's sole object was to paint from nature. There is no trace here of hostility or of a desire to idealise. The Miller is simply one of the most vigorous sketches of an unmitigated brute ever drawn by poet or painter:

The Miller was a stout carl, for the nones,
Ful big he was of braun, and eek of bones;
That proved wel, for over-al ther he cam,
At wrastling he wolde have alwey the ram.
He was short-sholdred, brood, a thikke knarre,
Ther was no dore that he nolde heve of harre,
Or breke it, at a renning, with his heed.
His berd as any sowe or fox was reed,
And ther-to brood, as thogh it were a spade.
Up-on the cop right of his nose he hade
A werte, and ther-on stood a tuft of heres,
Reed as the bristles of a sowes eres;
His nose-thirles blake were and wyde.
A swerd and bokeler bar he by his syde;
His mouth as greet was as a greet fornéys.
He was a Iangler and a goliardeys,
And that was most of sinne and harlotryës.
Wel coude he stelen corn, and tollen thryës;
And yet he hadde a thombe of gold, pardee.

Prologue, ll. 545-563.

Very different from these, and in that subtle vein in which
Chaucer is so eminently successful, is the portrait of
Madame Eglentyne, a model of good breeding and sensitive-
ness, tender with just a touch of affectation, very pious, of
course, but never quite forgetful of her looks, even in the
midst of her devotions:

> Ther was also a Nonne, a Prioresse,
> That of hir smyling was ful simple and coy;
> Hir gretteste ooth was but by sëynt Loy;
> And she was cleped madame Eglentyne.
> Ful wel she song the servicë divyne,
> Entuned in hir nose ful semely;
> And Frensh she spak ful faire and fetisly,
> After the scole of Stratford atte Bowe,
> For Frensh of Paris was to hir unknowe.
> At mete wel y-taught was she with-alle;
> She leet no morsel from hir lippes falle,
> Ne wette hir fingres in hir sauce depe.
> Wel coude she carie a morsel, and wel kepe,
> That no drope ne fille up-on hir brest.
> In curteisye was set ful muche hir lest.
> Hir over lippe wyped she so clene,
> That in hir coppe was no ferthing sene
> Of grece, whan she dronken hadde hir draughte.
> Ful semely after hir mete she raughte,
> And sikerly she was of greet desport,
> And ful plesaunt, and amiáble of port,
> And peyned hir to countrefete chere
> Of court, and been estatlich of manére,
> And to ben holden digne of reverence.
> But, for to speken of hir conscience,
> She was so charitáble and so pitóus,
> She wolde wepe, if that she sawe a mous
> Caught in a trappe, if it were deed or bledde.
> Of smale houndes had she, that she fedde
> With rosted flesh, or milk and wastel-breed.
> But sore weep she if oon of hem were deed,
> Or if men smoot it with a yerde smerte:
> And al was conscience and tendre herte.

Ful semely hir wimpel pinched was;
Hir nose tretýs; hir eyen greye as glas;
Hir mouth ful smal, and ther-to softe and reed;
But sikerly she hadde a fair forheed;
It was almost a spanne brood, I trowe;
For, hardily, she was nat undergrowe.
Ful fetis was hir cloke, as I was war.
Of smal corál aboute hir arm she bar
A peire of bedes, gauded al with grene;
And ther-on heng a broche of gold ful shene,
On which ther was first write a crowned A,
And after, *Amor vincit omnia.*

Prologue, ll. 118-162.

II

Chaucer's handling of his characters was not limited
to the drawing of these truthful and delicate portraits,
which by fixing the features, impart to them a certain
immobility. He takes each pilgrim down from his frame
and does not abruptly pass from the portrait to the tale.
He does not let us forget that the speaker is a living being,
whose gestures and tone of voice are peculiar to him. In
the course of their ride, he makes the pilgrims converse
among themselves, he shows them calling out to each other,
approving what one has just said and more often still
rating each other. They give their opinions on the stories
that have been told, and these comments reveal their
dominant thoughts, their feelings, and the objects of their
interest. A sort of comedy is being enacted throughout
the poem, which binds together the various parts; it is
only just outlined, it is true, but it suffices to show the
intentions and comic powers of the author. The gentle
knight soothes the angry ones with grave and courteous
words. Some pilgrims, whose natures or occupations

place them at enmity, exchange high words and nearly
come to blows. The sturdy Miller and the slender Reve
rail at each other; the Friar quarrels with the Somnour.
First the Miller and then the Cook get drunk. The
Pardoner and the Wife of Bath each deliver interminable
discourses before coming to their stories. The prologues
and epilogues constantly bring back the attention from the
tales to the pilgrims who narrate them or listen to them.
In this way, the characters who were at first described by
the poet reveal themselves yet again by their words and
actions.

As is often the case, when passing from the analytical
portrait to the direct and dramatic presentment, some of
the pilgrims become more complex and less easily com-
prehensible; the character is enriched by a number of
small traits, but loses its well defined contours. This is
the case, for instance, with the famous Wife of Bath, who
is certainly the finest creation of Chaucer's humour. And
this, not through the initial portrait, however vigorously
drawn, nor through the tale she relates—and it is a very
good tale, and perfectly adapted to the masterly woman
she is—but through the incomparable monologue of more
than 800 lines, in which she airs her grievances on the way.
As she speaks, she seems to loom larger before us, to break
through the precise contours set by the portraitist, and to
assume the proportions of a character in Rabelais.

She is a creation of the imagination, but not one easily
reconciled with logic, and although richly endowed with life,
she probably was never seen in actual life. She has more
attributes than logic could compass and put together in a
single human being. In fact, she embodies a whole literature—all the sarcasms against women and marriage
accumulated through the ages. Could there be so much

cynicism in the world? Is such a pest, such a combination of conjugal despotism, sensuality, garrulity, and
peevishness possible? But she pours forth such a flow of
spirited language that our objections are swept aside.
Moreover, there are certain accents in her voice, certain
expressions on her countenance, which force us to regard
her as a living person. In order to understand her, we
must piece together the little bits of information which
escape her in the abundance of her effusions, and also the
minute details supplied by the poet in a casual way. She
would not talk in that unbridled fashion, she would not be
so loud of speech, if she were not " som-del deef." The
way in which she speaks of her prowess as a domestic
tyrant, warns us at once that it should be put down to
boasting. She is anxious to startle and shock the other
pilgrims. All her confidences are a sort of game, for she
wishes to amuse her hearers. Moreover, if she is so wonderfully learned in all questions relating to virginity and
marriage, on the many pious and profane invectives addressed by man to woman, we get to know in the end that
she had it all from the clerk who was her fifth husband,
and who used to take a bitter pleasure in collecting verses
from Solomon, diatribes from Saint Jérôme, and sarcasms
from Jean de Meung—all aimed at woman. She recites all
these with indignation, in order to justify them by the
proofs which she adduces against them. On the whole, it
is a complex character, and we do not know whether what
she says of herself is true or exaggerated, or partly invention. In fact, she is so many-sided that every interpretation is possible. Nevertheless, an inexhaustible fund of
comic effects is supplied by the contrast between the
immorality of her sayings and the dogmatic tone in which
they are uttered, by her contention that women should be

supreme, whilst her whole life is a proof to the contrary. She must be put on the same rank with Panurge and Falstaff, but she comes first in the order of time.

This revelation of character, through a person's words and actions, is to be found elsewhere, but not on such a large scale, in the monologue of the Pardoner, for instance, or in that of the Canon's Yeoman. A better example, however, is to be found in Master Harry Bailly, the proprietor of the Tabard, referred to as " our hoste," for he is always present on the stage, and is the real centre of the comedy which is being enacted on the road. His portrait is not given at the beginning with those of the other pilgrims, and Chaucer merely introduces him in the Prologue by means of a rapid sketch:

> A semely man our hoste was with-alle
> For to han been a marshal in an halle;
> A large man he was with eyen stepe,
> A fairer burgeys is there noon in Chepe:
> Bold of his speche, and wys, and wel y-taught,
> And of manhod him lakkede right naught.
> Eek therto he was right a mery man. . . .
> > Prologue to the *Canterbury Tales*, ll. 751-757.

This merry companion gives unity to the whole poem, where he plays the part of the ever-present protagonist. He is never off the stage, and his character, which was at first just barely outlined, is gradually revealed to us in the course of the pilgrimage in a series of traits, which are different of course, but which combine to build up the portrait. It is by seeing and hearing him that we gain his acquaintance, and this from the very first evening:

> And after soper pleyen he bigan,
> And spak of mirthe amonges othere thinges,
> *Whan that we hadde maad our rekeninges.*
> > Prologue to the *Canterbury Tales*, ll. 758-760.

His practical sense is at once established, and we get further on another instance of it in the proposal he makes that a dinner should be offered at his inn to the best story-teller.

He not only looks after his own interests, but he excels in handling men. He is dictatorial by nature, and his profession only strengthened this disposition. He is the king of innkeepers, and knows how to start the fun, and how to moderate it. He has the airy manner required to fill the part of a leader, which he assumes or gets the others to thrust upon him with perfect impudence. Amongst all the pilgrims, who are strangers to start with, and consequently look askance at each other, he is the only one who feels perfectly at ease from the beginning, the only one to think of a plan for the journey. He has no sooner received his money than he forgets his dependence and assumes the manner of a rich burgher treating his friends. What cordiality in his voice, and what a clear-headed man he shows himself to be in the very first words he utters:

> Ye been to me right welcome hertely:
> For by my trouthe, if that I shal nat lye,
> I ne saugh this yeer so mery a companye
> At ones in this herberwe as is now.
> Fayn wolde I doon yow mirthe, wiste I how.
> And of a mirth I am right now bithoght,
> To doon yow ese, and it shal coste noght.
> Ye goon to Caunterbury; God yow spede,
> The blisful martir quyte yow your mede.
> And wel I woot, as ye goon by the weye,
> Ye shapen yow to talen and to pleye;
> For trewely, confort ne mirthe is noon
> To ryde by the weye doumb as a stoon;
> And therfore wol I maken yow disport,
> As I seyde erst, and doon yow som confort.
> And if yow liketh alle, by oon assent,
> Now for to stonden at my Iugement,

And for to werken as I shal yow seye,
To-morwe, whan ye ryden by the weye,
Now, by my fader soule, that is deed,
But ye be merye, I wol yeve yow myn heed.
Hold up your hond, withouten more speche.

Prologue to the *Canterbury Tales*, ll. 762-783.

From the moment he has been elected "governour" (Prologue, l. 813) he takes his part seriously, and knows how to
enforce obedience. But he asserts his authority with great
skill, with a rare understanding of the people he is dealing
with, and his uniform good temper helps him through.
Having mixed with people belonging to the various walks
of life, he can speak the language of each, from the most
courteous to the most trivial. The tone of his voice
changes according as he addresses the gentle Knight, or
the suave Prioress, or the drunken Miller, or the Pardoner,
who wants him to kiss his relics. When he speaks to the
Man of Law, he imitates the language of the law courts,
and one does not quite know whether he does it out
of politeness or simply to mock him, for he can be very
familiar occasionally. What respect he shows goes to real
merit, not to rank. His manner, disrespectful or kindly
in turn, by disregarding the condition of the pilgrims,
puts them on a temporary footing of equality: it invites
and enforces cordiality. Those he scolds most willingly
are people who, like the Monk, assume an air of gravity,
or the silent ones, like the poet himself. His love for a
jolly life and his business make him kindly towards
drunkards, and he honours Bacchus, who changes hate
into love. His profession left a very strong mark on him;
thence comes his curiosity, his cleverness in obtaining
information about people he does not know, and more
especially about the state of their purse.

But what is most characteristic of him is his tendency

to make fun of churchmen. He is, if the reader will forgive
the word, an " anti-clericalist " of the year 1386. He does
not mind that wily and jolly fellow, the Nun's Priest, who
tells risky stories. But a plague take those Lollards—the
Puritans of that period—who are so hard on people who
swear! On the mere suspicion that there is one standing
before him, swear-words roll off his lips by the dozen:
"for goddes bones" (*The Shipman's Prologue*, l. 1166),
"by goddes dignitee" (*ibid.* l. 1169). Moreover, these
Lollards are always ready to preach, and there is nothing
"Master Herry" hates so much as a sermon. When
a priest sermonises, he grumbles under his breath, but he
cannot bear it from a layman. He, of course, takes unto
himself the privilege now and then, but he will not grant
it to others.

This attitude of suspicion towards the secular clergy is
turned into open hostility in the case of regulars. He enjoys
hearing the Somnour divulge the doings of the Mendicant
Friar. He himself cannot resist the pleasure of jeering at
monks. He congratulates the Shipman for having exposed
one of them in his tale. He does not spare even the
pompous Benedictine of the pilgrimage, in spite of his
lordly airs; he chaffs him boldly to his face, and gives him
a summary of his ideas about monasteries and their inmates.
He mixes the " thou " and the " you " in the most comical
fashion when addressing him, according as he remembers
the man's importance or is only laughing at his massive
bulk.

His hostility to monks seems to be due to a personal
knowledge of their misdeeds:

Draweth no monkes more un-to your in.
The Prioress's Prologue, l. 1632.

Did dame Bailly's virtue ever suffer at the hands of one of

them? It is impossible to tell, for when "our host" speaks of her, his complaints are full of reticence. He may be a long way from the Tabard, where he left her, nevertheless he does not feel comfortable enough to say all he thinks. In fact, he gives one the impression that she must resemble somewhat Ben Jonson's wife, "a shrew, yet honest." What a dangerous tongue, and what a quarrelsome disposition! She must be an awe-inspiring creature with powerful arms, who fears no one, and before whom her lord and master, according to his own confession, is as meek as a lamb.

"Our host" has not only a large experience of matrimonial affairs and definite opinions about the clergy; he exhibits, in his position as judge of the pilgrims' tales, an aesthetic taste at once quick and sure. He is a literary critic, and whatever other faculties he may lack, decision is not one of them. He has wide sympathies, and most of the tales he hears gain his approval. The story alone attracts him, and he has an entire contempt for form. He has retained his freshness of impressions and laughs frankly when the story is amusing, while he waxes indignant when it relates the misdeeds of a scoundrel. The death of Virginia fills him with anger against the Judge Appius. He inveighs against this Appius like the spectator up amongst the gods pointing his fist at the traitor in a melodrama. He is heartbroken over the fate of the poor Roman girl, and has "almost y-caught a cardiacle."

But he possesses also a literary sense, which reveals itself in what he condemns. First of all the tale must have a meaning, that is, he abhors mere fantasy. The tale of Sir Topaz shocks his common sense and his practical mind. He thinks it is silly and a waste of time. It means nothing. There is too much rhyming and not enough reason in it.

He hates affectation of form, and at once taboos a pretentious style. He rebukes the Monk for his " figures " of speech, and fears lest the learned Clerk should treat them to a high-flown and pompous eloquence. Metaphors and long words bore him. Facts are the things that matter to him, or again, the useful moral that can be derived from a tale.

Thus, the character of " our host " is not lacking in breadth, and gradually we get to know quite a lot about him, about his moods, his tastes, his antipathies, and finally about his private life. The fact that the poet did not describe him analytically makes him the more living and real for us. Many other innkeepers have since been portrayed on the English stage or in the English novel, but no one of them can make us forget " Master Herry Bailly," the jovial guide of the Canterbury pilgrims.

III

We now can appreciate the lively comedy which forms the setting of the tales. But it does more than this really, for it penetrates them as well. As they constitute the principal part and the bulk of the poem, they might have split up this comic vein so as to render it insignificant. But on the contrary, they blended their substance with it, and the tales were for Chaucer a means of completing the portraits of his pilgrims. The tales he had at his disposal were ill-assorted. All the better! A clever distribution enabled him to make them contribute to the characterisation of the speakers. He chose for each one the tale which best suited his class and his temperament.

He did this admirably wherever he had time to do it,

and his success in this respect was such for the completed parts of his poem, that we can, nay, that we must, assume that he would have succeeded everywhere, had he brought the work to completion. His original plan was an ambitious one. Each of the thirty pilgrims was to have told two tales on the way to Canterbury and two on the return journey, which would have made a total of 120 tales. But Chaucer could not even give one tale to each of the travellers, and what is more regrettable, he was not always able, even for the twenty-four tales which compose the pilgrimage, to adjust the tale to the speaker. Several of these still show visible proofs that they must have existed before the collection was put together, or at any rate testify to the hesitations of the poet in trying to allot them to the proper person. The Shipman, for instance, seems to speak all of a sudden as if he were a woman, and the second Nun describes herself as an " unworthy sone of Eve." Further, the Man of Law promises to tell a story in prose and relates a legend in stanzas. We cannot therefore speak of the adaptation as being successful or complete in every case. But nevertheless, enough was done in this direction for us to appreciate the poet's intentions and to applaud his talent of execution.

In a certain number of cases the subordination of the tales to the all-enveloping comedy in which it finds itself included, is such that its original form is a little disturbed. More often still it is the meaning of the tale which is altered. For a tale may be considered from two different points of view. It may be considered for itself, and the writer's aim then is to derive the maximum effect from the way in which he distributes the parts, suspends or unravels the intrigue, co-ordinates the details with a view to the final surprise. The tale will be perfect if it has been cleverly handled, and if it is written in an elegant or spirited style. But the same narrative can be considered from the point of view of the speaker. In this case the author must conceal or sacrifice his own literary talent and his sense of proportion, in order to make room for somebody else who may be ignorant, clumsy, stupid, coarse, or moved by passions or prejudices which the poet does not share. At the same time the reader's interest is shifted from the story itself and its subject, from the niceties of plot and language, to the way in which the tale fits the fictitious character who relates it, and who, alone visible, holds the stage and seems to bear the responsibility of what he narrates. Chaucer applied this principle to the parts of his work to which he was able to put the final touch. He was very careful to let the speaker reveal himself in digressions which disturb the harmony of the tale, but which are an outlet for his knowledge, his gossip, or his particular mania. Indeed, the tale is no longer as good in the abstract, nor as swiftly and dexterously handled as it might be, and often lacks the witty sayings in which the author likes to reveal himself. It possesses no longer an absolute and individual existence; it is part of a whole, and can only be judged in relation to that whole. Thus, if we isolate the Wife of Bath's tale, it seems inferior for ease, cleverness, and brilliance to *Ce qui plaît aux Dames* by Voltaire. But the tale, as found in Chaucer, is not spoken by the poet himself, but by a gossip of a woman who pours into it her philosophy of life, and uses it as an argument to prove what she thinks ought to be the relations between husband and wife. Seen in this light, it assumes a richness and comic force which make the nimble verse of the French writer look thin and purposeless. Moreover, this tale is only a very small part —the least important and enjoyable—of the long confession of the Wife of Bath. Instead of being the principal item, it has become subservient to the whole character.

Likewise, the Pardoner's tale would be made considerably lighter by the suppression of that long parenthesis of 200 lines, which is a denunciation of drunkenness and games of chance. But this would mean losing the amusing recital of the practices of this dealer in indulgences, and the evidence of the skill with which he mixes the most orthodox sermon with the most impressive story, in order to further his own ends. How could country folk doubt a man who quotes scripture and attacks vices just like their own parson? But there is so much more spirit and colour in his indictment! For he boldly aims at burlesque effects with his description of the doings of a drunken man; and he has his own experience to draw upon, for, remember, he delivers his eulogy of sobriety on coming out of the drinking-booth. And here again we are tempted to prefer the digression to the tale itself, in spite of the latter's verve and vigour.

The tale of the Canon's Yeoman is likewise interspersed with indignant exclamations and reticences, which hinder its course and are destined to produce similar effects: for the speaker is a man of the people who is dying to let his tongue wag, but who realises the danger he runs if he says too much. Moreover, he is not quite sure whether he admires or hates most his master's scientific knowledge. Duped as he is, and reduced to poverty and bad health, he still clings to the illusions that kept him for years in the service of a wizard, capable of paving with gold the road "from here to Caunterbury." He feels that this mere claim to superhuman power sheds a sort of prestige over himself. He is dazzled and tries to dazzle his hearers with the names of all the instruments he has handled, of all the metals and salts which he has helped vainly to transmute into gold, of all the magical words used by his master. As he jogs along telling his story, he is tossed from one last delusion to anger, and from anger to common sense. The story can take care of itself; he is not only relating an anecdote, but also giving vent to all sorts of contradictory feelings.

But it is not always necessary for Chaucer to modify the story so deeply by introducing into it realistic traits destined to reveal the speaker's nature. In many instances the mere attribution of the tale suffices, with a few words thrown in, or even none at all. What a happy choice of his in the case of the poor Clerk, wrapped in his books and living in a sort of dream, and who is made to relate the misfortunes of Grisildis, a model of gentleness and a symbol of wifely obedience and resignation! The touching and unreal story, inhuman in the extreme, and half-allegorical, seems like the natural bloom of his solitary idealism. Yet the good Clerk with downcast eyes is neither blind nor foolish. In order to enjoy such a story of unfaltering abnegation, he does not pretend that it is necessary to believe it throughout, or to expect to find in this world many women like Grisildis. In the same even voice, neither depressed nor exultant, with only a glimmer in his dreamy eyes, as a scholar whose humour is all concentrated within, he warns the pilgrims that "Grisilde is deed," and that the time is past when men could try the patience of their wives, and women wrap themselves in humility.

Thus there hovers something like a smile over more than one of the five romantic stories of the book. We need only compare the portrait of the Prioress, so full of gentle irony, with the story that she is made to relate; or listen to the sing-song and pretty snuffling of the simpering dame, or remember her mincing grace and tearful manner, to see in the legend of the young Clerk killed by the Jews, of his devotion to Mary, and of the miracle wrought by the Virgin to unmask his murderers, less a truthful story taken from the Gospel than the exquisite effusion of a devout person with a gentle and sensitive heart.

This applies also to the miracle of St. Cecilia. The poet, who had related it first in his own name, puts it on the lips of a Nun, whom, unfortunately, he did not have time to describe; but are we not thereby authorised to imagine her as representing the average nun of all times? Then, the impassioned eulogy to virginity preserved even after marriage, the ironical and half hysterical outburst of the saint before a kindly judge, the intemperate virtue and holiness depicted to us—all this becomes, as it were, the expression of the fanatic Nun, and ceases to have an imperative significance outside her. It is less the truthful account of the life of a saint than the truthful revelation, by means of this account, of the feelings of a nun and of the atmosphere which reigns in a monastery.

Even the sermon spoken at the end by the good Parson, so full of a doctrine approved of and revered by the poet, who puts it on the lips of the most exemplary of his pilgrims, impresses us as a sermon, that is to say, a succession of pious words, a long affair, which often makes people drowsy, when we hear the voice of " our host " anxiously warning him before he allows him to speak

> " Beth fructuous, and that in litel space."
>
> *The Parson's Prologue*, l. 73.

We realise at once the distance that exists between the most beautiful moral teaching and the limited capacity of the average humanity to listen to, and obey it. And we are at liberty to remember the host's impatience while we listen devoutly to the village Parson.

But Chaucer goes even further, and gives us stories at which he allows us to laugh, nay, which perhaps he intends that we shall judge fastidious or ridiculous. The Monk tries to make up for his rubicund and jolly appearance, for his fat and sleek figure, by reciting in a chanting tone the most lugubrious complaint on the tragic ends of the mighty and illustrious people of this world. He of course is protected from these distant evils by his thickly padded indifference. But the kind-hearted Knight grieves over them and protests; the " host " yawns and declares that the tale " anoyeth al [the] companye " (the Prologue of the *Nun's Tale*, 1. 3979). The gloomy recital is not allowed to proceed, and the Monk is silenced, but not until his drowsy speech has convinced the pilgrims of his gravity. Nor is Chaucer himself allowed to finish his tale. The matter-of-fact host rebukes him for chanting a ballad of knighthood, in which there is plenty of rhyming but very little meaning. Asked to tell a story containing fewer assonances and more facts, he slily avenges himself by obeying him to the letter. He gives up verse and relates in prose the formidable and endless allegory in which Dame Prudence proves to her husband, with the help of all the Fathers of the Church, and all the teachers of stoicism, that he must endure patiently the extraordinary trials to which he is subjected. In the last three cases the reader would be very ill-advised if he sought his enjoyment in the tales themselves, instead of deriving it from their very absurdity or wearisomeness.

IV

Thus, their mere attribution to the proper persons modifies the tales, however visible may be the traces of their origin. But this is not the only improvement made, for inside the tales, quite apart from the digressions already alluded to, and which are not really part of the tales, a similar progress has been realised. The same influx of life which vivified the pilgrims, body and soul, penetrated the stories which they relate. Here, of course, Chaucer's contribution is not always of equal value. However legitimate the admiration entertained by English people for the poet who first gave them tender and graceful verse, it must be admitted nevertheless that in the serious part, that is, in the really poetical part of the *Canterbury Tales*, Chaucer shows very little originality. Take, for instance, the one story in which he introduced most alterations, Boccaccio's *Teseide :* he transformed what was almost an epic of chivalry in stanzas, into a sort of drama dealing with amorous rivalry, and it does happen that Boccaccio's story, crowded as it is, gains by the suppressions. But elsewhere Chaucer is merely a literal translator, as in the tale of Melibee, or an adapter who keeps close to his model, as in the Parson's sermon, the life of St. Cecilia, the " De Casibus " told by the Monk, the legend of Constance, and the legend of Grisildis. It is remarkable, of course, that he should have been able to relate in such faultless stanzas and in a language up to then so uncertain these last two stories. His gift for tender poetry is all the more obvious if we realise that the most pathetic passages in the work, those filled with the truest human kindness and exhibiting the most delicate and exquisite sensibility, are all—or very nearly all—precisely those additions which he made to the story. But of course these original lines form a very small proportion of the whole, and are only like some very pure drops of water imported into large rivers.

Some of his humoristic digressions are in less good taste, for they sometimes derange (without the justification of dramatic requirements) the purport, the unity of a story, which demands faith or enthusiasm. However much we may like his playfulness, we must confess that Chaucer does not sufficiently control his sense of the humorous in places where he ought to retain his gravity. Upon the whole, it is chiefly for his countrymen that he is great and novel as the poet of piety, chivalry, or sentiment. In this respect, if we except the *Prioress's Tale* and the delightful first 200 lines of the *Franklin's Tale*, the immediate source of which is still unknown, he did not contribute much to European poetry. His additions, as far as matter is concerned, are insignificant, and for the details rather restricted. His great merit lies in the treatment, which is often admirable, but translation then considerably reduces for foreigners the best part of his originality.

The comic and realistic stories, similar to the French *fabliaux*, are of a vastly different order. Here so much wealth has been added that one could almost use the word " creation." And this remains partly true even if we compare Chaucer to Boccaccio, who gave life and warmth to a style, which, before him, was dry and colourless. But whilst Boccaccio retains the original conciseness, and does not do much more than present vivid or lively scenes, Chaucer, less compact and passionate, initiates the study of characters, and in many of his tales pursues the attempt made in his epoch-making Prologue to portray individuals accurately. Boccaccio leads to the picaresque novel, Chaucer to Molière and Fielding. So much so indeed, that with him the intrigue, the original anecdote, which was everything in the *fabliau*, and was paramount in Boccaccio, loses much of its interest and is nothing more than a pretext. This is already noticeable in the *Miller's Tale*, as proved by the importance given to portraits, those of the student, of the clerk Nicolas, and of Alison. But the most characteristic in this respect is the *Somnour's Tale*. What matters here, that on which Chaucer bestows all his care, is the presentation of the mendicant Friar, his wheedling ways, his familiar manner, his oratorical efforts to extort money from his patient. When we reach the coarse joke of the early version, the tale is very nearly finished. What was the *raison d'être* of Jacques de Basieux's *fabliau* is here but the conclusion of a study of character, wonderful for its thoroughness and abundance of comic effects.

But this is not all. It is not possible to study a character beyond a certain depth, without falling foul of the convention on which this style is based. In the original state, the *fabliau* is intended to make us laugh at the ridiculous position of a deceived husband. What little sympathy it contains goes to the lovers. But, if in this traditional frame be introduced the least amount of truthful observation of life, it is exposed to burst out and break. Now, just as Molière baffles laughter when he puts before us the sincere attachment and profound grief of Arnolphe, likewise Chaucer is not far from eliciting our compassion and even our preference for old January in the *Merchant's Tale*. He is ridiculous, when in his old age he marries young May. He is grotesque when, a wrinkled and white-haired old man, he fondles his pretty wife, and the page Damian is much better fitted for the part. But that does not matter. His deep affection, saddened by the knowledge that age unsuits him for his young bride, draws from him such passionate protests, his appeals to May are so nearly lyrical; his distress when he finds himself betrayed is so heart-rending,

> And up he yaf a roring and a cry
> As doth the moder whan the child shal dye
> > (*The Merchant's Tale*, ll. 2364-2365),

that the reader cannot refuse him his sympathy, and, forgetting the blind egoism of the old man, inclines to condemn the cruelty of the young wife, indifferent to his grief, and solely bent on the satisfaction of her amorous desires. At this stage, it is no longer a mere comedy which is being acted before us, but a complex drama, without exclusive prejudices, alternating between pity and laughter. And yet the story is only the *fabliau* of the *Pear-tree*, a perfect example of the cynical style. All we need do, to realise the progress accomplished, is to read first the story of the *Enchanted Pear-tree* in Boccaccio or in La Fontaine, and to turn afterwards to the *Merchant's Tale* in Chaucer.

Constantly, whilst reading the *Canterbury Tales*, especially the amusing ones, we feel that something new is shooting forth. The leaven of observation and truth is at work, transforming these fixed styles, which had a perfection of their own, but have now become too narrow and obsolete. And these tendencies represent the first visible manifestations of a conception, out of which were evolved the drama and the novel of modern literature.

V

In writing such varied stories, Chaucer used the most varied styles, or rather he found for each an appropriate mode of expression, because he has no style, so to speak, if we understand by this an elaborate mould in which the author casts his material, or again a sort of added ornament by means of which he tries to enhance it. The preoccupation of style, with its advantages, but also with its dangerous seductions to which the greatest have fallen a prey—Shakespeare himself being no exception—only begins really with the Renaissance. The splendour and artifice of style, whether the latter be personal or conventional, were unknown to Chaucer. His language is that of prose, from which it only differs in the use of inversions necessitated by rhyme. He does not violate syntax: metaphors in his verse do not enrich nor disturb the meaning of words, except to the extent in which they do so in common parlance. Epithets are sparingly used, and the wiles of rhetoric are absent. It is only when he follows an Italian model that his language is sometimes ornate: generally, it is simple, even, and flowing. The pleasure he gives to the reader comes straight from the feelings he expresses or the facts he relates, or again, from the humour which he blends with his tales. The merit of style in his case is simply due to the appropriateness of the expression. He follows closely and simply his material, which, as we have seen, is varied in the extreme.

He may be said therefore to possess all the tones in the writers' gamut. With one exception, however. He does not possess naturally that pent-up vigour and condensed force which will distinguish other writers. If passages of strength are found in his work, and there are some, they are generally copied from a foreign model. The descriptions so often praised in this respect, such as the one of the temple of Mars in the *Knight's Tale*, come straight from Boccaccio, although it is still to be wondered at that he should have found the metallic tones capable of rendering his sonorous original. Likewise, when his ideas are expressed in closer and denser lines than is his wont, we may be sure that he is momentarily the mouthpiece of Boethius or of some ancient writer. It would be useless to cite examples, because they could only be translations, and as such would not help us to characterise him. His own genius was not bent that way, and moreover, it must be acknowledged that the language was an obstacle. The English language had not as yet attained its energetic conciseness: the strong, short syllables were not yet possible to it; it had first to rid itself of inflections, and then to gain that strong, nervous, spondaic movement which comes from the massive grouping of the heavily accented syllables.

But with the exception of this particular note, the whole scale will be found in the *Canterbury Tales*, and a few quotations alone can give an idea of their variety.

Chaucer's pathos is delightful. There is no poet, not even amongst the greatest, who surpasses him in the expression of tender feelings. Like Racine and Virgil, he merits that an adjective should be formed out of his name to describe a certain shade of refined and penetrating emotion. He excels in painting the sorrows of a woman's heart, and in finding touching words to render that peculiar yet real logic which underlies a woman's lamentations. I shall give as an example, the scene in which Dorigene, on the coast of Armorica, laments the absence of her husband. No doubt Chaucer owes to some lost Celtic lay, to which

he refers, the exact setting of this scene, the black rocks
strewing the seashore. He may be indebted to it also for
the inception of the feeling which pervades the woman's
complaint. But if we compare this passage to other
passages in his work, it is obvious that he drew largely
upon his own nature for the words he put on her lips, for
the expression and accent which are in them:

> Now stood hir castel faste by the see,
> And often with hir freendes walketh she
> Hir to disporte up-on the bank an heigh,
> Wher-as she many a ship and barge seigh
> Seilinge hir cours, wher-as hem liste go;
> But than was that a parcel of hir wo.
> For to hir-self ful ofte " allas! " seith she,
> " Is ther no ship, of so manye as I see,
> Wol bringen hom my lord? than were myn herte
> Al warisshed of his bittre peynes smerte."
> Another tyme ther wolde she sitte and thinke,
> And caste hir eyen dounward fro the brinke.
> But whan she saugh the grisly rokkes blake,
> For verray fere so wolde hir herte quake,
> That on hir feet she mighte hir noght sustene.
> Then wolde she sitte adoun upon the grene,
> And pitously in-to the see biholde,
> And seyn right thus, with sorweful sykes colde:
> " Eterne god, that thrug thy purveyaunce
> Ledest the world by certein governaunce,
> In ydel, as men seyn, ye no-thing make;
> But, lord, thise grisly feendly rokkes blake,
> That semen rather a foul confusioun
> Of werk than any fair creacioun
> Of swich a parfit wys god and a stable,
> Why han ye wroght this werk unresonable?
> For by this werk, south, north, ne west, ne eest,
> Ther nis y-fostred man, ne brid, ne beest;
> It dooth no good, to my wit, but anoyeth.
> See ye nat, lord, how mankinde it destroyeth?
> And hundred thousand bodies of mankinde
> Han rokkes slayn, al be they nat in minde,

> Which mankinde is so fair part of thy werk
> That thou it madest lyk to thyn owene merk.
> Than semed it ye hadde a greet chiertee
> Toward mankinde; but how than may it be
> That ye sweche menes make it to destroyen,
> Whiche menes do no good, but ever anoyen?
> I woot wel clerkes wol seyn, as hem leste,
> By arguments, that al is for the beste,
> Though I ne can the causes not y-knowe.
> But thilke god, that made wind to blowe,
> As kepe my lord! this my conclusioun;
> To clerkes lete I al disputisoun.
> But wolde god that all thise rokkes blake
> Were sonken in-to helle for his sake!
> Thise rokkes sleen myn herte for the fere."
> Thus wolde she seyn, with many a pitous tere.

The Franklin's Tale, ll. 847-894.

Here is another instance of his tenderness, similar and yet very different. Here emotion is less direct; it owes part of its source and effect to the intermediary placed by Chaucer between himself and his tale. The Prioress is the speaker with her half-naive, half-affected sensibility. Only a woman could find such words, and one feels that they must be uttered by pretty lips and spring from a heart with unsatisfied motherly instincts. She reminds one of a gracious lady without children who cannot help kissing the little ones she meets on the road. It is about the young clerk devoted to the Virgin who is killed later on by abominable Jews:

> This litel child, his litel book lerninge,
> As he sat in the scole at his prymer,
> He *Alma redemptoris* herde singe,
> As children lerned hir antiphoner;
> And, as he dorste, he drough him ner and ner,
> And herkned ay the wordes and the note,
> Til he the firste vers coude al by rote.

Noght wiste~he what this Latin was to seye,
For he so yong and tendre was of age;
But on a day his felaw gan he preye
Texpounden him this song in his langage,
Or telle him why this song was in usage;
This preyde he him to construe and declare
Ful ofte tyme upon his knowes bare.

His felaw, which that elder was than he,
Answerde him thus: " This song, I have herd seye,
Was maked of our blisful lady free,
Hir to salue, and eek hir for to preye
To been our help and socour whan we deye.
I can no more expounde in this matere;
I lerne song, I can but smal grammere."

" And is this song maked in reverence
Of Cristes moder? " seyde this innocent;
" Now certes, I wol do my diligence
To conne it al, er Cristemasse is went;
Though that I for my prymer shal be shent,
And shal be beten thryës in an houre,
I wol it conne, our lady for to honoure."

His felaw taughte him homward prively,
Fro day to day, til he coude it by rote,
And than he song it wel and boldely
Fro word to word, acording with the note;
Twyës a day it passed thurgh his throte,
To scoleward and homward whan he wente;
On Cristes moder set was his entente.

                    The Prioress's Tale, ll. 1706-1740.

One would not like to mention the word humour in relation to this piece.   Yet the connection between a passage
of this kind and many other passages remarkable for their
delicate playfulness, lies in the artistic subtlety displayed
by their author in both.   Chaucer's range is even greater
in the comic than in the tender vein, and two specimens
are hardly sufficient to give an idea of it.   But we shall

be careful to choose them, as far as can be done, at the extreme limits of his manner.

Here is first the preamble of the *Wife of Bath's Tale*, in which she makes the mendicant friars responsible for the disappearance of fairies, goblins, and incubi. There is nothing more maliciously roguish in La Fontaine himself:

> In tholde dayes of the King Arthour,
> Of which that Britons speken greet honour,
> All was this land fulfild of fayerye.
> The elf-queen, with hir Ioly companye,
> Daunced ful ofte in many a grene mede;
> This was the olde opinion, as I rede.
> I speke of manye hundred yeres ago;
> But now can no man see none elves mo.
> For now the grete charitee and prayeres
> Of limitours and othere holy freres,
> That serchen every lond and every streem,
> As thikke as motes in the sonne beem,
> Blessinge halles, chambres, kichenes, boures,
> Citees, burghes, castels, hye toures,
> Thropes, bernes, shipnes, dayeryes,
> This maketh that ther been no fayeryes.
> For ther as wont to walken was an elf,
> Ther walketh now the limitour him-self
> In undermeles and in morweninges,
> And seyth his matins and his holy thinges
> As he goth in his limitacioun.
> Wommen may go saufly up and doun,
> In every bush, or under every tree;
> There is noon other incubus but he,
> And he ne wol doon hem but dishonour.
>
>   *The Wife of Bath's Tale*, ll. 857-881.

It is much more difficult to give an idea of his power in narrative. The chief characteristic of this power is its fullness. It spreads and flows, like a mighty river, through tales of thousands of lines. It carries sometimes in its course a strange erudition borrowed from the schoolmen,

from the pious books, or the classical authors familiar to
his times.   But, just as it is impossible to judge of the
colour and rapidity of a stream from a cupful of its waters,
we cannot hope to give, by means of a quotation, an
adequate impression of Chaucer's richness in this respect.
Here is, however, a portion of the scene from the *Merchant's
Tale*, in which he describes the wedding of January and
May:

> Maius, that sit with so benigne a chere,   1742
> Hir to beholde it semed fayërÿë;
> Quene Ester loked never with swich an yë
> On Assuer, so meke a look hath she.
> I may yow nat devyse al hir beautee;
> But thus muche of hir beautee telle I may,
> That she was lyk the brighte morwe of May,
> Fulfild of alle beautee and plesaunce.
> This Ianuarie is ravisshed in a traunce
> At every time he loked on hir face;
> But in his herte he gan hir to manace,
> That he that night in armes wolde hir streyne
> Harder than ever Paris did Eleyne.
> But natheless, yet hadde he greet pitee,
> That thilke night offenden hir moste he;
> And thoughte, " allas! o tendre creature!
> Now wolde god ye mighte wel endure
> Al my corage, it is so sharp and kene;
> I am agast ye shul it nat sustene.
> But god forbede that I dide al my might!
> Now wolde god that it were woxen night,
> And that the night wolde lasten evermo.
> I wolde that al this peple were ago."

>   .   .   .   .   .

> He drinketh ipocras, clarree, and vernage   1807
> Of spyces hote, tencresen his corage;

>   .   .   .   .   .

> And to his privee freendes thus seyde he: 1813
> " For goddes love, as sone as it may be,
> Lat voyden al this hous in curteys wyse."
> And they han doon right as he wol devyse

Men drinken, and the travers drawe anon;
The bryde was broght a-bedde as stille as stoon;
And whan the bed was with the preest y-blessed,
Out of the chambre hath every wight him dressed.
And Ianuarie hath faste in armes take
His fresshe May, his paradys, his make.
He lulleth hir, he kisseth hir ful ofte
With thikke bristles of his berd unsofte,
Lyk to the skin of the houndfish, sharp as brere,
For he was shave al newe in his manere.
He rubbeth hir about hir tendre face,
And seyde thus, " allas! I moot trespace
To yow, my spouse, and yow gretly offende,
Er tyme come that I wil doun descende.
But natheless, considereth this," quod he,
" Ther nis no werkman, what-so-ever he be,
That may bothe werke wel and hastily;
This wol be doon at leyser parfitly.
It is no fors how longe that we pleye;
In trewe wedlok wedded be we tweye;
And blessed be the yok that we been inne,
For in our actes we mowe do no sinne.
A man may do no sinne with his wyf,
Ne hurte him-selven with his owene knyf;
For we han leve to pleye us by the lawe."
Thus laboreth he til that the day gan dawe;
And than he taketh a sop in fyn clarree,
And upright in his bed than sitteth he,
And after that he sang ful loude and clere,
And kiste his wyf, and made wantoun chere.
He was al coltish, ful of ragerye,
And ful of Iargon as a flekked pye.
The slakke skin aboute his nekke shaketh,
Whyl that he sang; so chaunteth he and craketh.
But god wot what that May thoughte in hir herte,
Whan she him saugh up sittinge in his sherte,
In his night-cappe, and with his nekke lene;
She preyseth nat his pleying worth a bene.
Than seide he thus, " my reste wol I take,
Now day is come, I may no lenger wake."
And doun he levde his heed, and sleep til pryme.   1857

The Merchant's Tale.

These are some aspects of his style, not all. We cannot, of course, quote any of the passages, where, dealing in risky subjects, his muse fills the echoes with her Silenian mirth, and sometimes becomes, as in the *Miller's Tale*, a jade delighting in the coarsest tales. Here the story-teller who a little while ago reminded us of Racine, now leaves far behind him the elegant and mincing licentiousness of La Fontaine, and becomes a worthy rival of Rabelais.

This comic vein broadened as time went on. Discreet at first, a mere streamlet of fine raillery, it became gradually the main river in which tender and serious veins were finally absorbed. The gentle court poet evolved gradually into a juicy humorist. Yet, it is characteristic of him that he did not lose anything on the way. He did not starve one faculty to benefit another. He did not follow Toinette's advice and put out his right eye in order to see better with the left. If we remember how insipid an exclusively sentimental style can be, or how inevitably dry is a style which is purely comical, we shall at once appreciate the broader and more truthful character of the *Canterbury Tales*. One of the attractions of the poem is the easy way in which it oscillates from the pleasant to the serious. In spite of his growing disposition to raillery, Chaucer retained intact all his life long his power to love and admire. This cheerful cynic always preserved a tender corner in his heart. Mockery, either discreet or uproarious, never withered in him the gift of poetry. The two travelled side by side, and in perfect harmony, like his Wife of Bath and his Prioress. Even when we hear only one of them, we know that the other is close at hand, and we cannot forget that the hum of life is, like the poem, made up of their intermingled voices.

CONCLUSION

IF we now survey at a glance the entire work of the poet, we shall see clearly the direction followed by him, from the beginning to the end of his career. Truth was his magnet. He had found poetry unnatural; people had got to think that fiction was its essence, and its task to present an ingenious transposition of reality, according to artificial rules. He began by obeying the accepted canons; like his contemporaries, he had dreams and saw allegorical figures, he invented imaginary incidents; or he borrowed from books the subjects and characters of his poems. All along, it is true, he had a desire to be independent, and to put into these conventions more life and observation than they seemed to warrant. Little by little he began to realise that nothing could equal nature herself in interest and diversity. Then it was that leaving his learning in the background, and freeing himself from dreams and allegories, he looked straight at the spectacle of life and men, and began to reproduce it unaided. The docility he had shown towards his favourite authors, he now brought to the service of nature alone. Instead of the *Roman de la Rose*, Boccaccio, or Ovid, Nature was henceforth the source of his inspiration and his law. He became according to his subject her scribe or her painter.

But this faithful presentation of reality may be, as is well known, harsh, morose, or bitter; and men, on beholding it, often turn away from life in disgust. Chaucer, without flattering his model, puts it in a pleasant light, in an atmosphere which is sweet to breathe. One cannot read him without feeling that it is good to be alive.

Our first impression, when we take up his work, is one of

freshness and health, which seems to come to us from every side. It is due first of all to the use of a newly-formed dialect, the words of which had hardly been used as yet for literary purposes. Like the soil freshly ploughed in April, it has then a perfume which it does not possess at any other time. Generally, this newness of the language goes along with a certain crudeness of thought, with an art childish as yet. But Chaucer, who stands at the beginning of English poetry, stands also at the close of the Middle Ages. He inherited the whole literature of France, enriched by the generous efforts of three centuries, elegant in style, abundant in stories, exhibiting already signs of fatigue and over-production. He realised that combination, of which there is perhaps no other example, of a spring-like language with an autumnal literature. Chaucer, very young, and yet very mature, combines the charm of new-born things with the experience of old age. His naive expression gave back the grace of novelty to more than one description, more than one idea, which had paled and faded in the language in which they were first written. English words, hitherto locked in a long winter of expecta-tion, gave out, in his already learned verse, their first perfume.

To this advantage, due to exceptional circumstances, he joins gifts all his own, the first of which is a wide sympathy. To this especially his poetry owes its friendliness and smiling affability. The joy of being alive or of beholding life, the pleasure of being amongst men, these are every-where in his verse. He entertains, of course, towards some of his fellow-men an affection or respect, but all the others seem nevertheless to arouse in him a curiosity akin to interest. No one is excluded, and aversion is a very rare thing with him. He does not treat with disdain those whose foolishness he has fathomed, nor does he turn away in disgust from the rascal whose tricks he has detected. These still have some curious or funny traits which can amuse a good man. Vice is interesting to study if only because it differs from virtue. Whilst quietly unmasking the rogues, he is grateful to them in his heart for the pleasure they give him, and which compensates for much that is evil. Moreover, he repudiates the somewhat childish conception which divides men up into good and bad. He knows that human character is a much more complex blend than it is usually painted. He has no delusions about himself, and realises without bitterness that he is not violently impelled towards good. He classes himself with the average humanity, and so finds himself in touch with the mass.

The reader does not find in him a mentor, but an equal, who would fain be looked upon as an inferior, a good-natured companion always ready to make place for some-body else, or to let him have his say first. Far from pretending to teach others, he listens with attention, some might say with respect. Humour does flash now and then from his eyes, which he purposely keeps half shut. But there is no need to be anxious, for it is obviously at himself that he is laughing. It is very difficult to catch him in the act of mocking laughter under cover of his air of modesty, for after all this modesty is not wholly feigned; it is based on a knowledge of the curious workings of human nature, and consequently of his own nature also. The consciousness of their common failings is what draws men together. Amongst writers of genius the one who strikes us soonest as a friend is Chaucer.

A sympathy of this kind, based on self-knowledge, is a form of intelligence. And perhaps if I had to express in

one word the advance made by Chaucer, I would say that
he represents a progress of the intelligence. It is marked
on the one hand by a weakening of passion, based on self-
confidence, on strong desires and aspirations, on love or
hate, and which leads to lyricism or satire; a weakening
also of the imagination as a faculty for transforming or
exaggerating reality and projecting it on a distinct and
partly arbitrary plane, thus making for epic, romantic, or
allegorical poetry. On the other hand, pride of place is
given to the pleasure of observing and understanding,
which is only possible when the personality of the author
has been subdued. This peaceful and loyal observation of
life did not exist before Chaucer, at least not in the same
degree. There were, of course, works more noble and
more essentially poetical, such as the *Chanson de Roland*
and the *Divina Commedia*, to take two widely differing
instances. There were more exquisite ones, filled with
quivering passion, amongst the works of the French song-
writers, which, beginning with the romances of the twelfth
century, lead to Rutebeuf, and thence, a hundred years
after Chaucer, to Villon, in whom they reach the apex of
their development. There was, moreover, in Petrarch's
sonnets a refinement of feeling and language scarcely attained
by Chaucer. But where shall we find, except in Chaucer,
a work where the principal aim has been to portray men
truthfully, without exalting or disparaging them, and to
present an exact picture of average humanity? Chaucer
sees things as they are, and paints them as he sees them.
He restrains himself in order the better to observe.

Thus this Englishman, who breaks through the darkness
which shrouded the literature of his country, and who for
two centuries remained without a true successor; this writer,
who is still hampered at times by an imperfect syntax,

who is saturated with scholasticism, whose memory is loaded with biblical or profane allusions, whose astrological sky is peopled with stars stranger to European eyes to-day than those of the South Seas; this docile translator of multifarious or often antiquated works—really opened up a new literary field. A graceful and tender poet, exiled for his sin of humour from the highest regions of poetry, curiosity was certainly stronger in him than faith, and the joys of the senses and of the mind more keen than the rapture of enthusiasm. The things he saw interested him much more than those he dreamt of. The speeches he heard always seemed to him somehow entertaining, and even truthful, were it only as adequate signs of the speaker's nature and breeding. He leads the group of amused and good-natured observers who will accept as a fact the motley fabric of society, without wishing to dye to a uniform colour the many strands that compose it. Doubtless certain colours seemed to him more beautiful than others, but it was on the contrast presented by them all that he founded at once his philosophy of life and the laws of his art.

APPENDIX

For the benefit of those who would like to form an opinion of M. Legouis' skill as a translator, we here give ten pieces, where he has been most successful, we think, in rendering, without any dilution, the thought and imagery of the Chaucerian line. The language is just archaic enough to give in French the same impression of quaintness which charms modern English readers of Chaucer

I.—Ballad of Griselida

Grisilde est morte avec sa patience,
Même tombeau les a vu réunir.
Aussi crié-je en publique audience:
Que nul mari ne fasse plus souffrir
Sa femme chère, en l'espérance vaine
Qu'autre Grisilde il pourrait découvrir.

O noble épouse à la haute prudence,
Humble et front bas, garde-toi d'obéir,
De peur qu'un clerc n'ait cause et diligence
De te chanter pour les temps à venir
Comme Grisilde, et de peur que te vienne
La Chichevache en son ventre engloutir.

Imite Echo qui ne fait pas silence
Et qui répond mot pour mot sans faillir;
Ne soit ton bec cloué par innocence,
Mais le timon hâte-toi de saisir.
Cette leçon que chacune retienne.
Cause commune à peine de trahir.

Sus! archifemme, et te mets en défense;
Plus que chamelle es forte et peux férir;
Ne souffre pas qu'homme jamais t'offense.
Et toi, fluette et faible à l'assaillir,
Plus aigre sois que tigresse indienne;
Fais-lui marcher ton cliquet sans tarir.

N'aie peur de lui ni pour lui révérence;
Fût-il armé tout de fer et de cuir,
Les dards aigus de ta prompte éloquence
Le perceront au vif, s'il ne peut fuir.
De jalousie enforce encor sa chaîne,
Comme la caille il ira se blottir.

Es-tu jolie? où gens sont en présence
Fais ta parure et tes yeux resplendir;
Vilaine es-tu? sois large en ta dépense
Pour attirer amis et retenir.
Gai comme feuille au vent, nargue la peine,
Le laissant, lui, pleurer, tordre et gémir.

The Clerkes Tale, Lenvoy.

II.—PORTRAIT OF THE OXFORD CLERK

Un Clerc d'Oxford était de notre bande,
Dont la science en logique était grande;
Tout épilé luisait son vieux manteau;
Plus maigre était son bidet qu'un râteau
Et lui n'était guère plus gras, j'avoue:
Sous un front grave il avait creuse joue,
Trop peu mondain pour gagner un office
Ou dans l'Eglise atteindre un bénéfice.
A son chevet aimait-il mieux avoir
Vingt livres grands vêtus en rouge ou noir,
Un Aristote et ceux de son école,
Que riche habit, belle harpe ou viole.
Mais bien qu'expert en la philosophie
N'avait pour ce la bourse mieux remplie.
Ce qu'il tirait de ses amis pour vivre
Il l'employait à s'acheter maint livre,
Puis ardemment soulait pour ceux prier
Qui lui donnaient moyens d'étudier.
L'étude était son amour et son soin.
Ne disait mot de plus qu'il n'est besoin,
Et c'était dit en forme et révérence,
Court et fécond et plein de sapience.
Il inclinait aux discours vertueux,
Joyeux d'apprendre et d'enseigner joyeux.

Prol. ll. 285-308.

III.—PORTRAIT OF THE LIMITOUR

Et nous avions un Frère en noble arroi,
Un Limiteur, à la mine riante.
Nul ne savait, dans la gent mendiante,
Autant que lui d'aimable et doux langage.

Il avait fait maint et maint mariage
De jouvencelle, avec sa propre bourse.
C'était l'orgueil de l'Ordre et sa ressource.
Chez la bourgeoise ou le riche fermier
Il était plus que le chat familier;
Paraissait-il? chacun de s'empresser.
C'est qu'il avait pouvoir de confesser,—
Mieux qu'un curé, leur disait le saint homme,
Ayant pour ce la licence de Rome.
Suavement oyait confession;
Charmante était son absolution.
Il imposait facile pénitence
Où l'attendait quelque bonne pitance,
Car faire don à pauvre confrérie
Est signe sûr qu'on a l'áme guérie.
Il affirmait pouvoir bien, sans mentir,
D'après le don juger du repentir.
Que de pécheurs, chaque jour nous l'enseigne,
Restent l'œil sec malgré que leur cœur saigne!
Or donc, au lieu de pleurs et de prières,
Il faut donner l'obole aux pauvres Frères.
Toujours ce Frère avait dans sa cornette
Broche ou couteau pour femme joliette.
Puis il sonnait mainte joyeuse note,
Chanteur exquis et bon joueur de rote;
Pour la romance il emportait le prix.
Plus blanc était son cou que fleur de lys;
Avec cela, fort comme un champion.
Dans toute auberge il savait par son nom
Chaque valet et la moindre servante,
Mieux que lépreux et mieux que mendiante.
Car pour un Frére entre tous distingué,
Il n'était bon, ni bienséant, ni gai,
D'avoir commerce avec ladre et pouilleux.
Qu'y gagne-t-on? Quel profit précieux
A trafiquer avec telle pauvraille?
Mieux aimait-il marchands de victuaille.
En lieux amis, sous tous les riches toits,
Il était doux, serviable et courtois.
Oncques ne fut homme plus vertueux.
De son couvent c'était le meilleur gueux.
Pour sa " limite " il payait un loyer
Et nul que lui n'y pouvait mendier.
Tel charme avait son " In principio "
Que n'eût-elle eu savate ni sabot,
La pauvre veuve, avant qu'il fît départ,
En s'excusant lui remettait un liard.
    Parfois folâtre autant qu'un jeune chien,
Les " jours d'amour " il avait beau maintien;

Il n'y montrait froc pelé, de la sorte
Qu'un studieux et pauvre cloîtré porte,
Mais ressemblait un docteur ou un pape;
De laine double était sa demi chape,
Et ronde comme une cloche d'église.
  Puis il blaisait d'une manière exquise
Pour mieux sucrer son anglais dans sa bouche.
Après chanter, lorsque du luth il touche,
Ses yeux levés scintillent, comme au ciel
Les astres font par claires nuits de gel.

                                    Prol. ll. 208-269.

IV.—Portrait of the Parson

Un digne prêtre était de ce voyage;
C'était un pauvre curé de village,
Mais pourtant riche en œuvres de bonté.
Vrai clerc d'ailleurs, il avait médité
Sur l'Evangile, et sa bouche fervente
Rendait du Christ la parole vivante.
L'âme bénigne et l'esprit diligent,
De son seul bien était-il négligent.
Il haïssait punir comme d'un crime
L'homme oublieux de lui payer sa dime;
Mieux aimait-il, certes, donner du sien
A quelque miséreux paroissien,
Et l'assister sur sa maigre pitance.
En peu de chose il trouvait suffisance.
Sa paroisse était vaste, aux toits distants,
Mais par tonnerre ou pluie, en tous les temps,
Il se rendait, à l'appel de la peine,
Vers la maison la plus humble et lointaine,
Allant à pied, dans sa main un bâton.
Il répandait cette noble leçon
De vivre bien pour instruire à bien vivre.
Il avait pris ce texte en le saint Livre;
Il ajoutait en langage plus clair:
Si l'or se rouille, est-il espoir du fer?
Car si le prêtre est pécheur qui nous mène,
Comment penser qu'un laïque s'abstienne?
Et pour l'Eglise est-il plus grand'pitié
Que brebis nette et pasteur conchié?
Le prêtre doit inspirer le respect
Par pures mœurs à la brebis qu'il paît.
    Louant sa cure ainsi qu'un pré qu'on loue,
Il ne laissait son troupeau dans la boue
Pour s'encourir à Londres, à Saint-Paul,
Gagner argent, bon vivre et coucher mol,

A dire messe en quelque chanterie.
Restait chez lui gardant sa bergerie
Pour que le loup n'y vînt soudain mal faire.
Pasteur était et non point mercenaire.
Et bien qu'il fût saint homme et vertueux,
Pour les pécheurs il n'était sourcilleux,
Ni sermonneur hautain et rechignant,
Mais très discret et doux en enseignant.
Mener les gens au ciel par belle vie
Et bon exemple était sa seule envie.
Mais s'il avait affaire à l'obstiné,
Lors, quel qu'il fût, misérable ou bien-né,
Il le tançait vertement, par ma foi!
De meilleur prêtre il n'est en nul endroit.
Il n'exigeait pompe ni révérence,
Ni n'affectait farouche conscience;
La loi du Christ et de ses douze apôtres
Suivait d'abord, puis la prêchait aux autres.

Prol. ll. 477-528.

V.—PORTRAIT OF THE MILLER

Maître Meunier était, je vous le jure,
Un fort gaillard et de riche encolure.
Osseux, noueux, ferme comme un pilier,
Dans toute lutte il gagnait le bélier.
Trapu d'épaules, sur ses reins tassé,
Il n'était porte où se ruant, lancé
Tête première, il ne pût faire brèche.
Sa barbe large avait forme de bêche
Et couleur fauve, entre truie et goupil.
Une verrue à son nez avait-il,
Tout au fin bout, avec touffe pareille
A ces poils roux qu'un porc a dans l'oreille.
Chaque narine était un grand trou noir;
Sa bouche ouverte, un four énorme à voir.
C'était un franc goliard et braillard
Qui dégoisait maint et maint dit gaillard.
Sur le froment que sa meule triture
Il s'allouait d'abord quelque moûture,
Puis prélevait sa part, et deux encor;
Ce, nonobstant qu'il eût jà pouce d'or.
    Portant la dague et l'écu sur la hanche,
Capuchon bleu dessus la cote blanche,
Cornemusant à force par la ville,
Il nous mena jusqu'au deuxième mille.

Prol. ll. 545-563.

VI.—Portrait of the Prioress

Et mous avions une dame Prieure
Dont le sourire était tout simple et coi.
Son grand serment était " par Saint Eloi! "
Elle chantait très décemment du nez
Les chants divins à la messe entonnés.
Dame Eglantine (on la nommait ainsi)
Parlait français le plus pur et choisi,
Comme on le parle au couvent de Stratford,
Car le français de France ignorait fort,
Qu'elle était donc à table bien apprise!
Jamais morceau n'échappait à sa prise
Tant savait bien le tenir en sa route
Sans qu'il en chût sur sa gorge une goutte,
Et n'enfonçait dans la sauce ses doigts.
De courtoisie elle observait les lois.
Elle essuyait si net sa lèvre haute
Que dans sa coupe on ne l'eût prise en faute
De laisser oncque une tache de graisse.
Elle rotait tout bas par politesse.
Certe elle avait mine majestueuse,
Autant qu'aimable et toute gracieuse,
Car se peinait à suivre les leçons
Et de la Cour copier les façons
Pour mériter qu'on la tint en honneur.
    Que vous dirai-je aussi de son bon cœur?
Si charitable était-elle et si tendre
Qu'elle pleurait, voyant au piège prendre,
Saignante ou morte, une pauvre souris.
Ses petits chiens par elle étaient nourris
De fin rôti, de pain blanc et de lait.
Qu'un d'eux mourût, elle se désolait,
Ou qu'il glapît, bâtonné durement,
Car elle était toute âme et sentiment.
    Sa guimpe était plissée à maint beau pli;
Avait les yeux gris clair, le nez joli,
Bouche mignonne et doucette et vermeille,
Mais grand le front, bel et large à merveille;
Il avait presque un empan, je vous jure;
La dame aussi n'était d'humble stature.
    Exquise était sa mante; un chapelet
De fin corail à son bras s'enroulait,
Chaque dizain marqué d'un gros grain vert,
Auquel pendait, portant un A couvert
D'une couronne, un brillant bijou d'or
Avec ces mots: *Quid non vincit Amor ?*

                    Prol. ll. 118-162.

VII.—LAMENT OF DORIGINE

De son castel la mer était tout près
Et ses amis pour calmer ses regrets
La promenaient sur la falaise haute
D'où pouvait voir voguer près de la côte,
Allants, venants, nacelles et vaisseaux;
Mais cette vue éveillait tous ses maux,
Car soupirait à part souventefois:
" Las! n'est-il nef, parmi tant que je vois,
Qui me rendra mon mari?   Lors mon cœur
Serait guéri de sa dure douleur."
      Un autre jour elle venait pensive
Jeter les yeux du rebord sur la rive,
Mais en voyant d'affreux rocs noirs sous elle,
Son pauvre cœur frissonnait de peur telle
Qu'elle sentait ses pieds se dérober;
Il lui fallait s'asseoir pour ne tomber,
Puis contemplait piteusement la mer,
Disant avec maint gros soupir amer:
      " Eternel Dieu, qui par ta providence
Mènes le monde en sûre gouvernance,
Il n'est, dit-on, chose qu'en vain tu crées;
Pourtant, Seigneur, ces roches abhorrées,
Que l'on dirait noire confusion
D'Enfer, plutot que la création
D'un Dieu si bon, si parfait et si stable,
Pourquoi fis œuvre ainsi déraisonnable?
A l'est, à l'ouest, au sud, au nord, en somme
Rien ne nourrit, oiseau, bête ni homme.
Nul bien n'en sort, je crois, rien que malheur.
Ne vois-tu pas comme elle occit, Seigneur?
Cent mille corps humains se sont rompus
Sur ces rochers, quoiqu'on n'en parle plus.
Et pourtant, Sire, on dit le genre humain
Le plus chéri des travaux de ta main,
Tant que d'amour le fis à ton image.
Or peux-tu donc, toi si tendre et si sage,
Pareils engins créer pour le détruire,
Qui rien de bon ne savent, rien que nuire?
J'ai bien ouï prouver aux clercs pieux
Par arguments, que tout est pour le mieux
Quoique pour moi la cause en reste obscure . . .
Mais que Celui qui fait les vents ait cure
De mon seigneur, c'est ma conclusion!
Je laisse aux clercs toute disputoison. . . .
Mais ces affreux rochers noirs, à Dieu plût

Qu'ils fûssent tous au fond pour son salut!
Ces rochers là navrent mon cœur d'alarmes."
Ainsi disait en versant maintes larmes.

The Franklin's Tale, ll. 847-894.

VIII.—Story of the young Clerk devoted to the Virgin

Ce petit clerc dans son école assis,
Courbé sur son petit abécédaire,
Ouït chanter *Alma Redemptoris*
Aux grands debout devant l'antiphonaire;
A petits coups, tant qu'il osa le faire,
Il vint près d'eux, oyant de telle ardeur
Qu'il sut bientot le premier vers par cœur.

Point ne savait ce que latin veut dire
Car il était tout jeune et tendre d'âge,
Si pria-t-il un plus grand de traduire
Ce chant pour lui dans le commun langage
En lui disant quel était son usage;
Il l'adjura d'y mettre mots connus
Par mainte fois, et sur ses genoux nus.

Lui répondit cet autre un peu plus vieux:
" Ce nous dit-on, l'air qui te plaît si fort
Fut composé pour la Dame des cieux,
Pour la bénir, et pour prier confort
Et secours d'elle à l'heure de la mort.
Je n'en connais pas plus sur la matière,
J'apprends le chant mais sais peu de grammaire."

" Ce chant est-il donc fait en révérence,
(Dit l'innocent) de la mère à Jésu?
Or, par ma foi, ferai-je diligence
De tout l'apprendre avant Noël venu;
Et me dût-on pour l'A B C mal su
Frapper trois fois par heure avec la verge,
Je le saurai pour l'amour de la Vierge."

Chemin faisant, tant qu'il le sût sans faute,
L'autre l'apprit à ce gentil clergeon,
Qui depuis lors le chantait à voix haute
Sans se tromper d'un seul mot ni d'un ton;
Deux fois par jour il lançait sa chanson
Allant en classe et rentrant chez sa mère,
Tant Notre-Dame avoit son âme entière.

The Prioress's Tale, ll. 1706-1740.

IX.—The Passing of Fairies and Goblins

Au temps jadis où régnait cet Artus
De qui Bretons vont prônant les vertus,
Tout ce pays était plein de féerie.
Souvent dansaient sur la verte prairie
Les gais lutins en ronde avec les fées.
Il s'est passé des centaines d'années,
Ce m'a-t-on dit, depuis ces temps lointains
Et nul ne voit à présent de lutins,
Car le saint zèle et les grandes prières
Des Limiteurs et autres pieux Frères
Qui vont plus dru par les champs d'alentour
Que grains de poudre en les rayons du jour,
Bénissant tout: la chambre et la cuisine,
Et le grenier et la salle où l'on dîne,
Ferme et manoir, étable et laiterie,—
De cela vient qu'il n'est plus de féerie.
Car où soulait rôder quelque lutin,
Un Limiteur récite son latin
Tandis qu'il va durant la matinée
Faire de porte en porte sa tournée.
Femme peut bien, sans péril et sans peur,
De çà de là, sous les buissons en fleur
Et dans les bois s'éjouïr aujourd'hui,
Il n'y demeure autre incube que lui,
Et ne voudrait lui faire déshonneur.

The Wife of Bath's Tale, ll. 857-881.

X.—Wedding of January and May

Et Mai siègeait si gracieuse à table
Que de la voir était chose féerique.
Esther n'eut oncque un regard si pudique
Pour Assuer, ni si doux et modeste.
De sa beauté je vous tairai le reste
Hors que chacun ce jour en fut charmé
Et que semblait un beau matin de mai
Où règnent joie et douceur à l'envi.
    Le vieux Janvier en extase est ravi
A chaque fois qu'il contemple sa face
Et dans son cœur tout bas il la menace
De la serrer en ses bras, la nuit vienne,
Mieux que Paris ne fit jamais Hélène.
Mais grand'pitié le trouble et grand ennui
Pensant qu'il doit l'offenser cette nuit:
" Las! (se dit-il) ô douce créature!

Veuille le Ciel que ta tendresse endure
Tout mon courage, il est si vif et chaud!
Pourras-tu bien en soutenir l'assaut?
Je n'y mettrai toute ma force, va!
Ah! plût à Dieu que la nuit arrivât
Et que jamais cette nuit ne prît fin!
Quand tous ces gens partiront-ils enfin? "

Il boit clairet, hypocras et vernage
Chaud épicé, pour croître son courage . . .
Puis prend à part ses amis éprouvés:
" Au nom du Ciel, sitôt que le pouvez,
Faites sortir poliment tous ces gens! "
A lui complaire amis sont diligents:
On a tiré la courtine fermée,
Au lit porté l'épouse mi-pâmée,
Puis quand le prêtre eut la couche bénie
Chacun s'éloigne et la noce est finie.

Notre Janvier tient dans ses bras enclose
Sa fraîche Mai, son paradis, sa chose,
Cent fois la baise et rebaise et cajole
Et de sa joue épineuse la frôle,
Rude au toucher comme peau de requin,
Car il s'est fait la barbe le matin.
Or, se frottant à sa doucette face:
" Hélas! (dit-il) il faut que je vous fasse,
Ma chère épouse, offense et grand souci,
J'ai peur, avant que je sorte d'ici.
Mais cependant considérez (dit-il)
Qu'il n'est au monde ouvrier si subtil
Sachant ouvrer à la fois vite et bien;
Cette œuvre-ci sans loisir ne vaut rien.
D'ailleurs qu'importe à nous le temps et l'heure?
Sommes-nous point mariés à demeure?
Béni le joug qui nous unit tous deux!
L'homme ne peut non plus pécher aux jeux
Qu'il prend avec sa femme, tard ou tôt,
Que se blesser de son propre couteau.
De par la loi avons congé d'amour."

Ainsi Janvier besogne jusqu'au jour,
Puis prend à l'aube une soupe au clairet
Et sur son lit s'assied tout guilleret,
Et le voilà qui chante d'allégresse,
Baise sa femme, à nouveau la caresse.
Il est joueur comme un poulain lâché
Et sans tarir bavarde comme un geai.
Autour du cou sa peau flasque tremblote

Tandis qu'il chante à tue-tête et chevrote.
Dieu sait si Mai le trouvait à sa guise
Ainsi siégeant sur la couche en chemise,
Le cou ridé sous son bonnet de nuit!
Moins qu'une fève estime son déduit.
Il dit alors: " C'est assez travailler;
Voici le jour, je ne puis plus veiller."
Sa tête tombe, il s'endort jusqu'à prime . . .

The Merchant's Tale,
ll. 1742-1764, ll. 1807-1808, ll. 1813-1857.

INDEX